MW00456534

America's
Most
Alarming
Writer

Also by Charles Bowden

Killing the Hidden Waters (1977)

Street Signs Chicago: Neighborhood and Other Illusions of Big-City Life, with Lewis Kreinberg and Richard Younker (1981)

Blue Desert (1986)

Frog Mountain Blues, with Jack W. Dykinga (1987)

Trust Me: Charles Keating and the Missing Billions, with Michael Binstein (1988)

Mezcal (1988)

Red Line (1989)

Desierto: Memories of the Future (1991)

The Sonoran Desert, with Jack W. Dykinga (1992)

The Secret Forest, with Jack W. Dykinga and Paul S. Martin (1993)

Blood Orchid: An Unnatural History of America (1995)

Chihuahua: Pictures from the Edge, with Virgil Hancock (1996)

Stone Canyons of the Colorado Plateau, with Jack W. Dykinga (1996)

Juárez: The Laboratory of our Future, with Noam Chomsky, Eduardo Galeano, and Julián Cardona (1998)

Eugene Richards, with Eugene Richards (2001)

Down by the River: Drugs, Money, Murder, and Family (2002)

Blues for Cannibals: The Notes from Underground (2002)

A Shadow in the City: Confessions of an Undercover Drug Warrior (2005)

Inferno, with Michael P. Berman (2006)

Exodus/Éxodo, with Julián Cardona (2008)

Some of the Dead Are Still Breathing: Living in the Future (2009)

Trinity, with Michael P. Berman (2009)

Murder City: Ciudad Juárez and the Global Economy's New Killing Fields, with Julián Cardona (2010)

Dreamland: The Way Out of Juárez, with Alice Leora Briggs (2010)

The Charles Bowden Reader, edited by Erin Almeranti and Mary Martha Miles (2010)

El Sicario: The Autobiography of a Mexican Assassin, with Molly Molloy (2011)

The Red Caddy: Into the Unknown with Edward Abbey (2018)

Dakotah (2019)

AMERICA'S MOST ALARMING WRITER

Essays on
the Life
and Work of
Charles
Bowden

Edited by
Bill
Broyles
and
Bruce J.
Dinges

University of Texas Press
Austin

Lannan
CHARLES BOWDEN PUBLISHING PROJECT

Compilation copyright © 2019 by the University of Texas Press
Individual contributors' copyright information is available on page
323.

All rights reserved
Printed in the United States of America
First edition, 2019

Requests for permission to reproduce material from this work should
be sent to
  Permissions
  University of Texas Press
  P.O. Box 7819
  Austin, TX 78713-7819
  utpress.utexas.edu/rp-form

⊗ The paper used in this book meets the minimum requirements of
ANSI/NISO Z39.48-1992 (R1997) (Permanence of Paper).

Library of Congress Cataloging-in-Publication Data

Names: Broyles, Bill, 1944 July 9- editor. | Dinges, Bruce J.,
editor.
Title: America's most alarming writer : essays on the life and work
of Charles Bowden / edited by Bill Broyles and Bruce J. Dinges.
Description: First edition. | Austin : University of Texas Press,
2019. | Includes bibliographical references and index.
Identifiers: LCCN 2019005753
  ISBN 978-1-4773-1990-1 (cloth : alk. paper)
  ISBN 978-1-4773-1991-8 (library e-book)
  ISBN 978-1-4773-1992-5 (non-library e-book)
Subjects: LCSH: Bowden, Charles, 1945-2014. | Authors, American—
20th century.
Classification: LCC PS3552.0844 Z55 2019 | DDC 814/.54—dc23
LC record available at https://lccn.loc.gov/2019005753

doi:10.7560/319901

*Peggy, Apparently, at one time
I went down the wrong road.
And, alas, remembered the
geography. Love, Chuck*

CHARLES BOWDEN
inscription to his sister Peg
in *Blues for Cannibals*

*I sensed that he wanted nothing
more than to write in some new
way about subjects no one had
addressed.*

DAVID F. ALLMENDINGER,
about classmate Charles
Bowden in 1972

Contents

WRITERS ON BOWDEN

CODA

America's
Most
Alarming
Writer

Introduction

BILL BROYLES AND BRUCE J. DINGES

On March 15, 2015, three hundred people filled an auditorium at the Tucson Festival of Books on the University of Arizona campus in Tucson to pay their respects to Charles Bowden, who had passed away the previous summer, and participate in a discussion of his life and legacy. The panelists included writers Jim Harrison and Luis Alberto Urrea and Bowden's editor at *Harper's* and *Mother Jones*, Clara Jeffery. During the question and answer period that followed, Harrison—who had once described Bowden as "America's most alarming writer"—observed that "it's interesting to see ... how the whole Chuck reputation is lifting, rather precipitously, and I'm wondering why do we have to die to get that kind of jolt?" Harrison thought it was more than just postmortem curiosity. "The fatalists among us ... , " he reminded the sympathetic audience, "have been trying to get you to read this for years."[1]

And here, in a nutshell, is the challenge: How do we introduce this profoundly American writer, with his distinctive voice, disdain for borders and conventions, and propensity to peer into the abyss, where most of us would prefer not to look, to a readership accustomed to precise categories and easy answers? Bowden, himself, acknowledged the problem when he wrote: "I've noticed in bookstores they never know where to put my stuff." To him it all seemed so annoyingly simple. Everything he wrote—the dozens of books and hundreds of national magazine articles—came down to one thing: "I ... believe with every bit of my being, that the

Charles Bowden, America's most alarming writer

future is going to be a collision between limited resources and unlimited human appetites."[2] Nature, ecology, urban sprawl, human greed, violence, drugs, politics all play parts in a global drama whose unfolding Bowden was committed to chronicling with a reporter's keen eye for detail and an Old Testament prophet's apocalyptic urgency.

William deBuys probably comes nearest to defining Bowden's place in America's literary canon. In his foreword to the reissue of *Desierto: Memories of the Future*, deBuys compares Bowden to James Agee, whose *Let Us Now Praise Famous Men* similarly left critics scratching their heads in confusion and wonder. Both were unconventional stylists with an insatiable curiosity to uncover and report how the world really works.[3] Because Bowden lived in the desert Southwest and wrote about bats, mountains, canyons, savings and loan scandals, corrupt politicians, drug lords, and assassins, it has been too easy to dismiss him as a regional writer. Chuck would say: Take a step back. Look at my body of work. Pay attention to where we are heading before it's too late.

Bowden's professional background as a writer was unusual. He was born on a small farm near Joliet, Illinois, on July 20, 1945. Three years later, his father, who worked for the Internal Revenue Service, moved the family to Chicago and then to Tucson, Arizona, when Chuck was twelve. Bowden attended Tucson High School, earned his bachelor's degree in history from the University of Arizona and a master's degree in intellectual history from the University of Wisconsin–Madison in 1967. He completed the requirements for a PhD but walked away from the degree after refusing to make revisions to his doctoral dissertation. Following a disheartening turn as an American history instructor at the University of Illinois–Chicago Circle, Bowden turned his back on academia and returned to Tucson, where he drifted between university research and grant-writing jobs. He also edited tech manuals in the San Francisco Bay area, and mowed lawns before landing an

Charles "Chuck" Bowden, high school graduation, 1963

entry-level reporter position at the *Tucson Citizen*. He had found his calling. Chuck rapidly rose to prominence on the newspaper staff. As a portent of things to come, the selection committee awarded Bowden the Pulitzer Prize for stories he had written on sexual abuse and border crossing, only to have their decision overruled. Publicly at least, Chuck sloughed off the slight. Nonetheless, he left the *Citizen* at the end of 1984 and a year later joined Dick Vonier to launch *City Magazine*, a brash, bold, hard-hitting publication that garnered enthusiastic reviews and a dedicated readership before it folded, due to financial problems. Bowden cashed his last regular paycheck in 1989. From then until his death, he depended on magazine contracts, supplemented by occasional grants and fellowships, to support himself while he wrote books.

By then, Bowden tells us in "Credo," a talk he delivered for the Tucson–Pima County Public Library, he had reached "certain conclusions" that would define the arc of his life and career:

> One was that the desert was a disease and that I was doomed to live within its bounds and would never be cured. Secondly, I decided that the best way to understand something was to go to the edge. This desert was the edge of natural resources as Americans understand the term, and here in its heat and persistent droughts I could make sense of all those dull terms like the "environment" or "ecology." I believed, and still believe with every bit of my being, that the future is going to be a collision between limited resources and unlimited human appetites. And finally, I came back for the border, for the energy of the only place on this earth where a First World economy rubs up against a dirt world of poverty.

His obsession was "to write a history of my times based on these beliefs or notions."[4] And he brought formidable tools to the task:

Charles Bowden at work in his writing studio, 2002

a graduate student's grasp of historical context, an investigative reporter's thirst for facts, and an in-your-face writing style that demanded attention.

Writing consumed Bowden's life. When a girlfriend complained that he wrote "all the time," Chuck tried to explain that he was "possessed by the writing demon," but she was having nothing of it. "That's unfair to me," she said, only to have Chuck reply, "How do you think it makes me feel? My life is never my own."[5] When he wasn't in the field interviewing and collecting material, he typically woke at 3 am, brewed himself a cup of coffee, and retired to the computer in the writing "shack" behind his house, where he wrote late into the morning, saving afternoons for business calls and research, and evenings for casual salons with friends and drop-ins. In this manner, he turned out more than two dozen books (including eight unpublished manuscripts) and a flood of articles for *Esquire, GQ, National Geographic, Arizona Highways,* and others. The sheer volume of Bowden's publication demands our attention. His ability to hit a word count and meet deadlines kept him in constant demand with harried editors.

Bowden led a peripatetic existence when he wasn't writing. Deadlines kept him on the road for long stretches during which he gathered material, interviewed sources, and then holed up at home or in some isolated cabin to write. In his busiest freelancing days, he sometimes spent two hundred nights a year on the road. His little pickup truck ran well past 200,000 miles; his uniform of blue jeans, cotton safari shirt (green, brown, or gray), fleece jacket or down vest, and running shoes or huaraches seldom varied whether he was covering a story in Mexico or North Dakota, going to the grocery store, or meeting an editor in New York.

Bowden wrote for newspapers and national magazines for the simple reason that they paid enough money up front so that he could afford to write the books that mattered to him. He explained the process this way: "*National Geographic* called and asked me to do a story. I said, 'I'm not interested.' They said, 'We pay $4 a word.' Now I'm interested. They fly me to somewhere for five days, I write for three days more, and they pay me $16,000. Then I can write my books."[6] Magazines, in turn, hired him because he was fast, easy to work with, and turned in solid—often brilliant—copy. The latter included "The Pariah," a gut-wrenching article in the September 1998 issue of *Esquire* about Gary Webb, the *San Jose Mercury* investigative journalist whose career was ruined, and who eventually committed suicide, after he exposed a CIA connection to cocaine trafficking in Los Angeles' African American community. Another was "Ike and Lyndon," in the March 2000 issue of *Harper's*, a biting critique of Lyndon Johnson and the Vietnam War that journalism students still parse for its style and organization. *Aperture* prized Bowden for his graphic sensibility, pairing him with national and internationally known photographers. The same is true for *National Geographic*, which teamed him with photographer Eugene Richards to examine climate change and depopulation in North Dakota. Bowden similarly wrote about the human toll of Hurricane Katrina on New Orleans and lower Louisiana for *GQ* and explored the post-hurricane Mississippi Delta with Gene Richards for an article he hoped *National Geographic* might publish, again highlighting land, climate change, economic displacement, and survival in the wake of natural and human disaster.[7] Bowden's pieces for *Mother Jones* earned him a contributing editor byline. Chuck may have said he did it for the money, but his magazine articles exhibit the same deep reporting and riveting prose that characterize his longer work.

Bowden published his first book, *Killing the Hidden Waters*, at age thirty-two, in 1977. Its argument that the desert Southwest is pumping groundwater that can never be replaced struck a resonant chord among ecologists, and the book has never been out of print. Subsequent books cemented Bowden's reputation in the environmental community. In *Blue Desert* (1986), he blends current events, ecology, and personal stories in a stream-of-consciousness narrative that he returned to often. In *Frog Mountain Blues* (1987), *The Sonoran Desert* (1992), and *Stone Canyons of the Colorado* (1996), he partnered with Pulitzer Prize–winning photographer Jack Dykinga, to highlight human threats to wild spaces. *The Secret Forest* (1993), with Dykinga and botanist Paul Martin, captures the culture and rhythms of a Sonoran community. It also introduced readers to Bowden's fascination with Mexico.

Charles Bowden promoting his book *Blue Desert*, Mount Lemmon, Arizona, 1986

Street Signs Chicago: Neighborhood and Other Illusions of Big-City Life (1981), Bowden's second book, is a raw shout-out, in distinctively Bowdenesque prose, that he wouldn't be easily pigeon holed. Conceived with the edgy working title, "Get Home Before Dark," Chuck and his activist friend and coauthor, Lew Kreinberg, urge the city to face up to facts: "If we are to make the good life, we must make it where we now stand, not somewhere else.... We do it here and we do it now or not at all."[8]

Bowden returns often to this theme of a city's relationship with its inhabitants, its environment, and its economy. In *Desierto: Memories of the Future* (1991), he looks pessimistically across a landscape where developers and drug lords vie with mountain lions and indigenous people to shape the future, and hopes he is wrong: "I will witness cities being built where there is no long-term basis for them, watch families and friends proliferate in a place where there will never be enough food for them, and watch the earth underneath all this activity grow weary, sag with fatigue, and slip into a coma that smacks of death. Sitting here, the fire crackling, I quietly watch the past flowing into a future that cannot accommodate it, or stop its intrusion."[9]

The 1994 North America Free Trade Agreement (NAFTA), depressing Mexico's agricultural economy and drawing workers to border town factories that thrive on cheap labor, confirmed Bowden's deepest fears. "What we fear is already upon us," he warns in *Chihuahua: Pictures from the Edge*, his 1994 book with photographer Virgil Hancock, "a force launched by birth rates, interest rates, and five hundred years of misdirection, pillage, and neglect. Now we live with it."[10]

Bowden tells us that we need look no farther than across the river from El Paso, Texas, to discern how it may all play out. *Juárez: The Laboratory of Our Future* (1998), with Noam Chomsky and Eduardo Galeano, provides a chilling dissection of the economy of a once-proud border city, now ravaged by murder and corruption, fighting for breath and a living wage. It was a story he couldn't turn his back on. In *Dreamland: The Way Out of Juárez* and *Murder City: Ciudad Juárez and the Global Economy's New Killing Fields*, both published in 2010, Bowden relies on human drama and personal interviews to probe the intersection of geographic reality, economic policies and trade agreements, living cultures, and greed.

Events and Bowden's instincts as an investigative reporter drew him deeper into cartel violence in Mexico. When young women went missing in Juárez, he wondered why. An American DEA agent, Kiki Camarena, was tortured and murdered by cartel assassins, perhaps with assistance from DEA-trained Mexican agents and a CIA contractor. Then journalist Gary Webb found credible evidence that the American government was complicit in drug smuggling, and he was blackballed for exposing it. A Mexican beauty queen was brutalized so badly that she lost her mind. And Bruno Jordan, the brother of an American drug agent, was murdered as revenge for his brother's police work.

Bowden tried to make sense out of chaos along the US-Mexico border. He made it his personal war and found allies and guides in photojournalist Julián Cardona and drug enforcement agents Phil Jordan, Kim Sanders, and Don Henry Ford Jr. In lesser hands books such as *Down by the River: Drugs, Money, Murder, and Family* (2002), *Blues for Cannibals: The Notes from Underground* (2002), *A Shadow in the City: Confessions of an Undercover Drug Warrior* (2005), and *Some of the Dead Are Still Breathing: Living in the Future* (2009) might fight for space alongside dozens of lurid true crime titles on bookstore shelves. But Bowden built his stories upon fresh approaches and unique organization. He wants desperately to show readers that there are rational explanations for the violence. That good people are capable of horrendous evil. That there are lessons to be learned about national identity and character. And that there is more than enough blame to go around (crime syndicates couldn't sell drugs if Americans weren't buying them, and without the drug trade the Mexican economy would collapse).

In some respects, Bowden never left behind the history seminars he attended as a graduate student in Madison. He never lost his passion for research or his faith that the past and present hold keys to discerning the future. Readers of *Blood Orchid: An Unnatural History of America* (1995), in particular, will marvel at the ways in which he disdains standard formats and citations, instead interweaving quotations and multiple narratives. In this he may have been influenced by writers like Eduardo Galeano, whom he admired and whose *Memory of Fire* trilogy weaves quotations from historical documents into complex-but-inviting narratives.

In similar fashion, Bowden's own trilogy—*Inferno* (2006), with Michael P. Berman; *Exodus/Éxodo* (2008), with Julián Cardona; and *Trinity* (2009), with Michael Berman—gathers many threads found in his other books into a panoramic tapestry. With a sweep of both arms, he summarizes the broad unfolding of southwestern geography, migrations, and civilizations.

Well into his sixties, Bowden recalled a time as a child when he rattled off the tired bromide "honesty is the best policy." His father exploded, threatening, "Don't you *ever* say that again. You're not honest because it's going to benefit you. You're either honest or you're a God damned liar."[11]

Chuck Bowden attempted to give an honest account of the world as he saw it. The picture isn't always pretty and the conclusions he draws may not be what people want to hear, but his insistent voice calls out to us. Whether about ecology, climate change, globalization, drugs, violence, or a reporter's life, his books entertain and challenge us. Bowden was a lousy pretender. He called out the gorillas in the room. He reminds us that extinctions, greed, love, misery, beauty, poverty, nature, crime, people fleeing their homes in search of better lives are not abstract subjects for classroom debaters; they are existential matters of life and death. The solutions are out there if only we have the courage to admit our failures and confront reality head-on.

For all the darkness Bowden exposed, he identified fear as humanity's greatest threat and remained an optimist at the end. Several years before his sudden death in Las Cruces, New Mexico, on August 30, 2014, he explained to an interviewer how "as a kid, I used to play pickup games of baseball every day after school in Chicago." Chuck reminded him that "you can't step up to the plate without thinking you're going to get a hit. Otherwise, why the hell would you pick up the goddamned bat. Of course I'm an optimist. I want to preserve human joy. I'm not a pessimist. I'm critical because I'm in a ship that's springing leaks and nobody wants to admit it. I want to fix the boat before we sink."[12]

That is his alarm to us, his SOS. And why he wrote until the day he died.

NOTES

Portions of this introduction are adapted, with permission, from "Charles Bowden: Historian of the Future," Journal of the Southwest, Spring 2019, published by the University of Arizona Southwest Center.

1. Jim Harrison, foreword to Erin Almeranti and Mary Martha Miles, eds., *The Charles Bowden Reader* (Austin: University of Texas Press, 2010), vii; Harrison quote from "Charles Bowden's Southwest," Lawrence Clark Powell Lecture, cosponsored by the University of Arizona Southwest Center and School of Information Resources and Library Science, Tucson Festival of Books, March 15, 2015. Video available at C-Span TV.

2. Charles Bowden, *Credo: Ground Zero* (Tucson: Tucson–Pima County Public Library, 2002), 6.

3. William deBuys, foreword to a reissue of Charles Bowden, *Desierto: Memories of the Future* (Austin: University of Texas Press, 2018), x–xi.

4. Bowden, *Credo*, 6.

5. Charles Bowden, conversation with Bill Broyles, 1990.

6. Charles Bowden, conversation with Bill Broyles, 2007.

7. Molly Molloy, e-mail to Bill Broyles, August 12, 2018.

8. Charles Bowden and Lew Kreinberg, *Street Signs Chicago: Neighborhood and Other Illusions of Big-City Life* (Chicago: Chicago Review Press, 1981), 194.

9. deBuys, foreword to Bowden, *Desierto*, 4.

10. Charles Bowden, with photographs by Virgil Hancock, *Chihuahua: Pictures from the Edge* (Albuquerque: University of New Mexico Press, 1996), 4.

11. Aengus Anderson, "The Conversation #54—Charles Bowden," December 12, 2012, Las Cruces, New Mexico, *Journal of the Southwest* (Spring 2019); and available in audio at findtheconversation.com.

12. Ibid.

BEGINNINGS

Charles Bowden and the family dog, Richard III, on the family's small farm at Joliet, Illinois, about January 1947

Over the Rainbow

PEG BOWDEN

I mark the time with my younger brother, Charles Bowden (or "Chuckie," the family moniker until the end of his life), by the music we listened to over the last sixty years. Big brother George always had the radio tuned in to the pop music station, WLS-AM in Chicago, when we were kids, and our baby brother would sweetly sing "How Much Is That Doggie In the Window" (*arf, arf!*) with Patti Page, unabashedly and unafraid.

I miss many things about brother Chuckie—the heady discussions, the family celebrations, the book sharing, his culinary skills— but our connection around music was a unique and powerful glue that cut through any arguments or sibling crises. Even though we lived on opposite ends of the country and often didn't see each other for years, our conversations on the phone usually spun around to this question: "So what are you listening to these days?"

Chuck and I were eager to listen to all kinds of music: pop, classical, jazz, folk, and on occasion some country and western. I was the performing musician in the family, playing the piano and pounding on timpani in orchestras and bands. Chuck never learned to play an instrument, but nonetheless was a keen and discerning listener of most genres.

A prized possession in our Chicago apartment in 1952 was a high-fidelity phonograph. Lying on the carpet in front of the speakers, the three of us listened, discussed, argued, and enjoyed many hours in the living room, handling the vinyl recordings like precious jewels: "Don't scratch the record! Be careful of the needle!"

During our childhood years in Chicago, Chuck and I signed up for a classical music course that I saw advertised in a magazine. As part of the curriculum, we received long-playing 33-1/3 vinyl records delivered to our door. It cost us ten dollars each month, and we split the payment. Pooling our allowance and doing extra chores around the house, we came up with the monthly fee. I was twelve years old and Chuck was ten. It was a big financial commitment for us, and I'm still amazed that we sent in our monthly ten dollars for one year.

We both wondered what made music great. Why were Beethoven and Brahms and Bach at the top of the heap? We would read the small booklet that analyzed music theory, though neither one of us really understood any of it. Then we would listen to the symphonies and concertos as we lay underneath the record player on the floor in the living room, turning up the volume as loud as we could. The year was 1954. Our mother barely tolerated our listening pleasure and usually admonished us to "turn down the noise."

One of my favorite memories was listening to Modest Mussorgsky's *Pictures at an Exhibition*. We loved the last movement, "The Great Gates of Kiev," which builds into a majestic crescendo during the finale. Placing our mother's candlesticks on the lid of the stereo, we would crank up the volume and watch the candles vibrate from the resonance across the lid of the old phonograph. My recollection is that big brother George came up with the candlestick idea. He played in his high school band in Chicago and was developing an interest in classical music. We could feel the music's vibration deep in our gut. Always we were spellbound at the power of the chords, and of course thought it was great fun to see the candlesticks march to the music.

The three of us were stopped cold by the impact of the music. We couldn't come up with words to describe the emotions emanating from the music. For Chuck, I think it was a seminal mo-

Jude and Bo
Bowden, 1964

ment. He was contemplative and quiet, which was unusual for my loquacious brother. The music stopped the mental chatter and redirected the neurons. We saw colors. We saw visions. We had feelings we couldn't explain. I guess we were high on the music.

In 1957 the family moved to Tucson; George went off to college and remained in Illinois. As Chuck and I entered adolescence, we were swept up in the rock 'n' roll of the late 1950s and the music renaissance of the '60s, with Bob Dylan, Joni Mitchell, Leonard Cohen, the Beatles, and Janis Joplin. Chuck went to the Monterey Pop Festival during the "Summer of Love" in 1967. He came back a changed man. He was twenty-two years old, possessed by the message of the music, the artists, the politics, and the blatant sexuality of the cultural revolution. One of his prize possessions was a poster he had torn off a wall during the festival, showcasing Janis Joplin with one breast peeking out of a black velvet dress, her hair cascading over her shoulder. The poster graced his living room wall for forty years.

Chuck bought vinyls of all the artists and literally demanded that I sit down with him and listen. He would search my eyes for a response, a comment. The evolution of the Beatles' music, from *Sgt. Pepper's Lonely Hearts Club Band* to *Abbey Road*, and the power of Grace Slick's voice singing "White Rabbit," would prompt discussion about what this music was all about. It was never background noise, but rather was something to be attended to totally. Like most things with Chuck, his intensity could be overwhelming.

And our attention was enhanced, of course, with some good weed that Chuck always managed to have in his back pocket. By this time, we were living independently and tasting our freedom as young adults. We would sit on my back patio in Tucson, look up at the stars, and dissect the poetry and songs of Leonard Cohen. Yes, we decided that Cohen beat out Bob Dylan as our favorite troubadour.

Leonard Cohen, gravelly voiced, would half-sing, half-recite his epic songs, such as "Suzanne" and "Blue Raincoat." "Y'know, it takes on a totally new meaning when it is sung by the composer," Chuck would muse.

During the 1960s, I was playing in bands and orchestras as a timpanist as well as studying piano at the university. Chuck came to many of my concerts during our teen and young adult years. We often went out with other musicians after a performance, and I remember Chuck's fascination with the discipline and commitment it took to play the classical repertoire. Often he sat offstage and watched the solo performers, curious about their pre-performance

Chuck, Peg, and George Bowden in Tucson, 1968

rituals and preparation. He marveled at the hours of practice and commitment it took to achieve excellence. He peppered the musicians with questions, and they in turn were intrigued with Chuck's curiosity about their musical habits.

There was always something playing on my brother's stereo or radio. When he was writing, Chuck listened to music, but not at the same time. One activity followed the other. Music was never a distraction but was instead an experience unto itself. He concentrated with a fervor that is rare. Becoming focused on an artist or song, he would listen obsessively to a piece that seemed to help illuminate or clarify whatever he was working on. Music took his restless mind to places of peace. And excitement. And inquiry. The music inspired the writing; the writing influenced his listening tastes.

Years later, after the marriages, the divorces, the children, the moves to different parts of the country, Chuck and I still had conversations about music. E-mails about family passages and gatherings were interspersed with new artists and music that caught our interest. Chuck tried to connect with opera, but just didn't like it. His tastes often surprised me. He was beginning to listen to late Beethoven and liked the string quartets. We talked about how the string quartets were often trial runs for the composer's symphonies.

Chuck's tastes were eclectic, ranging from Linda Ronstadt ("Jesus, she has a set of pipes") to Beethoven, Stravinsky (in small doses), and later, Eva Cassidy.

Eva was a favorite. How did this incredible artist escape our attention? He loved Eva's rendition of "Over the Rainbow," claiming she drew more nuance from that song than Judy Garland had. Once, he sent me a tape of ten versions of this song to prove his point. He was right.

Chuck could be quite a talker, often dominating the room with his ideas. But when listening to a piece of music that captivated him, he became quiet and often emotional. No words. No attempts to prove a point. Occasionally, he would tear up. He went to a different place in his heart.

PEG BOWDEN is Charles Bowden's older sister. Her first book, *A Land of Hard Edges*, captures the personal stories of the migration of desperate people across the Sonoran Desert. Her second book, *A Stranger at My Door*, a memoir about her experience with a migrant from Guatemala, will be released in 2019.

On Campus

DAVID F. ALLMENDINGER

Bowden must have arrived in Madison to start graduate work in the fall of 1966. I'm fairly certain of this. I was a student in Madison at the time and remember meeting him. He was the second Arizona graduate to arrive in two successive years. Both had studied American history in Tucson with Jack Wilson (aka Raymond Jackson Wilson and R. J. Wilson), then a recent Wisconsin PhD, who later taught at both Wisconsin and Smith College. The first of these two Arizonans was Susan Horsman, who had known Charles in Tucson. Susan arrived in September 1965; she and I married that December. Charles arrived the next fall. I have a memory of him staying in our apartment briefly, and I have a letter from Jack, written in April 1966, telling me that Charles was coming to Madison in the fall on a Woodrow Wilson fellowship, that this boy was a real find, and that all of us should take special care of him, though I didn't have to marry him. The key figure was Jack.

Charles and his dissertation got tossed around between three different advisors and two committees before the showdown. William R. Taylor must have been his first advisor, but Taylor left Madison around 1968. Jack Wilson left Arizona and was in Madison for the year 1969–1970, I think. Jack then became the real dissertation advisor through the final draft. He must have served on the first committee, perhaps even as its chair for a time. Jack left for Smith (his second appointment there) after one year at Madison, but certainly continued to read Charles's work.

Charles and his wife, Zada Edgar, came to Northampton (Massachusetts) for a year or two when Jack returned to Smith. They

Charles Bowden at the University of Wisconsin–Madison library

rented an old farmhouse in the hill town of Ashfield. Charles continued to work on George M. Beard and neurasthenia, and Zada took classes at Smith (in French?). This was when we really got to know Bowden, in 1970–1972. There was a lot of talk about dissertations and neurasthenia. So far as I know, in those years at least, Charles was not involved in organized antiwar or civil rights causes. He was an intellectual, radical in his own way, in his work. Even in appearance, to judge by his photographs, he never changed.

Jack must have tried to shape Charles's manuscript into a form the committee would find acceptable; he might even have wanted to approve the dissertation as Charles submitted it, though I don't know that. Neither do I remember who else was on that committee or when they issued their first verdict. Charles told me that he submitted the identical manuscript (before spring 1974) a second time to a committee at Wisconsin. They refused to consider it, he said; they would not even reject it again, he said. Daniel T. Rodgers, later of Princeton, was acting as Charles's handoff advisor. I doubt that Rodgers ever met the candidate. There may have been no other committee members. Madison was in flux.

Charles's unorthodox style—punctuation, capitalization, language, sentence structure—must have put the professors off. Charles suspected they (or Mr. Rodgers) took offense at his "unseemly thoughts," but I doubt that. I'd been hoping that he would give in on the punctuation, and so on, and get his degree, but he wouldn't. He dared them to reject him, and so they did. By the time he published *Down by the River*, I noticed, the offending style had almost disappeared, but his language and thought had survived.

The problem became his style. I don't know when he adopted it, but he had committed himself to it by the time he wrote the first chapter. I remember sensing that it meant trouble in Madison. I don't remember warning him. But he knew. He insisted on the trouble. (The profs in Madison weren't the last to object, by the way. Even some of his later reviewers complained about it, long after he had toned it down.) I think he became reconciled to not squandering his life in a university. His Pulitzer nomination must have been sweet. I wonder how the dissertation reads now.

Around that time, 1970–1972, we had a number of opportunities to talk. We took some day trips around New England, new territory for both of us. We drove to the libraries in New Haven and Boston. And we made some excursions into the hill towns of western Massachusetts—Ashfield, Chesterfield, and so forth. On those drives he would talk about Beard and neurasthenia, and what Charles was finding in his research. But we never talked about teaching, the historical profession, or our "careers" (hilarious irony). I sensed that he wanted nothing more than to write in some new way about subjects no one had addressed.

DAVID F. ALLMENDINGER attended graduate school at Wisconsin (1961–1967) and taught at Smith College (1969–1972) and the University of Delaware (1974–2003). He has written three books, including *Nat Turner and the Rising in Southampton County* (2014).

Taking History Off Campus

CHARLES BOWDEN

Excerpted from a Charles Bowden letter to David F. Allmendinger, May 6, 1974. Allmendinger explains, "He sent me a letter in which he thanked me for sending him a book, Michael Lesy's *Wisconsin Death Trip*. He wasn't taken with it. And he was teasing me about finding a job in the East and abandoning a fallback plan to head West and look for useful work. I don't remember him ever saying anything about teaching, one way or another, and didn't know until recently that he'd ever had that experience. Hard to believe he enjoyed it."

Allmendinger adds that Bowden "typed most of it on a single sheet of paper, front and back, maybe from a legal pad—maybe Zada Edgar's. He mentions friends Steve Nissenbaum and Jack Wilson, among others. On a second sheet from the same yellow pad, he added some thoughts in longhand about recommended readings, and on the outside of the envelope, he typed a couple of last-minute quotations:

"'They'll give you their bodies but never their minds. Chorus: I didn't know it was this way in Baltimore.'—Dance Hall Girls, a local ballad.

"'It frightens the horses.'—testimony of a Navajo against the strip mine at Black Mesa, Arizona."

At the time, Chuck and Zada were living on Lee Street in Tucson and Allmendinger on Amstel Avenue in Newark, Delaware. The following is typed roughly as Chuck did, mixing capitals and lowercases on proper nouns, titles, and first words in sentences, though his strikeouts are omitted. The letter foreshadows Bowden-the-e-mailer, who dashed off similar letters from his computer at a prodigious rate. If he ever tried texting, he must have felt stifled by its restrictive limits on length.

David and susan and kinder ...,
    what are you doing? who are you doing it with? why are you do-ing it? for that matter what is anyone doing? steve hasn't answered a letter or call for nigh a year. jack seems to have been struck dumb. and the milktrain doesn't stop here anymore. Are you teaching? are you being paid for teaching? are you enmeshed in some other contribution to the republic? do you work in a gunpowder fac-tory? susan, have you gone the way of all female flesh and entered law school? do you have a garden or do you have photochemical smog? have you published the connecticut valley death trip? i sup-pose i once grunted the fact that I used to live in black river falls, and thus the book quickened the pulse. it sort of haunts (except for the hateful think piece tacked to the end): what the fuck do historians do that normally locks these shack wacky faces out of history? Answer: they explain the past.

THE NARRATIVE METHOD

last summer I talked with a university vice president, a rich lobby-ist, and the dean of the college of agriculture, and talking my talk emerged a ghost. the condition lasted five or six months. i wrote a book defending the central arizona project for the lobbyist. i wrote it as a memoir in the first person. it's almost four hundred pages long. you see he had written the book first and he took it to many presses and they said, Man, this is dog shit. Now the same readers say, wow, this is the real stuff, so i'll probably be a pub-lished author only my name won't be on the book and the book won't be true and if anyone reads the book and believes it and acts on its conclusion they will contribute to the death of the american west. all this leaves me less than elated. but, remember how fellers would talk about their army bit—won't trade it for the world!—well i feel some of that. of course no one would trade with me. but it did give me a professional satisfaction, like the perfect crime. it also gave me a four or five month spell of manic depression and near starvation which has only lifted since mayday. for quite a while i felt i was on the enemies list, only i did not know whose list. while i was wasting my vital essence making money as a ghost and then working back toward a simple cadaver, zada pursued the law and wound up on law review and other spots of honor. she has just finished her first year and smacks of veniality. two things i hate: lawyers and doctors. of course i only consort with her in her female capacity. this morning she is downtown interviewing with the country attorney's office for a summer job torturing the communities miscreants.

while she was swallowing gobs of jurisprudence, i continued my lifetime task of trying to get a phd. but it seems i try too little. i sent back the identical manuscript they had rejected and lo and behold they refused to consider. thus they will not even reject it again. my new advisor—a soul claiming to be daniel rodgers—decryed the weird language and unseemly thoughts of the piece, but said if i tossed out half and followed his cogent clues for the rest, i just might prove worthy of the hallowed title. i failed to reply.

then come may i took a job at the Office of Arid Lands u of a. object: assemble a bibliography with explanatory essay on water and energy in arid lands. translation: stop the baddies from strip mining our mother earth. been on the job about three weeks and am a maniac. get up around dawn and read until my eyes and my liquor fail. the lusts and sputters of my life are coming together. i came back home to watch arizona die, and i'm going to get my chance. if things go as the pres and his urchins in the energy business plan, i'll say you can kiss the surviving remnant goodbye by 1985 or 1990. you can kiss the four corners area goodbye right now.

mr. peabody's coal company done hauled it away. anyway, i'm to put together this thing in five months and travel round the western states chatting with the mad hatters that are doing the deed. spend my time reading esoteric studies done by the office of coal research or the u s petroleum council or the eps boys or other such scum. and man they are. a teaser: to produce 100,000 barrels of syncrude from oil shale a plant generates enough solid waste (oil soaked rock) to cover a forty acre plot to depth of one foot, each day. they plan to fill "topographical depressions" i.e. canyons. the four corners power plant smoke was the only sign of human life visible in the southwest in the gemini photos—the plume was 230 miles long. the plant generates more filth than new york or la (some say both combined). they're building five more right now. by the year 2000 40% to 60% of the daily water runoff in the us will be needed to cool power plants. Babble babble. you see everything you ever hated about middle america middle class life is true: it's a death trap.

on the other hand I'm still mired in the joys of horticulture. bear with me: cucumbers (Armenian, and Ohio MF 17-pickling), beans (Cherokee wax and Japanese Yard long), squash (zucchini), peppers (Anaheim Chili and Yolo Wonder Ball), tomatoes (San Marazana [Marzano] plum and Delicious beefsteak), corn (Illini-Xtra Sweet and Butter & Sugar), cantaloupe (Heart of Gold), sunflowers (Russian Mammoth and Mexican-tithonia), morning glories (Heavenly Blue), passion vine, marigolds, (First Lady orange and yellow), daisies (Gloriosa and Shasta), zinnia (Giants), roses, (Don Juan, climbing), gardenias (vetchi [veitchii]), four o'clocks, naked ladies, mexican wandering jew, chrysanthemums (couple of dozen), oregano, fennel, thyme, tansy, and succulents, plus water lily, water hyacinth, and horsetail. plus bees, carp, and gold fish. Heir Ich stehe Ich kann nichts anders. i'd like to get chickens to keep Job [his dog] company.

the last time i spoke with you the plan was to pursue a westering pattern. i see by your new address you are practicing stealth. next year i suppose it will be bermuda, then san marino, the kurdish lands, bangcok, microoceania, pitacairns, and so on. this will be not help. true, you miss the smog engulfing the great plains, but watch out of oil slicks, leaks from coastal nuclear plants. I think you should reconsider.

enough nattering. thank you very much for the wish book. i recently went diving down on the gulf of california and I saw two rays (or skates or whatever you call them)—well, it looked like they were mating. thought you should know. Two other things I've learned recently. oysters can change their sex, and montezuma always had a hot chocolate before retiring to his harem. and oh yes, I read a nice line in an essay by a texan: "when I dance with that ole girl my dingus gets as hard as chinese arithmetic." what else? beer is selling at ten cents a bottle here. pinto beans—frijoles—run 75 cents to $1 a pound. And yes, I read the transcripts. I could not believe that anyone could degrade the presidency after lyndon johnson. Now that you've mastered book wrapping why not try something big like a letter or phone call?

chuckzadajob and a cast of thousands

A WORD FROM OUR SPONSOR [HANDWRITTEN ADDITIONAL PAGE BY BOWDEN]

Those Nader studies are impressive pieces of work and as a Westerner in exile (or flight or psychotic alienation) I think you should read some—you have? Well how was I to know? Try *Vanishing Air, Water Wasteland* or the *Damming the West*. A good book on energy is called Energy by John Holdren and Philip Herrera. Holdren is a physicist and he wrote the first half. This you should read. Herrera is a journalist and is best ignored.

If you crave reports on the real world there is a newspaper ($10.00 per year) called: *High Country: The Environmental Biweekly*, published in Lander, Wyoming by a man claiming to be Tom Bell. I've read three issues and it's not bad.

If none of this gives you a cheap thrill, I still recommend my old standby—*Never Cry Wolf* by Farley Mowat and/ or *The Congressman Who Loved Flaubert* by Ward Just.

And by all means watch Upstairs/ Downstairs on NET.

There. I've tried to help. And on all occasions deny that Patty Hearst has been brainwashed. Women must be taken seriously, even the rich.

Street Signs with Lew Kreinberg and Charles Bowden

BARBARA HOULBERG

I met Chuck Bowden in Madison, Wisconsin, where he was a graduate student. I was introduced to him by Lew Kreinberg, who wanted me to meet a fellow history student, brilliant—who had become a friend and seemed a "fellow traveler." I think I may have been introduced to Chuck at the 602 Club, a hangout for art, history, and English majors—primarily graduate students. Lew and Chuck were obvious "like thinkers" politically, and both had spent years in Chicago and knew the town well.

Chuck was married to Zada Edgar, a short, freckled redhead, funny, smart, and erratic. They invited us to dinner, and I remember an apartment of the natural sort for those days: fabric wall hangings, bed mattress on the floor and the same for the dinner table. Zada was a terrific cook. Wine was the drink of the day. It was hard not to be drawn to Chuck. Very tall, slim and with a slow, deliberate voice and presentation. I remember thinking that I would like to write down everything he said. I remember thinking that his feet were small for so tall a man. Zada laughed a lot, and her bursts of energy and enthusiasm were almost disconcerting. Lew called her "Zada potata."

Later, I remember Lew remarking that Chuck's doctoral thesis was rejected as his major professor said that "it read like a novel." Such horseshit. The man was a writer!

Lew and Chuck talked a lot about Chicago and Lew wanted to write a book about neighborhoods, the Mayor, and other things peculiar to Chicago. Lew *loved* Chicago. I think he convinced Chuck that it would be terrific subject matter. Lew had been working for years as a community organizer in Chicago, but he must have realized that he needed help; he couldn't write well, and he didn't have the kind of discipline needed for a project like this, alone. Lew could tell stories and was a great people watcher, and had a righteous sense of outrage at the inequities of power, money, and influence. He worked for the Jewish Council on Urban Affairs, a community organization. So, the two of them collaborated. Lew would write or tape and send it to Chuck in Arizona and Chuck would rewrite and retape and send it back to Lew. The upshot was that although Lew provided anecdotes and some ideas, Chuck wrote the book. It was a great gift that he gave his friend Lew and provided the validity for almost everything Lew did subsequently.

Lew and I visited Chuck in Tucson. I can't remember if my son Paul was with us for the first or second visit. But I do remember that Chuck and Zada had a goldfish pond with koi or goldfish in it and that they were raising bees. One of the marvelous things about Chuck is that he was constantly engaged by new research—bees, bats, scallops, cacti, and on. I think Paul learned about the joy of research and study, and certainly bicycles, from Chuck. In fact, Chuck was a role model for Paul and passed on his love of bicycles. Just as Chuck built his own bicycle, Paul altered and built several bicycles during his lifetime.

So we met Bo, Chuck's mother [Berdina], a large woman with just as large a heart. Quite a talker, as was her son. And we met his father, Jude. Bo called him Mr. Bowden. Mr. Bowden talked about apples. Seems that was the part of the Midwest that he missed the most. When he died I planted an apple tree at San Bar Beach, and called it "Mr. Bowden." It's still there. Years later, Bo told me that Mr. Bowden wanted to leave Chuck something toward his house in Tucson, thinking that Chuck might not make a lot of money.

Lew Kreinberg and Charles Bowden at a lakeside beach

Mr. Bowden, he wanted Chuck to have an anchor and knew he was not a businessman. I remember lots of ashtrays and cigarettes around Mr. Bowden, as he sat and read. Chuck's mother, Bo, was the kind of woman who had eternally outstretched arms that any-one could move inside of. She was fond of Zada, and probably of Kathy [Dannreuther], and most likely would not have been able to find fault with anyone.

I remember Chuck took us to Mexican restaurants in Tucson, and I could barely eat the food—Lew loved it. Chuck also had given me a book, *Yes Is Better Than No*, by Byrd Baylor, an author he knew. I *loved* the book and over the years have bought many copies of it.

Chuck came to San Bar several times, once after he had had valley fever and needed to sleep. He slept for days it seemed, many days, barely rising to eat or go down and dip into Lake Michigan. On one trip, he and Lew spent many hours on the beach drinking, I think, Tavola red and sunbathing. I remember seeing those guys sleeping in the sun, with their shirts off, and thinking how lovely that must be. On another recovery trip, Chuck had a broken leg that needed time to mend.

We once drove to Tucson in an old elegant car that had air-conditioning. Lew wouldn't let us turn it on because it used energy—the same reason he would never let me hook up my twelve-dollar washing machine when we lived on Rockwell. We had to conserve energy. So I suffered across the desert. I must have told the story because the next time Chuck came to Chicago to work on a book, he lugged a big old window air-conditioner with him—I really suffered during the summers in Chicago. As I recall, the bad wiring in the building wouldn't allow us to use the air-conditioner—ironic.

Some of us walk in pain and always will—mine from my son Paul's suicide. I suspect Chuck's pain came because he had the trait of sensing, feeling, what others feel.

Maybe it is evident, but I think Chuck is the most important man I have ever known, the greatest man, and he has been a critical part of my life, as well as Paul's. He introduced me to the most important books and authors I have read, and all of which Paul read as well: Ken Kesey's *Sometimes a Great Notion*, Wendell Berry, *Lonesome Dove*, *Yes Is Better Than No*, Zapata, *Zen and the Art of Motorcycle Maintenance*, *West with the Night*, Frankl, *Meaning of Life*, *Cry of Angels*, Aldo Leopold, and Ed Abbey come to mind immediately. And strangely, John Berger. Chuck found him before I knew about his writing—and my field is supposed to be Art. Chuck said Berger made more sense than anyone.

BARBARA HOULBERG, an artist and teacher, was at one time married to Lewis Kreinberg, who coauthored *Street Signs Chicago* with Charles Bowden. Bowden's elegy to her son Paul appears in a catalogue for the exhibition *Paul Dickerson, 1961–1997* at the American Fine Art Co. New York July 21–September 3, 1998.

Chuck Becomes a Reporter

KATHLEEN DANNREUTHER

When Chuck and I started dating in 1976, he asked me to read a manuscript of his that our friend Lawrence Clark Powell was shopping around to Alfred A. Knopf and the University of Texas Press. The manuscript, published by the University of Texas Press, became *Killing the Hidden Waters*, which has been in print since 1977. During the next four years, Chuck survived by piecing together some freelance work and serving as a consultant on several large-scale humanities projects that I directed for the Tucson Public Library (now the Pima County Public Library).

During this time, the *Tucson Citizen* published a feature article, written by Lifestyle editor Dick Vonier, on what a great institution the library was. To this day, after thirty years as a library manager, I haven't read a better article about the role an outstanding public library plays in its community. Chuck was down to pretty much his last $7.50 and beginning to realize that he needed to find a "real" job. So, I suggested that he talk to Vonier about becoming a feature, or at least freelance, writer for the *Citizen*. Dick assigned him a couple of freelance projects and then, smartly, hired him as a reporter in 1981. They had similar personalities, were intellectually compatible, and both appreciated fine writing.

It's almost too much to believe today, but the eighties were the heyday of Tucson journalism, with the *Citizen* and the *Arizona Daily Star* squaring off as rival newspapers. The *Citizen* boasted a stable of very fine investigative reporters and feature writers. After several months, Vonier gave Chuck carte blanche to choose and develop his own stories. As I predicted, Chuck became a star.

He was a favorite with the reading public as well as with his colleagues. His distinctive first-person style, a type of "gonzo" journalism in the best sense of the word (he greatly admired Hunter S. Thompson), became something other reporters tried to emulate. That, and his ability to make connections where none seemed obvious, made him a great reporter. The fact that he churned out this brilliant stuff at a fast clip made him much beloved by his editors.

Besides his admiration for Dick Vonier, Chuck was also a big fan of David Mitchell, the *Citizen*'s managing editor. When Mitchell accepted a job with the Vancouver, Washington, newspaper, *The Columbian*, he asked Chuck to move to Vancouver and work for him. Unbelievably, Chuck accepted, but he didn't want to go alone. I refused to move without a job or health insurance, so Chuck proposed, saying, "I really want you to come with me. Let's get married." I accepted and we were married at the Pima County courthouse, with Larry and Fay Powell as our witnesses.

Chuck went off to Vancouver to start his job, while I stayed behind to sell the house on Ninth Street and resign my job. Chuck's dad, who may have sensed that Chuck would never be financially successful, had given him the house before we met. I don't recall if it was an outright gift, or if his dad paid $10,000 and Chuck took out a $10,000 mortgage, which he paid off as quickly as he could. Either way, the house was free and clear, which gave Chuck a certain independence. Chuck called me from Vancouver one week— seven days—later, and said, "I've never seen the sun. I'm coming home." After living most of his life in the desert, he was depressed by overcast skies and constant humidity. "Okay," I thought, "it's a good thing I didn't quit my wonderful library job yet or sell the house." Chuck's buddies at the *Citizen* welcomed him back with open arms, no questions asked.

After some time back at the newspaper, Chuck started getting restless. He resented being married and asked me for a divorce. We split up amicably (I was his second wife, and he never remarried), remaining friends for a very long time, during which he often came to me for constructive criticism on articles and books he was working on.

Close to our separation, Chuck received a letter from the Pulitzer Prize committee notifying him that two of his articles had been nominated in the feature writing category. One was a four-page article on child abuse, entitled "A Mother Fights through Her Anger and Agony to Change System." The other nominee was another four-page article that required a substantial amount of background research, including a hike across the desert during which he pretended to be an immigrant crossing the US-Mexico border, from El Saguaro to Tacna, in one-hundred-plus degree midsummer temperatures. A ridiculous project, to be sure, but one for which Chuck probably deserved the Pulitzer simply for walking across those killing fields.

What followed was bizarre, to say the least. First, Chuck received a letter from the *Wall Street Journal* editor, who chaired the feature category committee, announcing that the committee had selected him to receive the Pulitzer. Then a second letter arrived bearing the awful news that the Pulitzer family had overturned the committee's recommendation. Instead of acknowledging Chuck's work on child-abuse victims and dying migrants, the Pulitzer was going to the author of an article on the new 747 airliner. I'll never forget the *WSJ* editor's apology in that second letter: "I'm so sorry. You deserved this."

Chuck was disappointed but undaunted. He was used to being turned down. His doctoral committee, for various reasons, had turned down his PhD dissertation at the University of Wisconsin. The University of Arizona Office of Arid Lands Studies had rejected the report that became *Killing the Hidden Waters*, calling it "unscientific" writing. Then the Pulitzer denial.

Chuck had the last laugh. He went on to write more than two dozen books and hundreds of articles appealing to readers all over

THE WALL STREET JOURNAL   DOW JONES & COMPANY, INC.

Publishers

22 CORTLANDT STREET - NEW YORK, N. Y. 10007

ROBERT L. BARTLEY
EDITOR

April 19, 1984

Dear Mr. Bowden:

I thought you might appreciate a note saying that those of us on the feature writing jury for the Pulitzer award had picked your pieces as the best of those we'd read. You were the only nominee who was on everyone's short list. On a personal level, you were my choice all along.

I haven't read the entry the Board moved in as the winner in this category, but you can at least have the small consolation of knowing that one group of professionals greatly admired your writing.

Sincerely,

[signature: Robert Bartley]

RLB:pb

Mr. Charles Bowden
Tuscon Citizen
Box 26767
Tuscon, Arizona 85726

Robert L. Bartley, chair of Pulitzer feature writing committee, letter to
Charles Bowden, April 19, 1984

the world. He became a hero to activists dedicated to preserving the southwestern landscape and lifestyle, and the symbolic heir to Edward Abbey's legacy.

KATHLEEN DANNREUTHER, a Tucson native, spent most of her career as manager and administrator with the Pima County Public Library. She also worked as a City of Tucson grants coordinator and as Dr. Andrew Weil's grants and development director.

Let the Tortoises Roll

NORMA COILE

I vividly remember Chuck Bowden's first *Tucson Citizen* newspaper story in 1981, an essay on Sabino Canyon, the Sonoran Desert oasis beloved by more than one million visitors a year, told through his memories as a Tucson teenager.

I can still picture it, feel it pounding in my chest: Chuck and his male friends, shaggy haired, dangerously sexy, cruising up the canyon with rock 'n' roll blaring, hurtling cigarette butts out the windows of some iconic '60s car into the black night.

Stop these good times, he insisted at the end of his riveting story; stop letting cars into this canyon.

I don't have to consult the paper's clip files to remember the last line: "Let the tortoises roll."

He'd burst into the *Tucson Citizen* newsroom, refusing to go to Human Resources, announcing to the city editor that no good writers get hired that way.

Assigned a desk across from mine, he looked at me through squinted eyes and asked, "Who sets the pace around here?" I pointed out a stenographer of a corporate reporter who produced reams of copy; don't worry, I added, no one can remember a thing she wrote yesterday. And over there, I noted, is our long-ball hitter, the mad dog with feet on desk and hands behind head, waiting for the rare target worth his investigation.

Chuck's gaze was dismissive as he immediately scoped out for himself the true competition in the room: Dick Vonier, the city editor with blazing talent, gently seductive wit, and self-professed boredom that led him to punch at barroom rivals much bigger than he was. Vonier had somehow arrived in low-key Tucson via the heyday *Milwaukee Journal* and *Life* magazine, where his features had included early tales of Mick Jagger and the Stones on the road.

Bowden and Vonier circled each other, went on a fishing trip, denied to each other (or at least to me) ever sleeping with the gorgeous exotic ex-Mormon reporter who had fled to the desert after throwing a Georgia O'Keeffe print at her husband in their DC condo. The two went on to give readers muscular, literary, cinematic, and unforgettable Bowden stories for the rest of Vonier's abbreviated life. Among them: a portfolio on child sex abuse ("kiddie fuck" was Chuck's working title for the story), border death, and drug violence that made it to the Pulitzer Prize finals for an obscure Gannett pm in Tucson, Arizona.

Chuck, who claimed for a time to have bedded every woman he'd written about, was a cynic whose searing descriptions of a brutal world cried out for humans to do better in this life.

His writing was so distinct, so powerful, and so Hemingwayesque that jealous newsroom wags held "Explain that Bowden lede" contests. "A herd of broken bottles had plowed across his face." A: he was a hopeless drunk; B: he was in a Coca-Cola bottling explosion; C: who the hell knows.

He said the secret to life was never believing your own press.

Soon the *Citizen*'s blowhard publisher called on him to headline a gangbuster pro-development, pro-freeway-building project so the publisher could sell more papers and get them to homes quicker. The story goes that he broke this news to Chuck while both were at a national Gannett awards banquet to collect Chuck's many prizes. Chuck quit in a flash, soon followed by Vonier, who was fired during a particularly extended drinking binge.

Let's start a magazine, Chuck said. The two mocked up a brilliant prototype, shopped it to a Tucson couple with DuPont family money, and *City Magazine* was born.

Charles Bowden, *City Magazine* editor, and Richard S. "Dick" Vonier, *City Magazine* publisher, about 1986

When Vonier moved to hire me, his off-and-on lover of five years, as the magazine's political writer, Bowden intervened by interviewing me alone at a cattlemen's club, the kind of place that in less-correct days would have had a bull's testicles nailed over the door. Chuck was in a kind of rapture, gushing, "You feel the chemicals pulsing in this room? It's the developers, working their million-dollar deals. It's so thick you can feel it on your skin. That's what I want you to write about. You always have the real story in your notebook, but you don't get it onto the page."

I suppose that was the time to reveal I didn't feel anything in that bar except the struggling air-conditioner, but I held back.

The magazine was the kind of place where Chuck might come in one morning and announce, "It cost us $60 in red wine, but I got the story," then stroll into his office to find novelist Edward Abbey waiting, or some scowling, sexist, bloated cops or politicos Chuck loved because they knew where the skeletons were buried.

During the magazine's short but fabulous run, I drove to Phoenix now and then to make sure the Arizona Press Club included alternative publications in its newswriting contests. There, reporters from *New Times*, the racy weekly that routinely brought down Arizona governors, worshipped at the altar of Bowden and begged to know how he wrote so beautifully.

I shared the few nuts and bolts I could—"You have to wake up really early to beat Chuck, he writes at 4 in the morning"—and then I'd insist: you can't learn to write, or think, like Chuck. Something, I never figured out exactly what, went so right in his childhood that he wasn't co-opted by the mundane, rote education system—or else, he was so original in his thinking and his voice that he miraculously transcended it.

I'm convinced you have to be born with a talent like Chuck Bowden's.

NORMA COILE has been a Tucson journalist for nearly forty years, working as a writer and an editor for the *Tucson Citizen*, then *City Magazine*, and now the *Arizona Daily Star*.

The Jimi Hendrix of Journalism

TONY DAVIS

I met Chuck Bowden in late summer or early fall 1981 and had no idea I was face to face with a budding genius. I must admit that despite his intellect, height, and imposing build, he didn't make much of a first impression on me. I knew little or nothing of his work—some loose talk about one or two books written and one column I'd seen on the op-ed page of the *Star* were my main exposure to the man, and they had left me cold. His column seemed a bit off the beaten path—an attack on Tucson's highly popular "Beat the Peak" water-saving program in which he argued that reducing the short-term costs of growth by holding down peak water consumption stopped the community from thinking clearly about the long-term costs of growth to the broader water supply. The water issue that was to become my life had flared briefly across my consciousness back in 1976, right after my move to Tucson, because the city council's liberal majority had been recalled for jacking up water rates in mid-June, but it had quickly receded into the background. I was the social services reporter, carefully chronicling the effects of Ronald Reagan's new presidency on the poor, and saw all journalism at the time through that lens. From all appearances, Bowden seemed like just the latest in a long list of feature writers to showcase their wares at the *Citizen* for fame and fortune, a path I'd decided to abandon years ago in favor of what I saw as hard-hitting reporting. That was one of my dumbest perceptions ever.

Bowden was assigned to the desk across from mine and gave little clue as to his own political leanings—I don't even remember what he said his political outlook was. All I can remember was that the pace of copy stepped up dramatically the moment he took over the seat. His stories were vital, had flair and color and wit and passion, and were unlike anything I'd read in a daily newspaper. In retrospect, he was the journalistic equivalent of Jimi Hendrix, a writer who broke all the rules and got away with it, with the daring of a riverboat gambler and the flourish of a Jimmy Breslin.

A history major in college, Bowden had no daily newspaper experience and had never attended j-school. He ranted and raved about whatever was on his mind and wore T-shirts bearing slogans like "Fuck Bechtel." He gave not a clue of the dark side that was to emerge later—the womanizing, the chain-smoking, the drinking, the egomania, the disdain in which he held most conventional journalism. He seemed unassuming, almost gentle in his intellectual presence. Strictly in hindsight, I wonder now if one reason he came to appreciate me as a friend was that I didn't automatically see him as the next Hemingway or Abbey, as many others did. He not only didn't suffer fools gladly, but he hated suck-ups.

Then, my life changed in a way that rocketed our worlds together. The environmental beat's previous occupant burned out, switched to the features desk, and I, feeling stale on the social ser-vices–poverty beat and seeking a new journalistic identity, literally ran into the deputy managing editor's office, begged for the job, and got it. I started the next day—the day that then interior sec-retary James Watt killed Orme Dam, a billion-dollar pipe dream boondoggle that would have flooded an Indian reservation north-east of Phoenix to store more water for the Central Arizona Proj-ect, a four-billion-dollar water project that may well have been a boondoggle but was no pipe dream. Already under construction, it was someday going to pump water 336 miles uphill from the Colorado River to Tucson. For years this dam had been a given for most of Arizona's water establishment (save Congressman Mo

Udall), which had assumed it could run roughshod over the small coalition of environmentalists and Indians who had opposed it, and now it was dead. Much of the credit for the change was being given to Steve Meissner, the *Arizona Daily Star*'s water reporter who had written a long, detailed, award-winning, but somewhat drab, series over the summer on how this dam would destroy an Indian tribe's culture by flooding the reservation. Bowden scoffed at that theory, saying that the dam was killed because of its high cost, not by a newspaper series, adding that Meissner's series was poor. "He just didn't have anything. No drama, no vision, nothing." That was my first real glimpse of the man's iconoclastic nature. He would rail in his columns against overdevelopment, persecution of Indians, the deaths of undocumented and illegal immigrants, the plight of striking copper workers, the subdividing of Tucson, and always, the city's unwillingness to deal with its scarcity of water by limiting growth. Then he would turn to me and say, "I only do objective reporting." Counterintuitive and devil's advocate to the core, he had views that were often surprising and occasionally dismaying. Although I'm sure he'd hate Trump today for ten different reasons, I can still recall him belting out what to me seemed like mindless populism when he sided with parents in a nearby Mormon community who were fighting to keep the likes of *Lord of the Flies* and *Of Mice and Men* out of their kids' classes. "Who do you want deciding what kids will read? Parents or bureaucrats?" sniffed Bowden after belting out eighty inches on the dispute. Shit, Chuck, I wanted teachers to make those decisions, but I might as well have been talking to a wall. Jane Erikson, the former *Star* reporter who in 1981 was covering the controversy for the Benson *News-Sun*, and won an award for it, tells me that "Chuck gave that story the best coverage of any reporter, except me, even though the [Phoenix] *Republic* and the *Star* attempted to cover it."

We would argue over minutiae; talk about books, music, and

movies; and rant together against the decline of the newspaper business that has seemingly never stopped. Chuck would alternately praise and disparage his work, calling himself a laborer in the "fluff factory," compared to "you heavy hitters" (such as me) who wrote long, tome-like, detailed analyses of issues and accounts of dry government reports outlining the ills of pollution and groundwater depletion.

He fed me with story ideas, most that I never picked up on for two months because I was so heavily into my own world. He lectured me constantly on the evils of groundwater pumping and untrammeled growth, suggesting that someday all Arizona civilization would collapse, the thought of which brought him unbridled glee. And he gently, and not so gently, poked at my liberal tendencies, even as he disguised his own ideology with ducks and dodges of my probing questions.

When we talked about journalistic objectivity, for instance, I mocked the idea that both sides always had to be given equal treatment, adding, "Would you give equal time to Adolf Hitler?" His quick response: "Wouldn't you have loved to have interviewed Hitler?" When Reagan ran for reelection against Jimmy Carter's former vice president, Chuck disparaged Walter Mondale as a near nonentity, never giving me a clue of whom he voted for. And on and on.

The context of our workplace was a newspaper that had rocked uncertainly between a writer's and an editor's paper for many years and was just on the edge of a long slide into economic and journalistic oblivion. Never a particularly gutsy operation, the *Citizen* was best known, when I arrived in July 1976, as a haven for drinkers and smokers and pseudocowboys, and a prisoner of its right-wing editorial page. My first day on the job, I overheard news editor Ted Craig (who would later try to downplay his growing conservatism by recalling his days as a vanguard of hard-hitting journalism at the *Arkansas Gazette* during the 1950s Little Rock school desegregation wars) say, "It used to be that it was easy here to find someone who wanted to go out and get drunk or get laid. Not anymore." As time passed, after Gannett bought the *Citizen* from local millionaire Bill Small in December 1976, the paper slowly professionalized and grew more honest, but its commitment to gutsy, edgy, long-term investigative or in-depth reporting never seemed consistent to me. It seemed to prefer writers to reporters and was often more like a literary magazine than a newspaper, making it a perfect haven for someone like Chuck Bowden. But I was always trying to push its envelope in a different way, trying to make it a vanguard for reporting on Tucson's current or looming problems with population growth.

Over time, I realized how much better a journalist Chuck was than any of the rest of us at the *Citizen*, how his insights penetrated more deeply into the human spirit and soul than did any of our conventional investigative efforts. He brought people and issues to life when we buried them in statistics and reports. He was one part poet, one part novelist, one part conservationist, one part dirt-digger, and one part bottom-feeder, scraping literary insights from the dregs of the earth. He walked through Cabeza Prieta National Wildlife Refuge in midsummer, over the objections of his bosses, to give us a feel of what it was like for Mexican immigrants to cross the border. He rode a semi from Tucson to Los Angeles to give us a feel for the life of a trucker. He spent days on the margins and in the heart of the 1983 copper strike to show how it had eaten into the souls of strikers and scabs alike. He devoted four pages to the story of a rape victim to, in his editor's words, "get at rape." He shunned the water issue I had glommed onto, not because he didn't wish to compete, but because he felt "water is only one story," and he had already written it years ago in his now-seminal book *Killing the Hidden Waters*. The day after the October 1983 floods, he caught the city's contradictory moods about flood destruction by noting the clapping of hands as condominiums fell into the

Rillito River, and the absurd theater of bartender Jim Anderson racing with gewgaws out of his apartment to save them from high waters. He took us to the scenes of destruction and conflict and made us feel as if we were there. He took us to the scene of Earth First!'s symbolic cracking of the Glen Canyon Dam and wrote the first big magazine-like piece on Dave Foreman as a combination of Merle Haggard and John Muir. Or, maybe, Hank Williams. He disdained the journalistic conventions of the time that we should send reporters to other cities to see how they tackled their growth problems, saying that the purpose of reporters was to tell stories, not write conventional accounts of urban affairs.

He verbally disparaged developers, consultants, engineers, road builders, and the public officials who fed the region's growth machine. He worked closely with the last genius editor I have seen, the late Richard Vonier, who knew how to shape literature with the same élan that he knew how to direct an award-winning, five-part investigative series. The two smoked and drank together like eighteen-year-olds, alternating talk of sexual conquests (my speculation) with journalistic ones. I, younger and a tad more naive, knew them and didn't know them. But we were all struggling against the same forces of darkness, the "Gannettoids" who saw journalism as nothing more than a series of circulation reports and ad lineage declines. The specter of budget cuts hung over our staff the entire time Chuck and I worked together, with rumors aplenty about how Gannett was planning to slash the body count from ninety-three to sixty-four because of continued circulation declines at the *Citizen* and most other afternoon dailies. We sniffed it, sensed it, agonized over it, and continued to push the limits of our skills until the bitter end.

The low moment of that era came during demonstrations by Earth First! protesting the twentieth anniversary of the closing of the gates at Glen Canyon Dam in April 1983. I had written a seventy-inch piece on the dam controversy, but Chuck drove to

Lake Powell to cover the actual demonstration and write daily accounts of the four-day rally. The only problem was that Vonier, an
off-and-on problem drinker and recovering alcoholic, went on a
bender, taking himself out of action during the entire demonstration. Chuck's story ran unexpurgated on day 1, but Dick's assistant
city editor, Mike Chihak, sliced Chuck's stories to fifteen inches
on each of the following three days, pissing Chuck off and giving
Chihak a reputation as a scold.

Funny, though, the line I remember most from Bowden's work
was not from one of his spectacular megapieces on Indians or copper miners. It was from an account of the 1984 county supervisor's
race between Ed Moore, a maverick Democrat, and incumbent
Bud Walker, a different kind of maverick Democrat. They were
both prisoners of the real estate lobbies, but Moore was less predictable and more impish. So he got the wary support of neighborhood activists and trounced the three-term incumbent in a primary.

"He was a beginner but he did not believe in luck," was Bowden's
lede the day after Moore's September 1984 win. Later, he quoted
Moore as saying when he took office, "We're going to get Neely," a
reference to Steve Neely, the county attorney whom no one trusted
but nobody could figure out how to get rid of. I was amazed at his
audaciousness and brazenness—Bowden's, not Moore's.

It all ended about a month later. Vonier had been fired from the
Citizen years earlier because of his drinking but had been given a
second chance. Suddenly, he was hitting the bottle over and over,
missing work shifts, and leaving others to line-edit stories; and his
days were numbered. He was being asked to do the impossible,
city editor and deputy managing editor at once, and it seemed to
us that he gave in to his baser instincts. His own account is that
he was so disgusted at what he saw as the paper's subservience to
development interests and its budget-hacking plans that he deliberately got himself fired so he could draw unemployment. Anyway,
one freakishly chilly October Saturday, I walked in and was told

Dick was gone forever. A couple of days later, our publisher told us that the staff was going to go through a period of attrition but the vacancies would be filled later. Every one of us in the room knew that was a crock and that the paper's golden days were essentially over. Chuck, disgusted at the impending loss of reporting jobs, quit soon afterward, deciding he would rather be broke than nitpicked to death with marginal assignments. Sometime in December 1984, his desk emptied and a void opened up in my life and journalistic heart. I never had a mentor again. No one who could challenge, coddle, nurture, annoy, or blast me with equal fervor. No one who knew more about politics, journalism, drinking, or anything else than I did. No one to inspire me, or piss me off, or make me think. The *Citizen* published for nearly a quarter-century more, but the twin departures of Bowden and Vonier gutted its soul forever.

Over the next twenty-five years, Chuck and I stayed in touch, but our journalistic mantras drifted apart. He grew increasingly obsessed with the corruption, violence, and border wars in Mexico, while I kept plugging away at the Southwest's growth and water wars that he'd inspired me to cover in the first place. Yet his home and delectable Italian cooking were always open to me, as was his sympathetic ear whenever I had gripes about the news biz, which was virtually always. More often than not, however, he would simply talk about the horrors he was watching unfold to the south, and I would sip my wine and listen.

Journalistically, Chuck went on to bigger and better things at *City Magazine* and in his book writing. But I've always felt that his daily newswriting contained some of the purest, rawest, most original and inspiring creations ever in our business, transcending the boundaries of journalism, reporting, literature, and essay into a hybrid that will never be seen again. It's easy enough to do that in a book or magazine article, but to transform the pages of a daily newspaper into a creative venture is something else again. Combine the old New York *Herald Tribune*, H. L. Mencken, Hunter

Thompson, *Mad Magazine*, and Waylon Jennings and maybe that would give you Chuck. He sprang spontaneously upon the page like a whipped-up soufflé, and when he disappeared from the *Citizen* his like would never again be seen in the daily press. Today, just as Hendrix would never be played on commercial FM radio were he to be starting fresh, Chuck would never get hired at a daily newspaper with all of its constraints placed on writers in the name of not offending readers. Of course, the way the biz is going today, neither would anyone else.

Since 1981, investigative reporter TONY DAVIS has worked on environmental, urban-growth, and land issues in the Southwest and West. He began with the *Tucson Citizen* and currently works for the *Arizona Daily Star*, covering the environmental beat, specializing in water issues. His award-winning articles have appeared in a number of newspapers and magazines, including *High Country News*.

BOWDEN'S SOUTHWEST

Stand My Watch

KATIE LEE

My first reaction when I think about Chuck these days is how scared I once was for him. Why he was still aboveground after all his researching, on-the-spot reporting, investigating, and publishing about the drug scene on both sides of our border with Mexico seemed nothing short of a miracle. Sometimes after putting down one of his articles or books, I wanted to run to the phone and call him—make sure he was still among us.

Vaguely, I recall a discussion we once had about "the razor's edge"—of explaining my dear deceased husband's years of track-racing in custom-built race cars—how it was like a drug he couldn't altogether stay away from. Hypersensitive-alert, you're here—one more inch, one more hair or heartbeat—you're gone. Riding that edge was like no other adrenaline rush, he said. Not the same as being pulled back across the border into the danger zone of drug reporting, or night-beat crime reporting for a newspaper, but similarities whisper to each other. It means that once you've experienced such a level, returning is almost a given.

Details of a first meeting with one who later takes a special place in my life are often lost in the ether—what was the occasion?— where the connection? The further it slips away, the less it matters where-when-how we met, since the connection I *do* remember has taken its place.

I read *Killing the Hidden Waters* in 1977.

Either our friend, Edward Abbey, introduced us—Ed gave me the book, and I was impressed enough to go bang on Chuck's door—or he came to some gig I had in Tucson and introduced himself. Whatever. I was hooked—on the style, on the message.

Tucson was my home long before Chuck was born—more than likely I also once lived on Ninth Street, but then I lived on every east/west street between Lee Street and Broadway, and several north/south ones during the 1930s depression. So, I experienced an unexpected shame after reading that book—should have been more aware of what had *really* happened to the Pantano Wash, and the Santa Cruz and the Rillito Rivers (where, as a teenager, I'd hiked, ridden horses) when they turned to bank-raging flash floods. His writing, his mind, was an extension from the prehistoric to now, with no interruption—as if he were one of the souls who lived here in the desert a thousand years ago and is now walking out of the rock, up through the ground, into the air, conversing about events as if they happened yesterday. He described these souls with astonishing intellect, humility, and depth of wisdom—thrusting what was there then, and is now, under our noses. Seldom do I quote other writers, but more than once I've used Bowden quotes to better state what I would never find the right words for.

When *Frog Mountain Blues* appeared (1987), he described boulder-filled canyons—places gaunt, graceful, wild, and treacherous I'd never *heard* of, let alone hiked to, hunted in, or dared trespass. Ramblings with buddies were confined to fairly mundane creases in the land compared to some of Chuck's Catalina Mountains cliff-hanging. And, of course, he tested, probed, and felt the pulse of that stretched-out, almost flat desert valley of creosote, catclaw, cacti, mesquite, paloverde, and cottonwood trees at the foot of those mountains; tested it with ever increasing intensity, along with testing himself; thereby deepening his respect for its perfection. Chuck's *art*, his talent for placing the reader beneath his treading boots, against the grainy desert granites, stemmed from a Spartan journalistic style, wherein a flow, a syncopated rhythm connects the dots—a subtlety the reader may be unaware of until neon flashes the message to the brain, long after the book is placed back on the shelf.

Sometime around 1988 or '89 he became editor of Tucson's *City Magazine*. I hadn't published anything about Arizona since 1976; he asked me for a piece for the mag, and I sent a sentimental tale I was sure he'd reject. Wrong. I was pleased to know about his being editor because I figured it could keep him away from reporting on the drug scene, at least for a while. Wrong again. But during that period I came to know more about his heartfelt intimacy with the desert—an intimacy that ultimately turns to love. Being in rapport with earth's sensuality is a quality few writers (especially males) are able to convey, even when they're aware of it. Not a problem for Mr. Bowden.

To know an author beyond the words in his, or her, books—like or not the writing or the subject—is to read a great deal more into those words than if you are not acquainted. In Chuck's case, the added richness is palpable. From *Killing the Hidden Waters*, when I didn't know him at all, through each of his books, to *Inferno*, I taste the greasewood, feel the sting, slap at the bites, know the heat, seek the shade, find the water, lie down and cool off beneath the stars. He writes of this often brutal terrain without a bitching thought about its scarcity; rather, delighting in the way nature has formed this desert and secretly pleased that not a whole lot of bipeds will invade and destroy its austerity in the near future.

To be honest, I'd given up on the lower Sonoran Desert until he pulled it back into focus for me. I'd returned home too many times, to see too many uglies tearing my desert to shreds. From our back adobe wall (off Harrison Road and Broadway) in 1955, we had a clear unobstructed view of the Catalinas thirty miles away, through flaming paloverde thickets, mesquite, and saguaro. When I came back in 1975, I was confronted with a block-long, four-story condo ten feet from that same wall. I turned away in tears, wanting to say, "Screw the bastards, let 'um have it!" But by then, having fought for, and not yet won back, Glen Canyon (drowned beneath Powell Reservoir), I fully understood the passion—to save whatever could be saved of the planet, *for the planet*—be it desert, mountain, forest, canyon, river, or ocean—not particularly for the human race, unless, or until, we wise up and begin undoing our mistakes—but for the beauty, integrity, and grace of *this unique blue ball.*

Some years ago Chuck was chosen to introduce me at an award ceremony in Tucson where he used the phrase "She has stood my watch." Ah, Charles, those words I certainly can't live up to. How I would love to say, "We stand each other's watch." You, with your books, your words, and our friend Jack Dykinga's photographs, are kingpins in saving a gorgeous chunk of our Southwest: the Grand Staircase-Escalante National Monument. And even if I've been unable, as yet, to move a stone for my Glen, I do not give up hope that one day we both can say:

"Mother Nature not only stood our watch, she fired the winning shot."

Actress, folksinger, writer, poet, and conservationist KATIE LEE was also a free-spirited river runner and staunch defender of the Colorado River and opponent of Glen Canyon Dam. She published dozens of essays, numerous songs, and five books—including *Ten Thousand Goddam Cattle, All My Rivers Are Gone, Sandstone Seduction,* and *The Ghosts of Dandy Crossing.* Kathryn Louise Lee died in 2017 at age ninety-eight. She wrote this previously unpublished essay in 2007.

Give Light to the Air

MOLLY MCKASSON

In my town, Chuck Bowden is a legend: Tucson homeboy makes good. He wrote a passel of great books, braved killer deserts, and eluded ruthless drug lords to get his edgy stories. But there's more. Over the years, Chuck Bowden honed an elegant argument for saving the Sonoran Desert and worked hard to get that message out in every way possible, including beautiful books laid out on fancy coffee tables in places where people might not otherwise care about desert pronghorn. When none of our elected representatives had the courage or vision to speak out against the nonstop urban sprawl that was destroying an acre of desert life every few minutes and taking the Old Pueblo's soul along with it, tens and thousands of us in the Tucson Basin saw Chuck Bowden as our real representative.

After our initiatives and campaigns failed to stop urban renewal or the blading of the upland canyons at the base of the Catalinas, Chuck Bowden became our balladeer—recounting the whole story, insuring that generations to come would know the depth of our loss. One of his first books, *Frog Mountain Blues*, became a classic the day it hit the bookstores in southern Arizona. While Chuck wasn't able to single-handedly stop Tucson from becoming like Phoenix, I see his imprint on regional land use policy over the last twenty years. The Forest Service was certainly listening to him when they made changes in the Catalina Mountain Range; his advocacy paved the way for the Sonoran Desert Conservation Plan; and someday his dream of a Sonoran National Park will be a reality. Chuck Bowden was an advocate for some of the most beautiful places on earth, and he was also my friend.

I forget exactly how we met—maybe it was a book signing back in the mid-'80s. He had that shy, lanky cowboy thing about him— sort of reminded me of Sam Shepard. Thank God I was wrong. He wasn't the strong-silent type, but he loved meeting folks and hearing new stories. He also loved to talk—about beautiful things, and about not so beautiful things. He had an omnivorous curiosity and seldom passed judgment.

I think we had our first real conversation at the Crossroads, a popular old South Tucson drive-in where they used to deliver beer and menudo to your car. We were eating inside when he asked me if I'd be interested in the job of arts editor for a new monthly magazine—large-format, black-and-white photos, uncensored editorial—which he and Dick Vonier, an old friend from his re-porter days at the *Tucson Daily Citizen*, had just started publishing. It was winter 1987, and I was overwhelmed with caring for my two-month-old son, but like everyone else in town I'd already fallen in love with *City Magazine*. At last we had a rallying point where the community's creativity and energy could come together and tackle important local issues. Although I was too selfish to think about it at the time, this whole enterprise was no small risk. Chuck didn't need the venue, as his career was already taking off, but both he and Vonier were willing to sacrifice in order to give voice to the rich imagination and diversity in our community.

Conversing with Chuck that day at the Crossroads was way more filling than lunch. It was a feast. Chuck talked like he wrote— with incisive passion, rich detail, quirky humor, and a constantly roiling sense of self-reflection. He had two habits that made his conversations dear to me: (1) he listened as well as he talked, and (2) his mind was always herding the details into a bigger picture without ever losing the inherent untidiness and unfinishedness that is reality. Sorry if it sounds condescending, but he was unique for a guy; he genuinely seemed to enjoy thinking and feeling at the same time.

I don't remember exactly what we talked about—outside of the job—but I'm sure we swapped hiking stories, probably some politics, very likely a favorite poem, and/or a recipe. These are typical but by no means inclusive of stuff that might get shared in a conversation with Chuck. Your subjects are as wide as the world when you hanker for a well-examined life. By the end of lunch, my face must have been flush as I accepted the job. Certainly my mind was rushing with new ideas and connections, so much so I almost didn't tell my husband about it. After all, a conversation in which there is a "communion of thoughts and feelings," commonly referred to as "intercourse" before the '60s, could be misconstrued. But from that day on our friendship was platonic, except that I suspect Chuck, like myself, favored Socrates over that other guy.

I didn't really know what I was signing on to that day at the Mexican food drive-in. Chuck wasn't big on creating parameters; he might not have even used the term "arts editor." Mostly he envisioned a job that included writing, or finding others to write, about local cultural events or people that turned me on. Review the circus? Sure. Interview a Tohono O'odham muralist? Absolutely. Advocate for the university to expand its dance program into a full-blown department? Why not? When I was hedging my instincts, he'd shrug and say, "Hey. I trust you." As long as I was passionate and got my details straight, it was fine by Chuck.

Within six months, *City Magazine* became a southern Arizona classic. Each month was new territory for me, a chance to experiment with different styles and new ideas, and Chuck kept encouraging more. Next to writing himself, he loved to nurture other writers. We used to sit down, usually over food, to tighten up my next installment. Before any specifics, he'd laugh and say, "Of course, we can take out the first paragraph." It was a rule of thumb he might have learned at the newspaper: the reader doesn't need

Cover of *City Magazine* featuring Charles Bowden and Art Carrillo Strong's story "El Nacho," September 1987

to be warmed up. He respected readers as much as he respected writers. "Your second paragraph gets right to it." I don't remember him suggesting "cuts" per se. What I do recall were suggestions about making a paragraph more like "beef jerky." But Chuck didn't

Cover of *City Magazine* featuring Charles Bowden and Dick Vonier's story "Charlie," about Charles Keating, August 1988

mean cram in more details. He taught me the poetic value of not trying to say everything in one article. Chuck Bowden was a great editor. All of us connected to *City Magazine* felt like we were really picking up speed.

Community support for the magazine kept on mounting. Just about everybody, save the developers, appreciated the love and intelligence Chuck and Dick pumped out every month. Artists and writers were clamoring to participate, and then suddenly it was over. Like a blazing 2+ comet. I always assumed that money was the root of the problem, though nothing is ever quite that simple. Twenty years later people are still reluctant to throw out their back issues; *City Magazine* is the chronicle of an amazing time in the life of our city. Fortunately, my conversations with Chuck didn't end with that era.

In 1989, I was recruited to run for the Tucson City Council, and after much soul searching, I signed on and was elected. My platform included growth control, more conservation and preservation, and a "greener" approach to city planning in general. Again Chuck was glad to lend his support to such a campaign. Over my two terms, we had some memorable conversations sitting outside on his patio discussing how best to wake up the community to the reality that uncontrolled growth doesn't mean economic boon—but is the literal definition of cancer. Of course, we also talked about making a perfect ragout, exchanging cereus cuttings, the relationship of saints and prostitutes *en la Frontera*, and other simple pleasures.

Ten years later, when I ran for mayor, Chuck and Mary Martha Miles were a huge help in a hotly contested, heavily covered campaign. Not only did they help fundraise, but Mary Martha kept my makeup and clothes straight for media events, and Chuck was always available for a political patio pep talk—spiced up with art, nature, and food. Sometimes Chuck would have a specific suggestion on how to frame an issue with keener clarity, and always he encouraged me to be creative, be myself, not to worry about image. He never said it, but I think he worried they would pull out all the stops to bury me, that it would get dirty and mean and that I'd get hurt. He was right, yet he and Mary Martha continued to help right up through my concession speech on election night. Fortunately, our conversations didn't end with that loss either.

Chuck continues to strike me as one of those rare folks who are not afraid to love the world, disorganized and brutal as it sometimes is. He didn't seem scared to have ideas fail him either. Maybe it's because it's the process, not the product, that interested him.

My friend Chuck had a good thing going; he regularly checked in with his conscience, his friends, his favorite shopkeepers, and then retired to his patio, as darkness came on, to watch the cereus blossoms open and give light to the air.

MOLLY MCKASSON served two terms on the Tucson City Council, from 1989 to 1997, and ran unsuccessfully for mayor in 1999. Her writing has appeared in a number of local magazines and other publications.

How's My Government?

RAY CARROLL

I am to see to it that
I do not lose you.

WALT WHITMAN,
Leaves of Grass

I had read the great Chuck Bowden long before meeting him. Eventually, I followed his long, angular shadow from our boyhood neighborhood in the South Side of Chicago to sunny Tucson, Arizona. Honestly, it was because of his work that I realized being a denizen of the bungalow belt was not a life sentence.

We became friends after our first official interview in 1997, shortly after I entered public office as a Pima County supervisor. Although he was a journalist and I an elected official, Chuck was always at ease and off the record, more intent on personal betterment and libations than on interrogations. I was an earnest political novice needing instruction on the fundamentals of the news business. He was my Socratic mentor.

His greeting to me was always the same, "How's my government?" I always smiled widely back at him, because it gave me more credit and influence than I deserved as a lowly first-term county supervisor. Any political leader worth his salt would have benefited from knowing Chuck Bowden. He always made me feel welcome by putting down his "crayons" and stopping his "scribbling" whenever I visited him. I envied his abiding-yet-engaging personality, his political acumen, and his simple life, his clarity of expression and comfortable style. He would reassure me that he understood me and enjoyed the company. "Do you follow?" he would ask.

Ray Carroll, Charles Bowden, and Arizona Senator John McCain, at a fund-raiser for the senator

Chuck had an inspired, and almost biblical, contrition over the way we used land in the 1980s. He had a message for the voters of Pima County and the people in power—"Stop killing the economic golden goose of our fragile Sonoran Desert!" Chuck softened the beachhead of "radical environmental politics" as we hiked and climbed much of my supervisory district and the threatened landscape he knew so well.

On the hoof in the wild, he was a grand champion of an outdoorsman, with awesome athleticism and hovering presence that kept most hikers half his age on edge. I enjoyed Chuck guiding me, and I admit, I sometimes could not make the grade. I paled in comparison and faltered in too many ways to number. He never quit challenging me to go out again, believing I could reach any summit.

Conservation of southern Arizona's historic ranches and cultural landscapes was the most fruitful accomplishment of the Pima County board of supervisors. Bowden was a good hand for advice; his sage guidance was to aim at the doable, not the impossible, dream, when it came to public initiatives and public support for open space and land policies. Like my own father used to tell me, "Pigs get fat and hogs get slaughtered." Pima County succeeded on a national scale and received our own Section 10 permit from the US Fish and Wildlife Service for the conservation of wildlands and threatened species. Chuck helped construct and sell a conservation system that best preserved our sense of place and protected in perpetuity our Holy Land 2.0, through a document called the Sonoran Desert Conservation Plan. Of course, I am grateful for the decades we shared as friends and his being a thorn in the side of injustice. He lived his life with a purity of purpose. I will always be thankful for the chance I had to share his vision and brotherhood.

I have known Chuck as a deeply spiritual person, whose favorite book was *The Little Flowers of St. Francis*. Although he had an abiding respect for the Lord's creation, and a profound knowledge of the Bible, Chuck wasn't at all religious. Yet here's the deal. His personal honesty (perhaps intentionally) transcended lofty sermons, and his devotion to protecting the Sonoran Desert was admired by the most dogmatic creationists. An icon of the Southwest from the southwest side of Chicago, Chuck Bowden had a Mike Royko-esque love of irony.

I know well the Chicago poets and authors he unraveled, felt, and loved in the public school libraries of Chicago. I loved them, too. Gwendolyn Brooks, Robert Frost, Carl Sandburg, I devoured them all, just like the young Chuck Bowden had. We marched the sidewalks and crosswalks to begin our day at Cook and Sheldon public schools, respectively. We shared the same fish-flopping and gasping out-of-water feeling as displaced midwesterners in the dry heat of our first 112-degree Sonoran Desert summer. We gradually made ourselves into hybrids of Chicago and Tucson by cross-pollinating our memories and new experiences in the beautiful Old Pueblo. Our shared history brought joy to each of our visits.

Pima County appropriately named its community center on Mount Lemmon after Chuck, for his love of the Sonoran Desert and the generous and benevolent protection he gave its friends. The strong and majestic Chuck Bowden Mount Lemmon Community Center is the town hall and the central gathering place for residents and visitors alike. He would love that. We built it out of the ashes of a devastating fire that laid waste to almost two-thirds of his beloved Santa Catalina Mountains. He loved these mountains. I think he would be immensely proud to know he's still keeping watch over them. His parents' ashes were spread near the center.

Chicago native RAY CARROLL served twenty years as a Pima County supervisor in Arizona, where he established himself as a champion of the environment and efficient government.

Discovering Chuck

WINIFRED J. BUNDY

Memories swirl around in my head recalling Charles Bowden. While researching for an arid lands course at the University of Arizona, I ran across Bowden's then-unpublished report "Killing the Hidden Waters," a chilling cautionary tale of people's use and misuse of groundwater, our most precious resource, and decided to locate the author. We met at the University of Arizona Library, where, between Chuck's emphatic slaps on the library table and my very vocal agreements with his arguments, we were immediately ushered outside. We decided to meet at his home, hidden by oleander bushes and guarded by a large "vicious dog" sign. Bowden's provocative and brilliantly written study so impressed me that I brought it to the attention of my friend and mentor, Lawrence Clark Powell. LCP shared my enthusiasm and retraced my path to Bowden's front door. He became the manuscript's champion, bringing it first to the attention of Alfred A. Knopf and then to the University of Texas Press, which published it in 1977.

I have owned and operated the Singing Wind Bookstore and Ranch in Benson for forty-three years during which time Chuck was a frequent guest at events I hosted for authors and readers. To accommodate my customers who couldn't attend readings and required home delivery, I often brought books into Tucson for Chuck to sign. While waiting for Chuck to appear, his mother and I became good friends. Dressed in a plain apron and seated at a linoleum-covered kitchen table, she told me how she had nurtured Chuck's writing in the face of his father's vocal insistence that there would be no writing career.

As Chuck signed, he told me about the books he valued most: Lawrence Clark Powell's *California Classics* and *Southwest Classics*, along with his essay, "The Southwest"; Conrad Richter's *Sea of Grass*; and Edward Abbey's *Desert Solitaire* and *The Monkey Wrench Gang*. Later, when Chuck's circle of friends broadened, he raved to me about Jim Harrison's *Legends of the Fall*, *Wolf*, and *A Good Day to Die*, and Sherman Alexie's *Reservation Blues* and *Indian Killer*. He also appreciated Gretel Ehrlich's *Heart Mountain*, a novel about the World War II internment of Japanese Americans at Heart Mountain, Wyoming.

Of all of Chuck's many books, my favorite is *Blue Desert*, which I believe expresses the essence of the desert and the spirit of the Southwest. It will remain a classic. His observation "I am in the boom and I try to catch the roar" speaks most profoundly to me.

WINIFRED J. BUNDY worked at Special Collections in the University of Arizona Library, and she has operated the Singing Wind Bookshop and Ranch in Benson, Arizona, since 1974.

Mr. Southwest

JOSEPH C. WILDER

The first time I met Chuck Bowden was probably in 1987. I had been editor of what became *Journal of the Southwest* for a year and had just been appointed director of the Southwest Center at the University of Arizona, as well. Chuck sidled up to me and my wife, Peggy, at Jim and Loma Griffith's annual summer party out in the desert near San Xavier Mission. He seemed to know who I was, and he was intent on letting me know that I was certainly *not* "Mr. Southwest." I suspect he had heard about me from Julian Hayden, someone Chuck idolized, and someone who had been a family friend of mine for decades (which he would not have known). That may have put me in the position of being a sort of competitor, perhaps even a potential rival. This was baloney, of course. Chuck had no need to worry. In his own way, *he* was Mr. Southwest—clearly the region's leading general intellectual. My ambition was to be a leading regional publisher.

I always liked and admired Chuck. In 1993, the Southwest Center published one of his early books, *The Secret Forest*, in its series with the University of New Mexico Press. Featuring fantastic photographs by Bowden's longtime collaborator Jack Dykinga and an important introduction by the distinguished botanist Paul Martin, it provided a sterling nonacademic take on the Alamos, Sonora, region and made a significant contribution to our regional bibliography. It still holds the reader's attention some twenty years later. The book quotes liberally from historical sources, while maintaining the first-person account that became Chuck's trademark. Missing from the book—to its credit—are other Bowdenesque qualities, such as the sprinkling of Bob Dylan quotes that always seemed to mask more than they revealed. The one Bowden essay I rejected for *Journal of the Southwest* led off with a long Jimi Hendrix quote that, it seemed to me, he included only to establish how hip and cool he was. Chuck was hip and cool, for sure, but he didn't need Hendrix to establish it. His own prose was quite sufficient, especially when he pulled back from that curious and irritating self-consciousness that can undermine the best of narratives.

In his best work, Chuck wrote deeply thought-out essays that captured an exhilarating exuberance and, ironically perhaps, were characterized by what I think of as a profoundly academic sensibility. In part, this played out in the extraordinary attention Chuck paid to sources—most, oddly enough, highly scholarly products of the academy. The combination of first-person description, integration of local perspectives, and the scholarship Bowden obviously admired and utilized usually resulted in a manuscript of utter originality, depth, and accuracy. If Bowden unleashed was a bridge too far, Bowden disciplined by his own code of formal truth-telling created the sort of work we never forget.

I drifted away from Chuck and his work as he increasingly wrote about the El Paso–Ciudad Juárez border and, in many ways, became his own character. I still admired the sheer verve of his writing—its energy and commitment—and I took him seriously. Chuck walked the walk, never made excuses, and was never untrue to himself or his vision. He ultimately wrote about himself, I guess, but in so doing, he vastly illuminated our beloved region. Losing Chuck, we end up losing a piece of ourselves—that piece bound up in place—and we are the lesser for it.

JOSEPH C. WILDER is director of the Southwest Center at the University of Arizona and editor and publisher of the regional quarterly *Journal of the Southwest*.

Chuck's Desert Garden

KASEY ANDERSON

Visiting Chuck at his house in Tucson was always a treat for me because it meant a walk through his backyard botanical garden. Chuck loved plants and had spent considerable time over the years selecting and planting trees, shrubs, cactus, and vines that he found interesting or attractive. It was an eclectic blend that formed a dense green space, which provided shade, beauty, and habitat for wildlife that happened upon it.

He liked the idea of attracting wildlife to the yard, especially birds. To that end, he had tall, spreading South American mesquites for nesting and cover and a native canyon hackberry tree (*Celtis reticulata*) providing seasonal nutritious fruit for finches, cardinals, mockingbirds, and others. Another native plant in the yard, special to Chuck, was the chiltepin pepper plant (*Capsicum annuum var. glabriusculum*). It is one of the oldest hot pepper plants known, and the fruit-eating birds just love it. Even though the heat of these small peppers is challenging for humans, birds are oblivious to it and eat their fill. Chuck also put out birdseed to supplement, of course, in case anyone got left out. For his favorite bird, the hummingbird, with its nectar-seeking bill, he planted shrubs with bright orange and red tubular flowers, including Mexican honeysuckle (*Justicia spicigera*), chuparosa (*Justicia californica*), and the South African cape honeysuckle (*Tecomaria capensis*). These plants, along with feeders full of sugar water, assured steady visitation by several species of hummers, and Chuck was very pleased about that. Not all the plants were for wildlife, though; many were about their form, flowers, or fragrance.

In the midnineties, Chuck took a fancy to Madagascar palms (*Pachypodium lamerei*). This is a striking semisucculent plant armed with needle-sharp spines covering the trunk from the ground all the way up to the palm-like leaves at the top. It's very drought tolerant and so was a good fit for Chuck's garden. Being from Madagascar, these plants are normally sold as container plants for patios and sunny indoor locations, because they are very sensitive to cold and need protection in the winter. Chuck scoffed at the notion of potting this exotic specimen and promptly planted several in the ground, just south of the big mesquite. They thrived and soon grew taller than him, even occasionally producing white flowers at the top. It was a great accomplishment for Chuck, and he was very proud of these plants.

Chuck was also quite fond of cactus. He planted many in a bed across from his office that he could easily view through the window. Many shapes and sizes were represented in that plot. The San Pedro cactus (*Trichocereus pachanoi*) was the most vertical and tallest of the group, and most interesting to Chuck because of its psychoactive properties. Apparently, it was used by indigenous people in Peru for special ceremonial events. Chuck never used it that way, but he liked knowing it was possible. Another columnar cactus in the group was Old Man cactus (*Cephalocereus senilis*). It is native to central Mexico and is unusual because of its grayish-white wooly hairs that resemble a beard. Moving down to a globular form is the golden barrel cactus (*Echinocactus grusonii*). This is also a central Mexico plant, and it stands out in the garden with bright yellow spines glowing in the sunlight and its nearly perfect spherical appearance. Next, the Torch cactus (*Trichocereus hybrid*)—the cactus with the most stunning flowers—occupied a prominent place at the front of the plot. These plants produced some magnificent floral displays during spring and early summer, and are very photogenic.

Another cactus Chuck was quite fond of and held in high regard was rose cactus (*Pereskia grandifolia*). It's native to Brazil, and what's unique about *Pereskia* is that its growth form is shrub-like and that it is the only cactus with leaves. It is thought that this plant represents the most ancient form of cactus. The plants have showy pinkish flowers in early summer, and the bees love them. The *Pereskia* is growing next to the east wall of the yard, situated near a very special paloverde tree called "Desert Museum" paloverde (*Parkinsonia hybrid*). This hybrid was discovered and developed at the Arizona-Sonora Desert Museum in the early 1980s. It exhibits characteristics of Mexican, Blue, and Foothill paloverde. It's a fast grower, strong, and thornless, and it produces abundant blooms that last into early summer. Chuck was among the first to acquire and plant one when it became available, and what a beauty it became. It was definitely the big show in the backyard during May and June.

The really big show most of Chuck's friends were familiar with was the blossoms of the exotic night-blooming *Harrisia* cactus. It's native to southern South America and has rope-like green stems, with small spine clusters. The stems grow along the ground and form tangled clumps. Chuck's clump was about 6 × 10 feet and stood squarely in the center of the yard. Bloom time for these plants was different each year. Fifty to one hundred buds would appear from June to early July, and the call would go out to friends and neighbors to come for an early morning viewing. Not everyone was a morning person like Chuck, but those who came were treated to a mass of large, white flowers and the wonderful fragrance they produced to attract pollinators. By about eight o'clock the six-inch blossoms began to melt as the sunlight found its way into the yard—gone for another year.

Charles Bowden showing his desert-plants garden in bloom

Chuck wasn't satisfied at having just one big flowering event in his yard, however. He found another night-blooming cactus with even larger white flowers, *Selenicereus grandiflorus*. Often called moonlight cactus, this plant is native to central Mexico/Caribbean Islands and produces up to twelve-inch blooms. In habitat it climbs trees, and Chuck was enthralled by the prospect of it winding its way up his favorite mesquite. He did have some success with this plant, training it up the mesquite trunk and installing drip lines to keep it damp, but I can only recall a few blossoms on a couple of occasions.

Continuing with the night-blooming cactus theme, one of the best outings I had with Chuck was in 1999, when I was a volunteer at the Nature Conservancy. The organization was preparing to move its Tucson office to an undeveloped site near Cherry Boulevard and Fort Lowell Road. I discovered six of our native night-blooming cactus—queen of the night (*Peniocereus greggii*)—growing among the other plants. It was decided to move the plants before construction began, and I got the job. Knowing Chuck's interest in night-blooming cacti, I asked him if he would help me excavate these plants and move them to a safe location. He readily agreed, and we met there the next weekend to take them out. Chuck came with his gloves and shovel and was very enthusiastic about the task at hand. The *Peniocereus* cacti have large, tuberous roots, so we spent several hours carefully digging around the plants' roots so as not to damage them. Chuck was very impressed by the subsurface size of this plant—aboveground it was hardly noticeable—and he was delighted to make contact with it.

Chuck's passion for plants was just one of many in his life, but it was important because the garden was his connection to nature in the city. His garden was actually a second living space, and he spent considerable time there watching birds and unwinding after many hours at the keyboard. I always enjoyed visiting with him there and discussing plants and nature. We connected on the botanical. Chuck actually listened without interrupting, sometimes, and not many of his friends can say that. Ya follow.

A second-generation Tucson native and lifelong resident, KASEY ANDERSON was Bowden's friend for nearly three decades.

Planting Trees

KIM SANDERS

I met Chuck Bowden in 1997, when I was a Dallas Police Department Narcotics detective assigned to DEA. He approached me at the direction of a retired DEA agent. He wanted to know about an informant who had passed away and had spent his life fighting the cartels that had ruined people he loved. I had known, worked with, and respected the courageous old man. About a year later, Chuck returned to Dallas when I was working undercover on a case related to a group of heroin traffickers. He asked me to tell him my ground-level perspective.

I had to be able to get a gut-feeling assessment of someone pretty quick in the business I was in. I liked Chuck pretty much right away. He had that air of a damaged soul and the eyes of a man who had seen too much pain and suffering, which I could relate to. I also knew that the years of tension and stress were destroying me, for I no longer believed in what I did, and knew I had to leave it or die. I took Chuck deep into the ugliness of what had become part of my world. In so doing, I came to learn that the tragedies and human suffering he had so deeply investigated, wrote about, and lived through were trying to destroy him, too.

Chuck had a unique ability to be almost invisible while he was scratching down his notes in his little pocket notebook. All I had to do was tell people, "He's with me." Many of the people he came across with me were not formally educated, and most of them had had their asses kicked by the hand that life had dealt them from the get-go. Though not formally educated, they were not stupid and had to survive on their instincts, which were honed on the mean streets. They could quickly size up the atmosphere of a person around them. Most of them had been hurt many times and in many ways and could tell quickly when someone wasn't comfortable in their world or had a superiority about them. Chuck fit in, and I know they sensed his own pain, which was from the years and years of going amongst the damaged, the neglected, the homeless, the victims, the terrified, and the hopeless.

You see, my friend Chuck had what we call in Texas "a good heart," and I know in my own heart that it was more than that—he had a good soul. He went to dangerous, dark places, where evil lurked—real evil. He went without weapons, and he never tried to hide his agenda, which was to be the advocate for human beings who suffer. His lot in life was to poetically jog the conscience of those of us that are lucky enough to be able to make a difference—to make that difference. Chuck knew that evil begins when one turns a deaf ear to the soft whisper in our souls—that there is something more—that our existence has meaning.

He was an amazing cook, and as he slowly cooked his signature osso buco at my house one night, we had a deep conversation about our lives and the paths we were on. That night he told me when he was young, his father told him that he planted trees to leave something good behind long after his own existence on this earth. We agreed that we had seen too much, been close to too much ugliness for too long, and it was inevitably fatal. We knew we both had to find a way to return to something—something that brought peace to our souls—a place of innocence. Chuck's sanctuary, the place he returned to, was the pristine desert and, once there, the millions of stars in the sky. He knew he had to go there, and he left for it the next day.

We stayed in contact. I soon went to Homicide and worked the rest of my career there as a detective. Chuck went to Mexico and did investigative reporting on the cartels' slaughter of so many, including innocent victims. When I lost my twenty-four-year-old son, Skipper, to a rare heart infection, Chuck came to Dallas and sat with me. I told him I believed the grief was going to kill me. Like always, he absorbed another person's pain and then he wrote the soulful truth of losing my boy. Grief almost did kill me, but I went back to the job of living.

KIM SANDERS was a Dallas police officer for over thirty years, working undercover narcotics investigations for more than twenty years, before retiring as a homicide detective.

A Man for All Seasons

PHIL JORDAN

For here we are not afraid to
follow truth wherever it may lead

THOMAS JEFFERSON

Chuck Bowden interviewed me at the El Paso Intelligence Center (EPIC) about the devastating loss of my young brother, Bruno, murdered by an undocumented kid from Juárez, Mexico. After explaining the purpose of his visit, Chuck convinced me that I should talk to him. He had a unique way of "disarming" people, and before long I felt like I was talking to a family member or a fellow DEA agent. Chuck soon became a part of my El Paso family.

Having spent my career working with the Federal Bureau of Narcotics (FBN) under the Treasury Department, and the Bureau of Narcotics and Dangerous Drugs (BNDD) and the Drug Enforcement Administration (DEA), both under the Department of Justice, I was convinced from the very beginning that I was talking to a genuine investigator. Chuck was looking for truth, supported by facts—something that I felt neither the El Paso Police Department nor the FBI had any interest in doing while investigating Bruno's death. Chuck single-handedly did more in solving my brother's murder than the El Paso Police Department, or any other agency. His talent for truth finding was born out of quiet persistence, intelligence, and ambition.

In all honesty, I feel that I learned more from Chuck than he ever learned from me. Chuck laid a solid foundation for the reality that is reflected in many of today's headlines—corruption exists at the highest levels of government. I believe that Chuck knew corruption was more widespread than what I knew and believed. He demonstrates that understanding in *Down by the River*, highlighting the FBI's entrapment of my cousin Sal Martínez. I strongly believe that the FBI targeted Sal in this fake investigation as retribution for my testimony against the agency in *Matt Perez v. FBI*.

I admired Chuck for his tenacity—his desire to uncover the facts, the truth—and for the unique and powerful way in which he wrote his stories. I personally witnessed his relentless pursuit of information and the way in which he assembled the facts in a compelling narrative. Chuck was a special writer and a unique human being.

PHILIP "PHIL" JORDAN served thirty-three years in federal and state law enforcement, rising to Special Agent in Charge of DEA operations in Arizona, Oklahoma, New Mexico, and Texas, and then director of the El Paso Intelligence Center (EPIC), located at Ft. Bliss, Texas. His brother Bruno's murder by the Juárez cartel was the subject of Charles Bowden's book *Down by the River*.

Chuck Bowden in the Twilight Zone

CAL LASH

"I didn't choose this course," he said. "It chose me."[1] This is my response to those who ask me, "Why did Chuck go to the Dark Side?"

I am a reader, not a writer; a cop, not a journalist. I am not formally educated and rely on my street-gained experience for survival and understanding. This is where Charles (Chuck) Bowden and I bonded. We both rose up out of the wombs of deep black midwestern soil in the middle of sweltering July heat.

Chuck's openness in sharing with others his knowledge and philosophy was, to me, an asset of his great character. In my opinion, he deliberately tried to avoid "fools," who he believed were an impediment to his work. Money allowed him to scribble incessantly and feed the birds, listen to music and drink red wine. Chuck walked in wilderness unknown to most and understood by very few.

Chuck referred to himself as a "reporter" and seemed to have some disdain for the term "journalist." I've been asked, "Would Chuck have been a good police officer?" The answer is "yes." Good cops and good reporters are on-the-ground investigators looking for facts, observing, mentally assessing, and putting these observations to paper. Bowden, writing about his friend Arturo Carrillo Strong, a Pima County drug enforcement officer, said, "But more importantly he had the eye.... For a while I worked for a newspaper and the main thing I learned was that most people are born blind and prefer to remain in that condition."[2]

Chuck would have been at the top of the law enforcement detective field, as he was as a reporter. However, it is my experience that law enforcement in general is a place where brilliant folks quickly become bored with the day-to-day repetition of human behavior called crime. Cops and reporters have similar reactions to their experiences. Alcohol abuse is one, along with high rates of divorce, heart disease, and suicide.

In the many conversations I had with Chuck, his biggest "confession" was that when he was just stretching out of his teens, he traded some guns for illegal drugs that he took to San Francisco to share with friends. Chuck shared with me past times when his humanitarian beliefs led him to commit acts considered illegal— providing assistance and financial aid and shelter to poor, downtrodden immigrants seeking refuge from poverty and death. One time, he found a starving South American refugee outside his house in Patagonia. Chuck took the man to Nogales, where, out of his own wallet, he outfitted him with American-style clothing and a cell phone. I will always cherish the photograph Chuck sent me of a tree sticking out of his backpack. He was about to smuggle the tree into Juárez for Father Hinde and Sister Betty Campbell, who operate a mission there.

I value the time I spent with Chuck at El Pastor's place for the destitute mentally ill. Located on the southeast side of the mountain opposite Juárez, it provides shelter for those who would otherwise die on Juárez's noncaring streets. A place from which you can see on the mountain the huge painting of a white horse commissioned by a Mexican cartel boss. It signals the landing spot for cartel planes and is guarded by the Mexican Army.

In my times with Chuck, including examining the shootout scene in Mexico between the Mexican Federales and one of "El Chapo" Guzmán's cartel lieutenants, I never saw any sign that Chuck was seeking thrills. He was on a fact-finding mission driven by curiosity and wanting to see for himself, not having a lot of faith in sound-bite news reports and government statements.

I didn't perceive Chuck's behavior as going to the dark side. I think he was capable of operating in the *twilight zone*, a moving line that separates the illuminated day side and the dark night side. He was reporting on the human condition. Chuck deeply sensed the principle of the cosmic order, and he felt the presence of the soil-ridden hands stretched upward from the desert sand of "some of the dead are still breathing."[3]

While I understood Chuck's deeply intense, driven behavior, I never perceived that his reporting, his documentation, or his publications were driven by thrill seeking. Chuck provided his own answer in *Credo*: "From time to time I have been accused of a dark interest in things, and I have no real answer to this charge."[4] Chuck wrote me: "You sensed what has driven me. My work on the border and on the drug wars is a kind of detour that happened because I was appalled by the denial of the murder of Mexico."[5]

In 2014, Chuck was in a hurry. I believe he sensed that he was on his last Red Line. Chuck wrote in *Mezcal*: "The desert, the big empty where humans do not dominate, is necessary to slow down my velocity, to rid the clutter from my brain. But it is too late for me. I am too long out of the Stone Age and I can only visit the past."[6]

The only time I saw even a hint of fear was in Chuck's last days, when he feared that he might die before he finished his current projects, which to my knowledge were "Blood on the Corn" and possibly "Dakotah: The Return of the Future."[7] Chuck and I had discussed the Gary Webb ("Kill the Messenger") story, and I knew Chuck felt badly that he had not been able to help defend him when Gary was persecuted by the federal government. The government still contends that Webb committed suicide, although it notes that he shot himself *twice*. Bowden's publication, with Molly Molloy, of "Blood on the Corn" was a sixteen-year project detailing Webb's exposé of the presidential- and CIA-run Iran/Contra affair and how the CIA conspired with Mexican Federales and Mexican cartels in the torturous murder of DEA agent Kiki Enrique Camarena. Chuck wrote: "But I knew Gary Webb got it right and that was the worst possible thing he could have done."[8]

I believe Chuck was misunderstood by many, particularly "academics," and possibly even family members. He never really belonged to the academic world, and as he grew older he kept moving farther away from people he considered were living in a world of denial. He was disappointed in some. Chuck was more comfortable hanging out at Nogales, Arizona, than in a university setting, particularly the University of Arizona. He told me on several occasions that he couldn't stand going to Tucson, but he needed to go there to resolve some legal matters. However, he didn't get there, because his writing came first.

From my conversations with Chuck, it seemed that as much as Chuck had in common with Jim Harrison, Jim really never understood him—or possibly it hurt to try and understand Chuck. I know that Chuck shouldered pain from his disagreements with Harrison.

As for academia's desire for Chuck to be "another Edward Abbey"—while they had a number of similarities (they both clearly understood that *they were living in a desert,*[9] and they both certainly gravitated toward entropy of resources), Chuck was no more like Abbey than Abbey was like Wallace Stegner. There was only one Chuck Bowden, and one Edward Abbey, and there will be no clones.

Now a semiretired private investigator, CAL LASH was a Phoenix, Arizona, police officer from 1968 to 1991. In 1972 he worked with what is now the Federal Drug Enforcement Agency, under DEA agent in charge Phil Jordan, who later introduced him to Chuck Bowden.

NOTES

1. Scott Carrier, "The Final Rhapsody of Charles Bowden: A visit with the famed journalist just before his death," March 15, 2015, motherjones.com /media/2015/03/charles-bowdens-fury.

2. Bowden quote in the foreword to Arturo Carrillo Strong, *Corrido de Cocaine: Inside Stories of Hard Drugs, Big Money and Short Lives* (Tucson and New York: Harbinger House, 1990), xi.

3. Charles Bowden, *Some of the Dead Are Still Breathing: Living in the Future* (Boston and New York: Houghton Mifflin Harcourt, 2009).

4. Bowden, *Credo*, 8.

5. Bowden e-mail to the author, December 3, 2010.

6. Charles Bowden, *Mezcal* (Tucson: University of Arizona Press, 1988), 99.

7. I phoned Chuck while he was staying at Jim Harrison's house in Patagonia, shortly before Chuck returned to Las Cruces and died. He said he had been out of touch for a few days due to a visitor recording a profile article for a southwest publication. Chuck said he was working on projects that "would kill him or be the death of him" (not sure of the exact wording). I took his comments to mean that he was working himself to death. And I believe part of it was trying to do right by Gary Webb.

8. Bowden quote in his introduction to *Kill the Messenger*, by Nick Schou. As a police officer who worked illegal narcotics, I was well aware of such matters and knew DEA agents involved in these areas. Gary Schou tells the story in *Kill the Messenger: How the CIA's Crack Cocaine Controversy Destroyed Journalist Gary Webb* (New York: Nation Books, 2006). Gary Webb stirred controversy with his exposé *Dark Alliance: The CIA, the Contras, and the Crack Cocaine Explosion* (New York: Seven Stories Press, 1998).

9. Bowden, *Credo*, 5.

The Most Fearless Writer in America

KEN SANDERS

Although it took me more than three decades of friendship, if I ever learned anything from the late Charles Bowden, and I did, the most important lesson he taught me was listening. Whether on a phone call or in person, Chuck would expound on a current event, a favorite new or old author, a piece of music, a place, a person, a thing ... it didn't matter what the subject matter was at all, Chuck would rhapsodize over whatever his current obsession was ... and your job was to listen. Chuck's soaring rhapsodies were almost always of substance, about something or someone important, whether you grasped that importance at the time or not. You follow? Like I said, it took me more than thirty years to get it.

Chuck's soliloquies could be about almost anything: the beauty and truth of the avian world—its denizens' care and feeding, their habits and habitats; the dazzling variety of hummingbirds—and on and on into the depths of minutia. These impromptu encyclopedic lectures could come up at any time and any place and were a dazzling showcase for the quickness and brilliance of Chuck's mind. You follow?

I certainly didn't, at least not at first. That hummingbird rhapsody that started out being about the importance of feeding birds, after discoursing down dozens of avian byways, was articulated in such a manner as to make you learn something, usually not something you expected. Chuck's point about feeding birds was that you did it, not because they needed you, but because you needed them.

You might gather from these informal lectures that perhaps Chuck was not a listener himself. You'd be wrong about that. These brilliant outbursts were the result of a lifetime of listening to people and the planet where we all abide. Often, after listening to one of my own tirades, Chuck would say, "You can think that, Ken, but you'd be wrong." I can only recall twice, in over thirty years, when Chuck admitted I was right about something, thereby admitting that he was wrong. I can no longer remember what I was right about.

From *Killing the Hidden Waters* in 1977 to *El Sicario* in 2011, Chuck wrote and published more than two dozen books and left behind eight manuscripts that will be published posthumously by the University of Texas Press. And for a goodly portion of that time, he created and helped run *City Magazine* in Tucson and was a full-time working reporter. He could write ten thousand or so words before breakfast and revise the manuscript and lose half of those words later the same morning. I know. I watched him do it.

HOW I MET CHUCK

I began my Dream Garden Press publishing company in 1980 and was bugging my friend Edward Abbey to let me publish an annual calendar based on his writings. In March 1981, I received a phone call from Ed telling me that if I wished to discuss that "silly calendar" he was going to be at Lone Rock, down at Lake Powell, for "some kind of spring rites," and I could meet him there. I had been planning a backpack into the Maze that spring anyway, so I left a few days early and drove down to Lone Rock. It was the year that Abbey and a then-unknown radical environmentalist group, Earth First!, dropped a three-hundred-foot plastic crack down the face of Glen Canyon Dam.

I became heavily involved with Earth First! and returned two years later, in the spring of 1983. The Park Service had announced plans to hold a twentieth anniversary birthday party for Lake Powell, so I decided to organize a funeral party for Glen Canyon. The

NPS had invited Secretary of the Interior James Watt and the governors of Utah and Arizona (Scott Matheson and Bruce Babbitt); we had Ken Sleight, Dave Foreman, and Earth First! Ed Abbey couldn't make this one, but we had a pirate ship and an airplane and Beach Boys mannequins surrounding a James Watt mannequin. We staged our own counterdemonstrations: EARTH LAST! and Mutants For Watt.

After a long night of drinking and what have you at Willie's Waterdog Saloon in Glen Canyon City, I was rudely awakened from my fitful slumber by a tall, lanky man standing over me, asking questions that were way too hard for that time of day. That was my introduction to Charles Bowden. I didn't take well to his line of relentless, probing, and far-too-intelligent questioning, and I was no match for his insightful ruthlessness. My answers were likely surly and short and not answers at all. This was not a good beginning. Chuck soon had his revenge with his portrayal of me in a chapter in his third book, *Blue Desert*. Despite our rough-and-tumble beginning, Chuck and I would go on to become good friends.

VISITING CHUCK IN TUCSON

In the 1980s, Chuck and a friend had created *City Magazine*, and Chuck worked as a reporter while freelancing stories and articles and working on *Blue Desert*. He had previously published a brilliant book on water usage in the West—*Killing the Hidden Waters*—and *Street Signs Chicago*, which drew a cover blurb from Studs Terkel. He wrote relentlessly. I often visited Chuck back in those days and stayed at his home, which was within walking distance of the University of Arizona. The house and yard were modest sized, and the backyard was crammed with cactus, succulents, and native vegetation, all designed to attract as many birds as possible. Wherever Chuck lived, there were bound to be a lot of birds. The only author I know who might have been Chuck's equal in conjuring up birds

is Terry Tempest Williams. The centerpiece of this highly orchestrated landscape was a towering, overwatered mesquite tree.

Chuck's bedroom was dark and cave-like, the windows completely blacked out, providing utter darkness when he slept. Abso-
lute silence and total darkness. Kind of like a room-sized sensory
deprivation tank, but this being the desert, no water, just full
up with darkness and silence. No matter how long I stayed with
Chuck, I avoided his bathroom. I'm not particularly fussy about
hygiene and cleanliness, but I was terrified of Chuck's bathroom.
I don't recall ever taking a shower there. I brushed my teeth in the
kitchen sink, and I usually peed out in the yard. I would reluctantly
use the toilet, all the time terrified of what might come out of its
depths and suck me down into the sewer system (assuming there
was one). Let's just say Chuck's bathroom in those days was a petri
dish of the unknown, with several dubious scientific experiments
occurring simultaneously. And I learned, to my chagrin, that as
a scientist I apparently am a coward. If rust never sleeps was the
motto of his shower and bath, mold never rots was the B side of
that single. I often slept outside on the patio, or on the couch in
the living room.

Eating with Chuck back then was also an adventure of sorts—
adventure being whether you would eat or not. There was always
lots of good strong black coffee, though. But food wasn't much on
Chuck's mind. He had appetites for other things, and a metabolism
much different from mine. Later on, Chuck discovered the joys of
cooking, took a Cordon Bleu cooking class in Venice, Italy, and
became a gourmand chef. Eating with him *then* more than made
up for the early days of deprivation.

BOOKSTORE DAYS

By the early 1990s, after years of financial chaos, my publishing and
book empires were barely hanging on. As was I. I was holed up in

an old building off an alley in South Salt Lake City that my family owned. I'll let Chuck tell the story: "I know this guy in Salt Lake City who says he's a bookseller, but when you go to his shop, he's never there and the door is always locked. Even when he's there, even if you knock, the door is locked and he won't let you in." Or words to that effect. As I said, those were some rugged, financially lean years.

At a long-ago barbecue I hosted for Chuck, an old friend came by early, before the party, and drank beer with Chuck. They discussed orchids while I tended to my barbecue. My friend couldn't stay for the party, but he called a day or so later to ask me: "Say, who is that Chuck guy and why does he know so much about orchids." My friend fancied himself an orchid expert until he met Chuck. Late that night, in a far corner, Chuck was holding court with a few folks who hadn't left yet. I went to bed. The next morning, as the sun was coming up, Chuck and a lone woman were still out there, their chairs pressed together, earnestly engrossed in an all-night dialogue. Chuck had that kind of power.

I invited Chuck to come up and headline the grand opening of my new downtown Salt Lake City bookshop in the fall of 1997. Old friends Trent Harris, Alex Caldiero, and Scott Carrier also read or performed. Chuck wrote a piece especially for the event, "Book Collecting: The Last Refuge of the Illiterate," designed to offend my audience. Of course, I subsequently published the essay as a signed limited-edition collector's item. In the following years Chuck would return numerous times, usually in conjunction with a new book, but sometimes just to hole up at Forest House, my current abode.

Chuck loved reading and was a champion of authors and their books. But he had no use for first editions or rare collectibles. As Chuck would say, if one of my books is rare and collectible, it just means that the publisher didn't print enough of them in the first place. Ed Abbey was the same way. Both of them would make fun of me when I would give them piles of books to sign. But they always signed.

Like Abbey before him, Bowden developed a lifelong lust for the southwestern deserts and canyons. He lived in or moved around in the Sonoran and Chihuahuan Deserts of the southwestern United States and northern Mexico, with occasional forays into the Canyonlands country of the Colorado Plateau. He fell in love with the land and its people. Well, some of them. Scott Carrier and I once spent a day taking Chuck out into the western Utah desert and salt flats. With an F-16 swooping down on us on the bombing range, Chuck wasn't impressed. Or pretended not to be. He commented that our desert was too lush for his taste. The lying bastard!

ALAMOS

Chuck had, I think, a deep psychological need to always have a bolt hole, known only to a few, where he could escape. And he did so regularly—to write in isolation, to rest and recoup and contemplate what came next. One of the first of these bolt holes I ever knew about was Alamos, Sonora, a four-hundred-year-old colonial Spanish silver mining town high up in the Alamos Mountains about four hundred miles south of Tucson. The *camino* into town dead ended at the town plaza, and narrow winding cobblestone *calles* wound their way into the *barrancas* and the forests surrounding the village. At the edge of town there is an old tequila factory,

Charles Bowden at Alamos, Sonora

where it is rumored that during the Mexican Revolution Pancho Villa's men got so drunk the townspeople, armed with only sticks and stones, easily chased them away. It was here that Chuck first encountered future cartel boss Amado Carrillo Fuentes.

One of Chuck's criteria for selecting his bolt holes was remoteness; and he seemed to prefer a location in a transition zone of sorts. Alamos, being at the southernmost range of the Sonoran Desert, where it meets the northern edge of the tropics, was perfect. It boasted cactus and mutant vegetation transformed by the tropical moisture, like nowhere else. There were also orchids. Chuck wrote about this place in *The Secret Forest*, accompanied by lush photos by his pal Jack Dykinga. Here, I encountered for the first time kapok trees, whose large air-filled seeds used to be gathered and sewn into old "Mae West" style–life jackets.

Chuck was attracted to Alamos for the first time by his Tucson friend Merv Larson. Dubbed by the *Smithsonian Magazine* "the Picasso of concrete," Larson reportedly had amassed a large fortune and in the 1960s was involved in the movement to reform zoos by getting animals out of cages and into natural habitats. Merv had acquired a large tract of jungle land on the outskirts of Alamos that included the ruins of an old hospital. He was pouring his fortune into building a resort there, providing a serious income for the locals and drinking up the rest. The Secret Forest Hotel, built to incorporate the old hospital ruins, rose up out of the forest, with its second story unfinished, nothing but rebar and concrete basking in the sun and the rain.

Chuck, of course, holed up there and wrote.

ARIVACA

Arivaca, a sleepy town on the US-Mexico border, is home to a large national wildlife refuge that encompasses one of the largest avian flyways in the Americas. The locals simply call it "the bog."

Far from civilization and any kind of structured law enforcement, Arivaca shelters an unusual cast of characters—the usual dropouts from society, people on the fringe, folks on the lam, murderers and others on the run, sometimes from society, sometimes from themselves. The denizens hereabout police themselves. Or not. Most nights older, heavily laden trucks running without lights creep through the bog with engines groaning and gears clashing. Occasionally, a truck makes a wrong turn and dawn breaks over bales of marijuana spilled over the road and ground. Folks around here tend to keep to themselves and not ask a lot of questions. Like Alamos, it is good to have a guide here, someone who knows the lay of the land and is known, and hopefully tolerated, by the locals.

Chuck once introduced me to the town murderer in a bar. I shook hands with him. It was only later that Chuck told me about the murderer part. A friend of Chuck's had a ranch in the bog that wasn't being used much. Something about a bad divorce, I believe. Chuck, and his guard rattlesnake, Beulah, became the caretakers for a few years. Beulah lived under the back stoop. Byrd Baylor, a children's author, lived nearby. Early one morning after a late night, with the Carpenters playing on the stereo and a case of empty wine bottles strewn about, Chuck convinced me that Karen Carpenter was the best anorexic chick singer in the world. He was right.

PATAGONIA

Chuck's final bolt hole was in Patagonia, Arizona. Again, not far from the border, and again, right in the center of a bog. This was Jim and Linda Harrison's place, a private inholding with a river that runs through it, surrounded by a large family ranch and a preserve run by the Nature Conservancy. The Harrisons wintered here and moved out in the spring, when the landscape warmed up. That's when Chuck moved in. He summered there. He liked the heat.

Charles Bowden and a gray hawk, San Pedro River, Arizona, 1986

Chuck transformed the Harrison place into a birder's paradise. Dozens of feeders and thousands of birds. He blew through a hundred pounds of seed monthly. I know. I helped him haul it in. And as much nectar as the hummingbirds demanded. They were a thirsty bunch. Sitting on the front patio with Chuck at dusk, us drinking wine, the hummers drunk off the nectar, the rest of the "avians" spilling more seed on the ground than they consumed (no worries, the roadrunners and the rodents would take care of the spillage), Chuck and I would relax and talk and watch the birds flitter and the sun go down. It takes a while to hold a conversation with dozens, or hundreds, of hummingbirds flying about your face and eying the red of your wineglass as if it were more nectar.

We hiked daily in the bog and Chuck took great pleasure in showing me the treasures he found there. One of these was the oldest (and largest) living cottonwood tree in the world, or at least by our standards. And of course, the birds, and the bird nests, and the raptor aeries high up in the copse of trees.

RETURN TO ALAMOS

Chuck Bowden was the most fearless writer in America. To understand why, we must return to Alamos. A Mexican man was having a wedding party in a secluded spot down the river road, not far from the Secret Forest Hotel. This wasn't the man's first wedding party. He was fond of hosting them. He never actually got married. He just liked the parties—and the women. The man's name was Amado Carrillo Fuentes, a name that meant nothing to anyone then—just a small cog in the Juárez drug cartel.

Chuck became interested in Amado Carrillo Fuentes after he learned that Carrillo Fuentes had buried a friend of Chuck's alive up to his neck in the desert sand and left him for the sun and insects and critters to finish the job. Chuck was very loyal to his friends. So, he pursued Carrillo Fuentes through his rise to the head of the Juárez drug cartel. Chuck wrote stories about Carrillo Fuentes when nobody on this side of the border had ever heard of him, or cared—not the police, the DEA, the FBI, the CIA, nor any other shadowy government organizations. This was the early 1990s, the time in Chuck's life when, for better or worse, he descended into Juárez and Mexico to witness the drugs and madness and poverty. There he was befriended by Juárez journalist/photographer Julián Cardona and El Pastor, who tended to the insane and the unloved in an outdoor asylum on the outskirts of the city. And so many others.

Chuck kept writing about what he found: the murdered women in the trash heaps of Juárez, the tortured and the murdered and

L i e s I n T h e D e s e r t

Charles Bowden

That's what I do. I put words down on pieces of paper. I may not be the best person for the job, but frankly, I've never seen the job listed in the classified ads. I kind of made up the job as I went along. I use this place, this desert, as my springboard because here the past is rich, the ground is honest and the future is as naked and plain as the broken fence we call our border, as naked and plain as the dead rivers, as naked and plain as the butchered desert disappearing under pavement. You can live here and lie, but still, it is not as easy to lie here. Here lies are more naked, the earth itself rebukes the lies. Here you can see what is happening. The light is very bright here and you either look at things clearly, or you turn your back and pull the shades. But you can hardly say you don't know what is going on. That is the blessing of this place. And in the end the duty this place imposes on each and every one of us who lives here.

Chuck Bowden

This broadside is created for the opening of the new Salt Lake City Library, February 2003
Text © 2003 by Charles Bowden • Published by Ken Sanders Rare Books • Illustration © 2003 by Eddington and Makov

Letterpress broadside: "Lies In The Desert," by Charles Bowden, 2003

KILLING IS FUN

Words by Charles Bowden
Drawings by Alice Leora Briggs

THEY FIND THEM in the bright light of morning. Five men wrapped in blankets. The blankets are made in China since global trade has wiped out the Mexican *serape* industry. Two of the men have been decapitated and their severed heads rest in plastic bags. Beside them is a sign indicating that they died because they are "dog fuckers."

KILLING PEOPLE IS FUN. There is a feeling of power in slaughtering other human beings. And for many in Juárez, a feeling of power is a rare thing. The men beat their women, and that helps, but it is hardly the same rush of exhilaration that comes from killing another person. If wife beating was really a decent substitute for slaughter, murder would be all but absent in Mexico. But this is not the case.

NO ONE KNOWS how many assassins live and thrive in Juárez. There are an estimated 500 street gangs—but our knowledge of these facts is limited since the city police's expert on gangs was executed in January at the beginning of a killing season that is humming along at more than one hundred corpses a month. Still, assume there are 500 gangs, assume full membership requires murder, be conservative and say there are only ten members in each gang, and then you have 5000 young and frisky killers. To be sure, the Aztecas, one premier gang, has 3000 members—but why exaggerate the number of killers? Let's just say 5000. This tally ignores the world floating about the gangs, the land of police and soldiers and cartels where many other murderers find wages and niches.

YOU'RE GOING TO BE STRAIGHT, get that job in an American factory in Juárez, work five and a half days a week for sixty or seventy bucks, going to do this even though no one can live on such a wage in this city, going to do this even though you know the turnover in the plants is one hundred to two hundred percent a year, going to do this even though as you were coming up in the barrios you saw the men and women slowly devoured by the plants and then noticed that around age thirty they were tossed away like old junk, yeah, you're going to do this, you're going to be straight.

OR YOU ARE GOING TO TAKE THAT RIDE, join a gang, learn to flash the sign, do little errands for guys with more power, get some of that money that flows through certain hands, snort some powder and have the women eating out of your hand for a few hours in a discotheque, and you'll wear hip-hop clothing, have a short, burr haircut, never smile, stuff a pistol in your over-sized britches. A big SUV rolls down the *calle*, you hop in, the windows are darkly tinted and the machine prowls the city like a shark with its fanged mouth agape, and oh, it is so sweet when you squeeze the trigger and feel the burst run free and wild into the night air, see the body crumple and fall like a rag doll, roll on into the black velvet after midnight, and there'll be a party, fine girls and white powder, and people fear you and the body falls, blood spraying, and you feel like God even though you secretly stopped believing in God some time ago, and they tell you that you will die, that your way of living has no future, and you see the tired men and women walking the dirt lanes after a shift in the factory, plastic bags of food dangling from their hands, and you caress the gun stuffed in your waistband and life is so good and the killing is fun and everyone knows who has the guts to take the ride.

DYING IS THE EASY PART.
KILLING IS THE FUN PART.
TAKING THAT FIRST RIDE
IS THE HARD PART.

"Killing Is Fun" has been issued in a letterpress edition of 126 prints of which 100 numbered & 26 lettered are for sale by Ken Sanders Rare Books in June of 2009. Printed at Scrub Oak Press. Design by Alex Deckard. Artist and Writer are collaborating on: Dreamland, University of Texas Press 2010. Copyright 2009. All Rights Reserved.

Letterpress broadside: "Killing Is Fun," by Charles Bowden, art by Alice Leora Briggs, June 2009 the disappeared. Chuck went on to write a half dozen books about these grisly subjects. They would consume him for the rest of his life.

Through it all, he doggedly pursued Amado Carrillo Fuentes. He wrote an article for *GQ* magazine and published the first known photograph of the cartel jefe. Carrillo Fuentes retaliated by publishing Chuck's Tucson address on the front page of the Juárez newspaper. Chuck drove to the Carrillo Fuentes compound and stayed outside all night in his pickup truck, chain smoking cigarettes. Fuentes was definitely paying attention. Chuck kept writing. Amado Carrillo Fuentes died on a plastic surgeon's operating table, getting a new face. Bowden was still walking around. You follow?

THE END

Chuck died peacefully of a heart attack while taking a nap at his partner Molly Molloy's home in Las Cruces, New Mexico. I believe it was because his heart was too large. It had been absorbing the pain and suffering of all those desperate people he met and wrote about, until it finally just wore out. It wasn't empty, it was overfull. You follow?

KEN SANDERS is a lifelong bookman, vinyl junkie, river runner, activist, publisher, would-be author, and so on. He had the privilege of knowing Charles Bowden for more than thirty years, and Edward Abbey since the 1970s. He is proprietor of Ken Sanders Rare Books in Salt Lake City, Utah.

PUBLISHING CHUCK

Writing in the Moment

MELISSA HARRIS

"I was waiting for your kind to call." A sonorous voice at the other end of the line: deep and gravelly, with a hint of skepticism. He'd been white-gloved one too many times perusing various treasures at his hometown's Center for Creative Photography to embrace a call from a photography editor—without an eye-roll.

The December 1996 issue of *Harper's* had just come out, and within days I'd received a cluster of phone calls from colleagues— several photographers, and my friend Burt Joseph, a First Amendment lawyer—about a devastating article titled "While You Were Sleeping," by Charles Bowden. In that text, Bowden had focused on a group of young, unknown Mexican photographers who were risking their lives daily in the border city of Juárez to confront and combat *narcotraficantes*, rapists, murderers, and corruption— including in the government and police forces. They were bearing witness to it all with their cameras. Along with its exceptional reporting on a subject that had been largely ignored up until then, Bowden's piece placed front and center photography's searing ability to insist that attention must be paid.

Chuck was prescient, as always. This was years before Juárez would be regularly covered in the US press, before it would enter the public eye. He was also courageous—both physically, and in terms of his convictions, which were not always popular. And he was bilingual in words and images, understanding how those two languages can "brush up against each other" (as he might put it), realizing a power together that neither might achieve alone.

"While You Were Sleeping" resonated with urgency. I wanted Aperture to make a book with Chuck and the Juárez photographers immediately. That was the reason for my call, which he had apparently anticipated.

Chuck knew of Aperture, but didn't see Juárez as a subject for a typical Aperture photobook. I wanted to assure him that we could do it fearlessly and with integrity, so I sent him a copy of Eugene Richards's book *Cocaine True, Cocaine Blue*, which Aperture had published in 1994. The subjects of impoverished families and communities being ripped apart by addiction was familiar territory to Chuck: he had reported on these issues himself many times over the years. He found Gene's book to be wrenchingly honest—and I think that is what convinced him that Aperture had the chops to make his book on Juárez.

Later, I would introduce Chuck and Gene. It turned out to be the best gift I could have given either of them. Their processes and approaches were very different, but their intensity and sense of purpose—inspired by a vision of social justice, of fairness and human decency—bound them inextricably, heart, mind, and spirit. Some years later, in the "Phaidon 55" monograph *Eugene Richards*, Chuck would write this about Gene—but I think the words apply equally to Chuck himself:

> He's kept the faith. One that he cannot quite say but one he feels, and that faith is to get the world down with a camera, to tell stories with pictures, to paint scenes magazines do not want.... It is a calling.... And the call is coming from the people inside the photographs.

Also like Gene, Chuck had seen too much violence, too much poverty, too much injustice. What alleviated the darkness for him? Hummingbirds—in fact, all birds. A beloved tortoise, a cherished dog. Hoyt Axton's "Snowblind Friend," Leonard Cohen's *Ten New*

Songs. Red wine, shots of espresso, cooking a new osso buco recipe, night-blooming cereus, and desert walks, among other pleasures—pleasures that often made their way into his writing in one
form or another.

Other intense encounters. The Sicilian photojournalist Letizia
Battaglia has spent a lifetime combatting the Mafia with her cam-
era. In 1999, I showed Chuck the dummy for Aperture's book *Letizia Battaglia: Passion, Justice, Freedom*, which came out later that
year. He devoured the book, instantly recognizing in Letizia's guts
and humanity a kindred spirit. (When they eventually met, in
2001, they smoked, talked, and consumed espresso, riffing off each
other's fervor in ever-crescendoing excitement. It was volcanic.)
Chuck was also taken by one of the book's texts, by Palermo-based
anti-Mafia prosecutor Roberto Scarpinato, whose essay opens
with this quote from Edgar Lee Masters's "George Gray," in the
Spoon River Anthology. This spoke to Chuck:

I have studied many times / The marble which was chiseled for
me— / A boat with a furled sail at rest in a harbor. / In truth it
pictures not my destination / But my life. / For love was offered
me and I shrank from its disillusionment; / Sorrow knocked at
my door, but I was afraid; / Ambition called to me, but I dreaded
the chances. / Yet all the while I hungered for meaning in my life.
/ And now I know that we must lift the sail / And catch the winds
of destiny / Wherever they drive the boat. / To put meaning in
one's life may end in madness, / But life without meaning is the
torture / Of restlessness and vague desire— / It is a boat longing
for the sea and yet afraid

Chuck's book *Juárez: The Laboratory of Our Future* was published by Aperture in 1998. The book joined those by Gene Richards and Letizia Battaglia in its raw and brutal plea for a human

conscience. Chuck was a brilliant investigative journalist, whose honesty and passion were combined with a free-spirited defiance of gratuitous intellectual, political, and moral authority. He was always ready to challenge such givens. It all added up to an exhilaratingly simple provocation to his readers: *Take a stand. Make a difference.*

His presence? Large. In terms of both size and charisma, he owned any space he entered. One time when Chuck was in New York, he came over to my apartment to meet my Lhasa Apso puppy, Ella. Ella has always been a bit dubious of men, and when Chuck strode through the apartment door, his sheer height set my eleven-pound defender off into an outburst of growls. Chuck immediately lay down on the floor. Ella, still unconvinced, climbed onto his stomach and paced up and down his entire body many times, thereby establishing her dominance over him (at least, that was what Chuck told me her intention was). Hilarious as the performance seemed to me, it was plainly a very serious ritual for the two of them.

Chuck connected to people, creatures, and landscapes, and to a dazzling array of ideas and disciplines. The speed and agility with which he digested all he experienced were rivaled only by the explosion of ideas those experiences inspired. He was viscerally, uncompromisingly *awake* and ready to engage.

In 1999, after nearly five decades in existence, Aperture's quarterly magazine underwent a reconceptualization and redesign. Formed in 1952 by a group of photography proponents—including Dorothea Lange, Ansel Adams, Barbara Morgan, and the gurulike founding editor, Minor White—*Aperture* magazine has always been a mission-driven publication. At end of the century, I was its editor. Photography was undergoing radical changes, both technically and conceptually. I wanted to end the monographic or thematic approach—exploring a single idea, country, or ethnicity—

that had dominated the magazine's evolution. Our publication had become exclusive, not in the arrogant sense but in that it was leaving out much good work just because it didn't fit a given theme. With typical generosity, Chuck offered to lend his voice to ours. He was my pen pal and co-conspirator, having been a magazine editor himself, with deeply held beliefs about the magazine as a vehicle. A few days after he saw the first issue of the reconceived *Aperture* in 2000, an unsolicited "rough promotional manifesto" for the magazine appeared in my inbox. It was from Chuck, and it read, in part:

> The camera may lie, cheat, and steal, but it never has to stay home. Let's team the fresh eyes with the best writing and let them play like musicians in an after-hours club. Let's have harmony, dissonance. Let's improvise. Let's have no rules or schools or borders. Let's take the white gloves off. Let's be happy, let's be riveted, let's be sad, let's be the ocean blue, and let's be alive to what light and film can do to our souls.

With Chuck, there were "no rules or schools or borders" when it came to his work in *Aperture*. Over the twelve years that I was editing the quarterly, we had the privilege of publishing eight articles by him. Interlaced through all Chuck's pieces were sensuous considerations of time, life, death, love, and beauty, and the intoxicating wonder in being.

His certainty that images and words could coexist with parity— that one did not have to be subordinate to the other—made him an extraordinary ally. And with Chuck, sometimes it was in fact unquestionably the *words* that drove the piece. Although this balance might have perplexed some of our subscribers, to our delight, photographers were almost always willing to play, allowing their work to be pulled out of its usual context in order to connect with Chuck's subjects and sensibility.

A powerful example of this is Chuck's article "Blue Mist," which appeared in *Aperture*'s summer 2000 issue. It is a stark, vivid argument against capital punishment. It gave us the chance to speak with Bill Eggleston and Adam Fuss, to ask them if we might use their work in this somewhat incongruous context. It led to conversations I would never have had otherwise with these photographers. Their unqualified agreement was liberating for all of us.

We published Chuck's "The Lives of Saints" in our winter 2011 issue. It is a riveting, poetically woven piece about the violence still permeating Juárez, moonrises, hummingbirds, St. Augustine, Italian meals, and the American landscape (in every sense). Alongside Chuck's words, we used David Wojnarowicz's images in a context I know David would have appreciated, given his own nonlinear, controversial tapestries of words and images addressing AIDS, politics, religion, and the natural world. The piece closes with Gregory Crewdson's magical fireflies, and this passage by Chuck:

> I have decided to learn from appetites. I will slobber and drool and chew and inhale. I am done with dainty feeding.... / I am not a camera. / I am not a theory. / I am a hunger.

Chuck Bowden had no patience for conformity, no interest in power except to effect change. He often wrote of an *"is-ness"*—a term I've borrowed several times. I take it to mean a *presentness*, an *in-the-worldness* that makes everything vital and electric—like Chuck himself.

MELISSA HARRIS is editor-at-large of Aperture, where she has edited over forty books—including Charles Bowden's *Juárez: The Laboratory of Our Future*. She was editor-in-chief of *Aperture* magazine during 2002–2012. *A Wild Life*, her biography of photographer Michael Nichols, was published by Aperture in 2017.

The Big Kick: Editing Chuck

REBECCA SALETAN

I had the mind-expanding adventure of editing Chuck Bowden on only three books (*Blues for Cannibals*, *Some of the Dead Are Still Breathing*, and *A Shadow in the City*), but once he entered my awareness he remained an outsized presence there—emotionally, morally, aesthetically. In person, we met less than a handful of times, only once or twice in New York. I don't recall a single business lunch. Once, he camped with my family in the Coronado State Forest when we made a trip west, stoically tolerating two chattering four-year-olds and our lack of appropriate gear, despite an insanely overpacked trunk, for the sudden change in weather that broke over us on a day hike from desert scrub to alpine forest. A couple of years later, on a trip to California, I made a quick round-trip to Tucson and finally got to see the fabled garden, to taste the gumbo Chuck had been perfecting—we both loved to cook, and we debated the fine points of roux and okra and filé—and to see at last the lair from which that torrent of words emanated.

Mostly, though, we had a history of meeting by nonmeeting. Once, I returned to my office to find a magnificent bottle of red wine on my desk with a note—but no Chuck. He'd been and gone. He made no secret of his disdain for most of New York media culture and his even greater disdain for DC's political culture. To this day I cannot visit the capital without his description of it as "a city of people barely past their teens clowning around in suits" ringing in my ears. When we were approaching publication of *A Shadow in the City*, I called him to see when we might converge in Dallas so that he could introduce me to the DEA agent who was the subject of that book, in hopes of earning his trust and willingness to participate in publicity. "Oh, you don't need me there," Chuck said. "He just needs to meet *you*." I spent a day shadowing that remarkable cop, who had me impersonate a New York drug agent "who works with the Russians," so that I could sit in while he questioned a CI (confidential informant) in a Starbucks, and then a restless night in an equally nondescript motel where informants from out of town were put up, so paranoid I could barely bring myself to call my husband on my cell phone. "I like to stay in the ones with the hidden cameras," Chuck drawled, when I gave him my report. "They're in the alarm clock." It hardly mattered if he was kidding or not.

He'd sneer if you referred to his "career," but, a former editor himself, he unfailingly took in the minor twists and turns in mine, and he sent encouragement and sympathy just when I needed them most. When I became an editor-in-chief, he wrote me (in his characteristic uncapitalized style—he believed hitting the shift key was a waste of time and energy):

> becky
> maybe i once sent you this quote. if not, here it is. i found it a great comfort when i edited a magazine. it also applies to books, i believe.
>
> chuck

> *I note what you say about your aspiration to edit a magazine. I am sending you by this mail a six-chambered revolver. Load it and fire every one into your head. You will thank me after you get to Hell and learn from other editors how dreadful their job was on earth.*
> H. L. MENCKEN to William Saroyan, January 25, 1936

I returned to my office one afternoon to a note, not from Chuck but from the great narrative nonfiction writer William Langewiesche, to whom I'd sent a galley of *A Shadow in the City* with some trepidation. I hoped for a blurb, but I worried that Langewiesche, who wrote a gorgeously lean and understated line, might not appreciate the Bowden genius for more-is-more. Would Hemingway embrace Fitzgerald? In his younger days, Langewiesche had piloted a small plane in the border region and had written about the place in his first book, *Cutting for Sign*. His note was uncharacteristically effusive—he was thrilled to have discovered Bowden's work. Many writers could provide information about the border, he said; what blew his mind was Chuck's ability to capture the smoke-and-mirrors *feel* of the place, to render that "elusive underworld in the perfect tones of a dream." As Chuck himself said, in an NPR interview: "I decided the very experience, this kind of unreality I was living in, was the book, because this is a lot of our relationship to Mexico and this is the drug world."

I'd tasted Langewiesche's deep thrill on my own first encounter with a Bowden book, *Blood Orchid*, not long after it had been published in 1995. Early in its pages, Pancho Villa emerges among the cottonwoods to hike alongside Chuck. You could do that in nonfiction? There was something addictive about this writing, and something mesmerizing, charismatic, prophet-like (as others have said) about the persona on the page, the guy who wrote (as, Bowden-inspired, I'd later write in jacket copy for *Blues for Cannibals*) "scripture for an age when bushes no longer burn."

I learned things about writing from Chuck, and I loved to introduce other writers to his work—especially young writers who need courage to follow their wilder impulses. It's hard to derive "rules" from a writer who appeared to break them willfully, but here are a few:

Follow the line of a feeling to evoke a greater whole, rather than the straight arrow of time along a single narrative line. Many writers are afraid to jump around chronologically, or from storyline to storyline. Bowden couldn't help it—for him a story was only the sum of its disparate parts. *Blues for Cannibals* is a gumbo of "red wine,

Moby-Dick, human brutality, the suffering of other species, the obdurateness of paradox, the ambush of love, beauty beyond comprehension, the immensity of loss implicit in our planetary crimes," to quote the reviewer Donna Seaman, who loved and trumpeted this and many other of Bowden's books.

Describe from scratch. Bowden's evocations of place are masterpieces of synesthesia, meticulously observed and composed. From *A Shadow in the City*:

> Listen as the air brakes jack the ear on the big roads lacing the city and moving its blood like sludge, hear the horns, the choppers— whomp whomp whomp—overhead on their secret errands, the shout of children racing through the back lanes, the chirp and crackle of birds stalking the crumbs and garbage, the click of keys in the towers, the hum of overhead lights in the caves of work, the soft rich vowels of Spanish in the back rooms of businesses, the chords of a blues guitar asking for someone to consider the question, long sigh of a zipper down the back before the dress melts to the floor, the bark of angry dogs, the slippery song of knife sliding into flesh, blade warming itself with blood, the lights at night fighting the prairie, beams, shred, slabs, towers, beacons of light that only seem to underscore the loneliness as people pull the shades in their houses and lock doors and scurry down darkened walkways and pray for dawn.

His flights of figurative speech are judiciously deployed, and even at his most baroque he is not over the top because the figures emerge from connections seen and felt: "Executives with casting-couch faces, starlets with the blank eyes of fawns and the hearts of great white sharks" (*Blues for Cannibals*).

Be willing to offer yourself up in order to implicate the reader. Bowden is a master observer, but he never lets us forget there's a human—a human with both powerful hungers and a relentless conscience—doing the witnessing. An early chapter in *Blues for Cannibals* opens on the back of the head of a woman. We quickly come to realize she is sitting at the funeral of her dead toddler, killed by her boyfriend who "most likely held him by the legs and swung him like a baseball bat" against the wall of their motel room while she was at her job lap-dancing at a "gentleman's club." Sensing we will want to flee in horror, Bowden reels us back:

Now I am studying the back of the mother's head as she sits in a separate alcove off to the side. She has fine hair, a kind of faint red, and I knew a woman with hair like that, and as I stare I can smell this other woman, and feel my hands tracing a path through the slender strands. I can smell the soap, the scent of the other woman, the small smile and fine bones and clean even teeth. In my memory, the coffin is open, the boy's face very pale and blank and he is surrounded by donated teddy bears that have poured in from a town that told itself these things were not supposed to happen.

We are not only seeing what Bowden sees, but yeah, we knew a woman with hair like that too, and before we can make our escape, we too are feeling it slide through our fingers, bathing ourselves in her scent, unable to turn off the sensory stream and detach.

Go all the way. Evoking and describing are not enough. Take the leap, connect story and meaning, show *and* tell, pronounce. Dare to think and feel—even exhort and instruct—from the page:

We wish to live forever and because of this desire we hardly live at all. (*Blues for Cannibals*)

We waste too much time on arguments about nothing. It happened, we are what became of it. There is no Eden to save, not now, not in 1492. (*Blood Orchid*)

If I had my life to live over, I would live very, very little of it the same. When people say they would change nothing in their life, I think they are either liars or fools. Life is about learning, and if you respect life and learn from it, you would of course not do things the same way. (*Blues for Cannibals*)

Apply seat of pants to seat of chair. For all the mad energy and reach of his writing, Chuck was one of the most disciplined writers I've ever edited. "To sleep in is a grievous sin," he believed, and he adhered to a punishing daily output. ("Is poet really a full-time job?" he once quipped to me.) When I quit a job that had made me miserable, he wrote to console me, recalling the turn his own work had taken after a magazine he'd poured his heart into editing had folded years before: "I went back to ... what had always provided me with my best sense of self. Since that time, I have never worked for another human being or belonged to anything. I became in my own strange way a kind of control junkie who wrote and peddled the writing." But while his books were sacred to him in a way he claimed his journalism was not ("Now I am finishing some magazine gigs ... because I want to do a book on southern Louisiana, on a place I sense is living in the future that awaits us all")—and he sometimes fulfilled his vision of them in what sounded like a fugue state, holed up in the most anonymous motel room he could find—once he had produced a draft he was remarkably egoless about it. He was almost gleeful when I sliced into his prose—"Attagirl!" he'd egg me on. He joked that he would be happy if the editing reduced a particular book to the size of a matchbook.

Along with the Mencken, he sent me this from Hemingway:

It's this way, see—when a writer first starts out, he gets a big kick from the stuff he does, and the reader doesn't get any; then, after a while, the writer gets a little kick and the reader gets a little kick; and finally, if the writer's any good, he doesn't get any kick at all and the reader gets everything.

I have both quotes tacked above my desk to this day, and every time I look at them I yearn to be on the receiving end once more of the tremendous kick I got from editing Chuck.

REBECCA SALETAN is editorial director of Riverhead Books, an imprint of Penguin Random House. Over more than three and a half decades in publishing, she has also held positions at Yale University Press; Simon and Schuster; Farrar, Straus & Giroux; and Houghton Mifflin Harcourt. In 2018, she received the Poets & Writers Editor's Award.

Of Rock 'n' Roll and Corn Laws: A Few Words on Charles Bowden

GREGORY MCNAMEE

Chuck Bowden once brought me a beguiling, befuddling manuscript. It was thick, knotty, printed in one of those horrific fonts that the early generations of Mac computers offered back in the middish '80s. I could make neither hide nor hair of the thing at first glance, but I carted it off to my office from our conference room—two lawn chairs, that is, in the middle of his poured-concrete-floored living room, surrounded by a pile of beer cans as the afternoon wore on, our talk punctuated by repeated spins of the latest records by Bob Dylan and Townes Van Zandt, back in those days when records were records and Apples were new.

A couple of weeks later I went back to Chuck with the manuscript. "I think I get it," I said. "But I think you need to reorganize it chronologically. The narrative would make more sense that way."

Chuck looked at me balefully, taking a long pull on one of his endless straights, and said, "Ah, fuck, McNamee. Chapter organization. That's just marketing."

I went away, and he went back to his Apple. Silence. Then, a few weeks later, Chuck was back with a manuscript that made eminent sense, if sense in a kind of loopy, deranged, Hunter Thompson-esque way. *Mezcal*, it was called, and it aimed to erect a concrete mausoleum over a culture that refused to acknowledge that its corpse overlay a place of aridity and austerity: "For my entire life I have hungered for the smell of earth and lived on carpets of cement and asphalt," Chuck wrote. He added that whatever gods there were in this overheated, underwatered place were dead and gone, and though he no longer quite believed in them, neither did he disavow them. I think he was being merely rhetorical on that score, for Chuck well knew that I'itoi, the Tohono O'odham creator, reigns in this place still. The traditional desert people believe that anywhere I'itoi's rocky home atop the mountain called Baboquivari can be seen is part of their world, and from Chuck's roof, Baboquivari lies in plain view—which means, of course, that I'itoi could see him, too.

Chuck preceded *Mezcal* with two more or less straightforward books that I edited for the University of Arizona Press, *Blue Desert* and *Frog Mountain Blues*, both books in which I'itoi plays his part. I have to confess, with due bias, that the first is my favorite of all his books, one that best captures the essence of a bleary-eyed cynic who secretly embodied everything that some wise person once remarked of the kind: that a cynic is really nothing more than a disappointed romantic.

That romanticism countered the one of old, the near-cliché of the desert of the John Van Dyke school that exalted in the pretty pink colors and far distances, that took the fact of distance and isolation as an affirmation of some sort of moral cleanliness that would have pleased T. E. Lawrence. No, for Chuck Bowden, the desert was a place that tested souls, to be sure, but always found them wanting: the desert, he insisted, was a place of which we were eminently unworthy, as every bit of our bad behavior ever since arriving here proved beyond question. In that insistence, Chuck was himself of a very old kind: a desert prophet who, having wandered as a stranger into a strange land, wondered why everyone was busy digging into the ground instead of digging the sky.

Chuck often wore a baseball cap, by way of Earth First!, with the legend "rednecks for social responsibility," but he had to go to grad school in order to attain that redneck status. In one of our earliest conversations, he asked me what I could tell him about the Corn Laws. I must have paused for a second too long, wondering if he was adverting to something to do with the Whiskey Rebellion. My pause gave him the expanse he needed to embark on a disquisition that, inside of a few beers apiece, took in the class struggle in nineteenth-century agrarian England, Wat Tyler's rebellion, the resistance of Dunkards and Lollards, and various other emanations of medieval and early modern Europe. All of this was odd enough considering that his academic hero, back when, yes, he was really and truly in grad school, was the radical Americanist historian William Appleman Williams, whose sense of resistance to things as they were was fueled by a fair dose of countryside rebellion of his own, out in the populist farm communities of southwestern Iowa where rednecks and intellectuals alike were socially responsible, mistrustful of anyone who hadn't done an honest day's work in his or her life. Chuck Bowden professed scorn for academics, that is to say, but he lectured as much as talked, and he would have made a fine addition to any campus as the kind of curmudgeonly prof who would have put the fear in an undergraduate but inspired the best term paper he or she ever wrote.

Chuck, who did his share of the dirty jobs, was fueled by many things. One was a kind of simmering anger that put me to mind of something the Scottish Marxist poet Hugh MacDiarmid wrote of in his memoir *Lucky Poet*, the necessity of cultivating a Viking-worthy *riastral*, a berserker-like rage to face the world around him. The other was a soundtrack that would sound like a classic rock station today, except with the deep cuts and as interpreted by a blend of MacDiarmid and Diogenes, using music as a tool in Chuck's ongoing critique of the world. It did not surprise me in the least when Chuck came into my office one day and announced that he was working on a book that was nothing but quotes from Bob Dylan and Jimi Hendrix in dialogue with each another. Fascinating, I told him, but getting permission to use the lyrics would bankrupt anyone short of Steve Jobs. The project did not go far, but it had

Charles Bowden, "Rednecks for Social Responsibility," 1987

its allure. He could have run with some of their ideas about lonely watchtowers and voodoo curses and woven them into a narrative featuring A-10 fighters, tainted water supplies, collapsed desert empires, civilizations vanishing before our eyes.

The other fuel was a damaging one, in the end, and that was the alcohol, and the cigarettes, and maybe a few other substances from time to time. I say this not moralizingly, for I did my best to keep up with Chuck, as a good editor was thought to have to do with a good writer back in those hazy days. I mean, Reagan was president, after all. One of my favorite inscriptions in my whole collection is one Chuck wrote in my copy of his book *Killing the Hidden Waters*: "To Greg, who would never kill water as long as there was a beer available." I couldn't do it, just as I could never keep up with Jim Harrison or, in his headiest moments, Ed Abbey. I count that a failure of a kind but a victory of another, for I—at least at the moment—still walk the earth. Moderation in all things, including moderation, as my doctor says.

Julian Hayden, a grand old man of the desert who gave Chuck and me and many another desert rat guidance and inspiration, once pointed to a corner of his yard littered with gallon jugs of Gallo wine, back in the day when Gallo made nothing short of rot-gut, and said, "Chuck stayed here for a couple of nights last week." A bartender at a Vietnamese restaurant at which we held, ahem, editorial conferences from time to time marveled, "I've never seen anyone who can drink so much."

All that was means to an end, and very much of a time. Our model was not Raymond Chandler, a man of mild ways, but Humphrey Bogart, who made cynicism and resisting authority and smoking unfiltered cigarettes with a rock and rye in the other hand seem very cool indeed. Bogart, of course, died a terrible death, but as for the rest of us, well, we were immortal.

Chuck was not just immortal but single-minded. No one could drink so much and work so hard—not even Hunter S. Thompson, whose work faltered long before he died. When Chuck had had a good night of it, he slept a few hours and then got to work, banging away at his computer for hours on hours, printing and marking up draft after draft, guzzling good coffee (and this back in the day when good coffee was not a given or a God-given birthright in America), and sucking down a pack or two of squares—and then, six weeks later, six weeks later just about every six weeks the calendar could record, producing another book. Yep, that'd be riastral rage: fifteen thousand words a week, not counting discards, all to the end of setting the wobbly historical record of our life and times straight at last.

I edited four of Chuck's books in the 1980s, as I say, books that were lightning-hot and fierce cries of love and pain, each a great leap forward from the one before it, a startling evolution of form whose central message remained constant up until the end: the world is a catastrophic mess, Chuck told us, and we are all complicit in its destruction—some more than others, some more thoughtfully than others, but all of us guilty. At the same time, he continued, the world is a fine place, and though none of us is worthy of its heartbreaking beauty and though we will probably lose in the end, it is our job to do whatever we can to save it from the monstrous machines that are devouring it. With which *we*, beg pardon, are devouring it.

We parted ways as editor and author when, after the three epochal books published in Tucson, he got the attention of the New York trade world and took the fourth manuscript we worked on together off to the land of fame and fortune. That book spoke of danger—of, for instance, the cocaine trade in Tucson, which he and I and friends such as Arturo Carrillo Strong had investigated in our own ways, and it forged links that Iran-Contra would prove in time. It spoke of bars full of people with mirrored sunglasses and mirrored teeth who would sooner see you—see anyone—dead than be bothered with a question.

Chuck Bowden asked questions. A few books down the line, having dealt with the likes of the saint-cum–con man Charles Keating and other assorted episodes of mayhem on the Sonoran Desert side of things, Chuck crossed watersheds and began to work the territory that would be an obsession forevermore, the binational killing field that was the Rio Grande in the more dangerous corners of El Paso and Ciudad Juárez. He would write of dead prostitutes and dead innocents and dead assassins and dead places: he would become the poet laureate of the dead and of all of those of us in the desert who are limping, ineluctably, into death's domain, whether having committed horrific crimes or just been in the wrong place at the wrong time.

Chuck Bowden was an original, and that is no cliché: he found a new way to write about the borderlands, and then the whole heart of the American empire, with a pure burning spirit that no one had captured before. He found a nonromantic way of writing about the desert, its literature full of purple emanations about alpenglow and pronghorn, while infusing it with a brand of romanticism all its own: lying in a sleeping bag on a gunnery range and counting satellites floating by in the sky, after all, is not so different from crossing near-virgin ground and happening on a long-abandoned pit house or a discarded suit of conquistador armor. Our mutual friend Ed Abbey had gotten off a nice ding or two about cops and tanks and the freedom that comes from walking naked in the screaming hot desert, but Chuck turned those offhand comments into a cri de coeur that was sometimes a college seminar and sometimes a coyote's howl. The academics have retreated into the aridity of post-postmodernism, the desert rats into a kind of quiet gnawing-at-the-edges activism, all of which makes Chuck's absence all the much more noticeable. But even absent, he speaks more than most, and he still has much to say.

Thirty years after his death, Ed Abbey is getting attention from a new generation, which may, pray the gods, bring that activism, environmental and literary and humanistic, to the fore again. Those gods know we need it: we need a purifying fire to scorch the greed-heads off this land, which indeed we do not deserve. It may take another thirty years before a new generation of literary journalists discovers what you can do given the formidable steel of a Charles Bowden. It's not that hard: all it takes is a command of the whole sweep of human history, a gimlet eye, and knowing every verse of Townes Van Zandt's "Pancho and Lefty." You don't even have to smoke cigarettes or drink bad red wine in order to pull it off, though there are days that I think the recipe, adjusted for modern abstemiousness, might be just the thing that a skilled practitioner of righteous indignation and unauthorized maintenance on big yellow machines might want to put to work.

Chuck had revenge of a kind, by the way, when he asked me to write for *City Magazine*, which he founded with longtime partner in crime Dick Vonier in 1986. One of my fond hopes is that the magazine, which lasted about three years and was the sort of thing that Manhattan or London would be proud of, is digitized and made widely available, for it's the kind of incitement that ought to set a hundred schools of thought contending and a thousand flowers blooming; the young radicals and desert rats of today ought to get something like it going again, filled with smart writing and scornful rage and other such things to *épater* the bourgeoisie. Bowden edited telegraphically, but he sure could make a magazine sing.

I wrote the piece he asked for—I no longer recall on exactly what, but one that probably tried to intellectualize something that didn't need it, like a punk rock band. He read it, then handed it back to me and said, "It needs more spin." Spin? I thought. Spin? Then I replied, "Ah, fuck, Bowden. Spin. That's just marketing."

GREGORY MCNAMEE is a Tucson-based writer and editor with more than forty books and more than six thousand periodical pieces to his credit. He is also a contributing editor to *Kirkus Reviews* and *Encyclopaedia Britannica*. Over a long career as an editor, McNamee has worked with hundreds of writers, including Jim Harrison, Edward Abbey, and Charles Bowden.

Sketches of Chuck

TIM SCHAFFNER

> *I'd also like to thank Tim Schaffner,*
> *my agent, who woke up one day and*
> *decided to find a different line of work.*
> *He never complained about the unseemly*
> *manuscripts I would leave at his door*
> *like scat. And we never had a contract.*
> *Or a disagreement. If you think this is a*
> *common experience, ask around.*
>
> CHUCK BOWDEN

I was Chuck's literary agent from 1988 to 1993, and, come to think of it, his first literary agent, too. The above acknowledgment appeared in the back of his book *Blood Orchid*—the last book I had the pleasure to work with him on, over twenty-five years ago. During this time, I represented him in the sales, negotiations, and creation of, in chronological order, *Red Line, Desierto, The Sonoran Desert* (with photographer Jack Dykinga), *The Secret Forest* (also with Jack Dykinga), *Trust Me: Charles Keating and the Missing Billions* (with Michael Binstein), as well as the aforementioned *Blood Orchid*, though—if memory serves me correctly (which it sometimes does)—I was no longer active as agent at the time of that book's publication in 1995.

I first became aware of Chuck and his writing when visiting Tucson with my soon-to-be first wife and her family in the late 1980s. On one of these early visits, I came across a locally produced publication called *City Magazine*, a wonderful tabloid that was a cross between the *Village Voice* and the *New Yorker*, yet with a decided irreverence as well. It was in those pages that I was introduced to the columnist Iggy the Iguana and its creator and cofounder of the magazine, Charles Bowden. Later that month, back in my hometown of New York City, I read a review of Chuck's just-published book, *Mezcal*. On my next visit to Tucson, I bought a copy at the Haunted Bookshop—an independent bookstore tucked away in the wilds near Tohono Chul Park on Tucson's northwest side— and read it in one gulp.

After my return to New York, I wrote Chuck a fan letter addressed care of *City Magazine*, inquiring if by chance he was interested in working with a literary agent for any new work he might have. A few weeks went by. Embroiled in other matters, I had all but forgotten about my letter when a package arrived with a rubber-band-bound manuscript titled *Red Line* and a terse note that read in part: "Here you go. And good luck dealing with those 'demons from hell ... ' publishers, as [Edward] Abbey calls them."

I consumed *Red Line* that night—riveted by Chuck's account of his solo walk from Tucson west through the Cabeza Prieta desert that he described in a matter-of-fact tone that underscored the deeply moving personal story of crossing the "red line" in his own life—and sent it off to a few editors who, I felt, would be attuned to Bowden's voice and resonate with his dead-eyed perspective. Gerald Howard, newly landed at W. W. Norton from Viking, was one such editor: he loved the book and made an offer in the low four figures. As I recall, Gerry's opening remark was, "Where'd you find this guy?"

My first phone call to Chuck was to convey the news. It was the first time I was to hear his basso profundo voice. He enjoined me to see if we could raise the ante a little, but suggested that I first "go to the bathroom and do a couple of lines, or whatever you guys do, and then go ask for more money." I promptly called Gerry, albeit without the enhancement of that particular stimulant, and asked for a higher advance; Gerry returned with a new figure. Chuck accepted, and we were off and running.

I had the chance to meet Chuck on another family visit to Tucson shortly after that, and so began a working and personal friendship that continued for several years and several books, and beyond. What I remember most about Chuck and our author-agent relationship were those times, generally around 9 am, when we would begin our day at the office. Just as Mr. Coffee was making its magic gurgling and the aroma of fresh-brewed java was wafting through the air—as if on cue—I would hear my assistant Jennifer's signature greeting: "Hiya, Chuck!" And there he'd be, looming in the doorway in his usual battle dress: a somewhat careworn down vest, a blue or pink denim shirt (or sometimes an olive-colored shirt adorned with many pockets, out of which sprouted multiple pens), jeans of course, and, it seemed for most of the year, the perennial huaraches.

Immediately the cigarette would appear, a no-filter Lucky Strike, and his monologue would begin, as if it had been carrying on in his head for the past several hours, which most likely it had, given that he was the earliest riser I've ever known (3 or 4 am was generally his waking hour, and his chosen time to write was from then until about 7 am). With coffee cup in hand, he'd call out to me, "Didja read the pages I sent you yesterday? Don't bother. It's shit."

"I threw all that out. Sorry you had to read that crap, if you did. I'll get a new draft for you later." (And, sure enough, a new manila envelope containing completely rewritten pages would be awaiting me on our doorstep that evening.) Then, after some lively conversation with Jennifer, generally of a political nature— national, local, world, you name it—he would be off with his customary "Adios" to return to his copious revisions, clattering out the driveway in his Toyota pickup truck with the bumper sticker "Nature Bats Last." I'd like to think we provided a kind of anchor, a shelter from the storm that was Chuck's life and world, in between his various peregrinations, whether Mexico, Argentina, or the northern Pacific. We also provided a sounding board of sorts to his nocturnal or predawn musings, as we shared cigarettes, coffee, and many laughs.

Later on, when I had disbanded the agency and was somewhat adrift, he provided shelter from my own storms on a couple of occasions. During this time he was working on *Blood Orchid* on a ranch outside of Arivaca. He invited me to come hang out there with him. We took long walks into the hills behind the house that were pocked with abandoned mines and other detritus of a bygone West. It was during one of these walks when he turned to me and said, "Look, as far as I'm concerned, you can sit on a rock for the rest of your life, and I won't think any the less of you."

To some this might seem like a snarky backhand compliment, but coming from Chuck, I knew it was sincere. Another observation he made while I was casting around for what-to-do-and-be-next-in-my-life was that everyone has an arrow within them that drives each individual, and that this inner compass is somewhat predetermined or instilled from a very early age; understanding oneself occurs with the knowledge of just what that arrow is. Of course, he didn't extrapolate; that was my task to discover, but I felt that, right here, was someone who understood what I was going through. It was as if he knew me better than I knew myself—which he probably did.

Client, friend, mentor. Chuck was all of these. For a young literary agent newly settled in Tucson and the Southwest, he was a guide as well to this land far from the chaos and claustrophobia of New York City. He introduced me to other writers, photographers, artists, cops, and journalists, some of whom became clients too. As he said in his acknowledgment, we never signed a contract, and never had a disagreement, rare back then, still rarer now.

At the end of his acknowledgment in *Blood Orchid*, Chuck wishes me well in my "new life." To which I can only say, "Adios, Chuck, and I wish you well in yours."

TIM SCHAFFNER, a resident of Tucson for over twenty-five years, worked for New Directions Publishing and Harcourt Brace Jovanovich before joining his father's literary agency, John Schaffner Associates, in 1983. After several years teaching in public high and charter schools, he founded Schaffner Press in 2001.

Assembling a Bowden Bibliography

WALT BARTHOLOMEW

Somewhere in 1999, I got into the idea of binding books. I have no idea why I started doing that. I didn't even read a book on binding. I went over to Bookman's and got a one-dollar hardback that had the sewn binding, and I just tore it apart and deconstructed it like an engineer. Then I said, "Okay, this is how you do it." So, I looked up bookbinding supplies. They sell these things at craft stores, the thread and whatever—book board is the big thing. It's not standard cardboard. It's between hardboard and wood, and you have to cut it with a box-cutter knife. And I was ready and said, "I need something to bind, now."

So I started writing letters to authors, thinking, "They're not going to answer me." It would have to be a limited edition. I can't do five thousand copies. That would kill me. Let me do a hundred of something. I am sort of a research nut. I had gotten addicted to the whole microfilm thing—that is entertainment to me. It's an OCD thing. And one time, when I went over to my friend Chuck Bowden's house, I said to him, "I'd like to do a little bibliography of you." It promotes him in a way and makes it seem as if somebody has taken him seriously. I said, "I will take this absolutely seriously and do my best." It's a fancy list is what it is. That's up my alley.

He said, "Oh, I don't know."

It took about two years. Chuck told me that he had written some newspaper articles. He didn't know how many but said there's over five hundred. I would go over to the University of Arizona Library, but there's no index of the *Tucson Citizen*, so I went through the microfilm. Every single roll. And every time I came across Chuck, I took the title and page number. And I read everything as I went. And then the magazines. There were over a hundred magazine articles. I do remember making twenty-three trips to the library to get all of the newspaper articles. And his books. I did everything, measuring them and studying how they're bound, in extreme detail. That's how bibliographies are done. I looked up Virginia Woolf and stuff that was done decades ago. I said, "I want to do this in a classic format." And I added my little touches, and put little notes in brackets, and added things that I came upon.

He definitely said, "Now, this is just my work. Nothing personal." I said, "It's a bibliography, Chuck. I'm not going to put a footnote about your personal life, I promise you." The problem is, though, once someone starts saying stuff like that, they start volunteering information. The bibliography was all about his writing, and just his writing, but he was worried that I might investigate him, or paw through his trash can for secrets.

When I went through the microfilm, I had to go through every single one and find everything, so I had to make twenty-three trips, four hours each, to do this. I went to Chuck and said, "I found your very first article." One of them was about Santa Claus, 1981, and they sent a reporter over to cover it and talk about kids sitting on his lap. Chuck would never want to write about that. It really embarrassed him, and he said, "You know, they sent me out on this stuff, stuff I'd never choose. They paid me for it. I needed money. I was mowing lawns, living on someone's couch." It only took about a year before he started writing long specials. They weren't really inserts, but they were extended, sometimes full- or multiple-page, articles. He started doing something on child abuse and getting into serious issues. So, that research took two years.

I finally typeset it, printed the pages, made twenty-six hardcover copies, A through Z, and he signed them as an autographed edition. Then I printed a hundred in the paperback edition. The result was *Charles Bowden: A Descriptive Bibliography, 1962–2000*, under my press, Sylph Publications, in 2001. I have a few of the paperbacks left. I even have notes beyond the year 2000. There's a lot of his work beyond that. Thinking possibly of a second edition, I kept adding every time something came out.

After reading more Bowden than possibly anyone has, I think Chuck really identifies with the '60s generation—when you think about it, all his stuff is very stream of consciousness. Almost like a Beat Generation thing, with his heroes such as Jack Kerouac and Bob Dylan. These are heroes to him, really influenced him, and he's very proud of that time period. In 1968, he was in San Francisco. The poster of Janis Joplin he had in his living room he got from Janis Joplin, when she was handing them out from the bed of a truck. That culture is a very big deal to Chuck and that's in his writing, but his writing is not like anything from that time period. Chuck isn't a hippie, but it's in him. Janis Joplin is a hero. He admired her.

I do think he's an original. I keep saying he was a cross between Edward Abbey and William S. Burroughs, but he's neither of those people. He's some of all of it, but he's not like anyone I've read. It is a distinct voice, and I think that was his goal. He wants to be distinct, and that's Chuck. You don't have to meet Chuck to understand. You can just read his books and realize there isn't anyone like this. Not even any regional writers. Who writes like Chuck? And about what he writes about?

Did I hear that voice in the very first material that I read? The very first material, no. *Killing the Hidden Waters* is the first published book. He told me, "Don't read that book. It's too dry." Aha, the man has a sense of humor. *Blue Desert* is pretty straightforward. It wasn't till *Blood Orchid* that he got bold. "If people are going to pay me for this … " I think that's what he really wanted to do from the beginning, but he was a newspaper writer.

He did get an award. He was nominated for a Pulitzer. And I knew Chuck could do this early on, but he just wasn't allowed to. He needed room to do this. Once he had the space, the final thing would have been the finances to be free to do this, unless staying hungry is what he needed to be able to write like this, to really put himself into this, and that's when he was really good. *Down by the River* was probably his ultimate long piece, where he spent three years on something, a lifetime, living in motels and following that story.

He called himself a reporter, even near the end. He said he was a reporter who wrote books. I think he considered himself a journalist. We had conversations about the difference between being a writer and an author, of which he was very critical. I said, "Well, what is the difference?" An author is a writer who becomes a celebrity.

This essay was adapted from Walt Bartholomew's "A Bookman Remembers Charles Bowden," Journal of the Southwest, *Spring 2019.*

WALT BARTHOLOMEW is a bookman and sole proprietor of Eliot Books and Sylph Publications in Tucson, Arizona. These days he spends the majority of his time sculpting and oil painting and preparing to live well into his eighties.

Lessons from Anger and Love

CLARA JEFFERY

*Clara, I still live ... The story here is
simple. The silence is not.*

That he died in his sleep, and not at the hands of the cartels, or the
coyotes, or dirty cops on either side of the border, is something.
There were times when he'd sit with his back to the door and travel
with a former member of the Federales for protection. But in the
end, it wasn't one of the long line of people he pissed off and laid
bare that finished him off. A flu likely did, probably with the help
of hard living: the chain smoking and the sequential all-nighters
and the alternating binges of black coffee and red wine. Charles
Bowden was sixty-nine.

Chuck—never Charles—didn't write for money, one reason he
wrote for me so often at both *Harper's* and *Mother Jones*. He didn't
write for fame, either, though he's revered among people who
cover the border and crime, and among writers who like voice and
metaphor and can forgive occasional romantic excess. He would
sometimes take an assignment an editor dreamed up, or one
you'd discussed along the way, but just as often he'd dump twenty
thousand words on you out of the blue. Sure, you had to cut it in
half somehow, and ground passages where the jazz got too free.
But he was gracious about editing—"Oh hell, do what you want, I
trust you"—and fact-checking (no small undertaking). He was a
champion of the underdog, which included the migrants and dirt
farmers, the *maquiladora* girls and asylum seekers he wrote about,
but also the writers, poets, filmmakers, photographers, or artists
whose careers he helped. He respected hard work, which could be

work that was dangerous or epic in scope, but also hard in another way: tricky, gutting, soul baring, a high-wire act.

Chuck was gifted to me by Colin Harrison, then deputy editor of *Harper's*. They'd worked on a piece before I came to the magazine in late 1995. "But I think a woman would be a better editor. It'll be interesting, anyway," I recall Colin saying. And maybe that's true—Chuck's writing *was* better when a few layers of machismo were pared away—but also Colin warned me that no conversation with Chuck came in under two hours. Once, I finally pulled the old-style receiver from my ear only to find that a vacuum seal had formed around it. "Bowden ear," I warned the fact-checkers.

But oh! Those calls! He'd range from how the rain sweeps down an arroyo to the works of Weegee to the proper preparation of veal bolognese. Gangsters, classical poets, the Keating Five, Fannie Lou Hamer, Gary Webb, things he'd covered or read or heard about, all coming together in one glorious baritone rumble punctuated by deep drags and sips of coffee or wine, depending on the time of day. If you devoted yourself utterly to following along, you might get about 80 percent of the allusions—wait … Nikola Tesla? Davis, meaning Miles or Angela or … —"Look, you follow? Look, you follow?" It was hard, sometimes, to say, "Uh, not really."

The first piece we worked on was "While You Were Sleeping." It begins with him contemplating a picture of a mummified corpse of a maquiladora worker likely raped, certainly killed, and dumped in the desert outside Juárez. Chuck was one of the first American writers to document the women hunted by person or persons unknown as they made the long journey from their homes to the US factories brought into being by NAFTA. His writing is heart wrenching, but it was his decision to tell the story through the eyes of the street photographers—Manuel Saenz, Jamie Bailleres, Gabriel Cardona, and Julián Cardona (who would later accompany him on other reporting trips)—documenting the carnage ripping through Juárez that gave the piece real power:

Over the past two years, I have become a student of their work, because I think they are capturing something: the look of the future. This future is based on the rich getting richer, the poor getting poorer, and industrial growth producing poverty faster than it distributes wealth. We have models in our heads about growth, development, infrastructure. Juárez doesn't look like any of these images and so our ability to see this city comes and goes, mostly goes.... These photographs literally give people a picture of an economic world they cannot comprehend. Juárez is not a backwater, but the new City on the Hill, beckoning us all to a grisly state of things.

When editors say stuff like "find your Virgil, find the figure that will help you tell the story behind the story," writers should take a page from Chuck Bowden, who had a novelist's eye for characters that could stand in for so much more. Take "Ike and Lyndon," perhaps the most esoteric piece of his I ever edited. In it he somehow used a man institutionalized for murdering his grandmother who spends his days painting portraits of the presidents to tell the story of a doomed president and the ghosts of Vietnam that haunt us all. Well, you'll just have to read it.

If I had to describe Chuck to somebody, not physically, necessarily, but the essence of him, it might be something like part Bogart, part Sam Elliott in *The Big Lebowski*, no small dose of Matthew McConaughey in *True Detective*, the kind of guy who would regale you with tales in a dive bar, and then walk you to your car—"always walk a woman to her car, no matter the time of day or night"—and then tell you where to get the best tacos before leaving you with a journalistic koan. Long before he'd made the border his life's work, he'd covered dark, dark things and was scarred by them. In "Torch Song," which was included in *Best American Essays*, he wrote of covering sex crimes and murders of little kids (for which he was a 1984 Pulitzer finalist), and how he retreated into a world of sex and drinking and suicide hikes through the desert, and discovered that the line between commonplace betrayals and kinks and those deeper, darker horrors is not as brightly demarcated as you'd thought, knowledge that was something you can never recover from, not really:

> Somewhere in those hours my second marriage ends. I know why. I too, tend to say yes. The marriage ends because I do not want to live with her anymore, because she is a good a proper person and this now feels like a cage. I do not want to leave my work at the office. I do not want to leave it at all. I have entered a world that is black, sordid, vicious. And actual. And I do not care what price I must pay to be in this world.

That piece is largely about how people can't bring themselves to face the realities of rape and abuse, despite their being the hidden backstory of so many lives. It was hard to edit; I sometimes dreaded our calls. I didn't have a child then. I tried to read it through yesterday and couldn't.

It is, of course, reporting on the border for which Bowden is best known. His book *Down by the River* (one of many) recalls how two DEA agents search for the truth behind the murder of their brother at the hands of a thirteen-year-old from Juárez and destroy their family in the process—all while telling the story of Amado Carrillo Fuentes, the (now dead) kingpin of the Juárez cartel who haunts so many of Bowden's stories. In *Exodus*, which first appeared in *Mother Jones* and later became a book, he traveled back and forth across the border to tell the story of the migrants:

> Here is the basic script: You get off a bus you have ridden for days from the Mexican interior, increasingly from the largely Indian states far to the south. This is the end of your security. On the bus, you had a seat, your own space. Now you enter a feral zone. With

money, you can buy space in a flop ($3 a night) and get a meal of chicken, rice, beans, and tortillas (about $2.50). You stare out on an empty desert unlike any ground you have ever seen. Men with quick eyes look you over, the employees of coyotes, people smugglers. On the bus, you were a man or a woman or a child. Now you are a *pollo*, a chicken, and you need a *pollero*, a chicken herder.

You will never be safe, but for the next week or so, you will be in real peril. If you sleep in the plaza to save money, thugs will rob you in the night or, if you are a woman, have their way with you. If you cut a deal with a coyote's representative (and 80 to 90 percent do), you still must buy all that black clothing and gear, house and feed yourself. Then one day, when you are told to move, you'll get in a van with 20 to 40 other pollos and ride 60 miles of bumps and dust to *la línea*. Each passenger pays $25. The vans do not move with fewer than 17, prefer at least 20, and do, at a minimum, three trips a day. A friend of mine recently did the ride and counted 58 vans moving out in two hours.... In this sector of the line, the 262-mile-long Tucson Sector, a few hundred will officially die each year. Others will die and rot in the desert and go uncounted. A year ago, a woman from Zacatecas disappeared in late June. Her father came up and searched for weeks to find her body in the desert, a valley of several hundred square miles. He stumbled on three other corpses before finding the remains of his own child.

In "We Bring Fear," his last piece for *Mother Jones*, he told the story of Emilio Gutiérrez Soto, a Mexican journalist fleeing north for his life, not from the cartels per se, but the Mexican Army units working with them. In "The Sicario," his last piece for *Harper's* (edited by the amazing Bill Wasik), he told the tale of a former cartel hit man who would dismember and bathe people in acid while keeping them alive via adrenaline shots just to torture them a bit more. There was the story for *Esquire* where he attempted to and largely succeeded in redeeming Gary Webb, the journalist who came under attack after claiming the CIA had aided inner-city drug dealers in a ploy to help fund the Contras. (Despite that piece and others vindicating much of his reporting, Webb killed himself, something that Bowden never got over.)

Bowden got all these people to open up to him because he liked a good story, even if it came from a "bad" person, and, besides, there's no good or bad on the border; "there is only this fact: We either find a way to make their world better or they will come to our better world."

I got the call from Scott Carrier on Saturday, near midnight. Scott, who's a writer and radio producer—if you've ever heard "Running After Antelope" or any of his other *This American Life* pieces, you'll remember them—and Chuck had been friends and mutual admirers for years. He'd once interviewed Chuck talking about writing in a short film by Lisa Miller; every writer should watch it. I'd seen Scott just a few months before. Had he seen Chuck recently? I'd asked then. Scott hadn't. He'd been dealing with some hard times, he explained, and didn't want to burden his friend. I told him I'd heard Chuck was not doing well, and maybe Scott would go see him? I put this to Scott because I knew he'd do it—when my car broke down as I made the cross-country trip moving to California, he drove me from Salt Lake City to San Francisco, took a nap, and turned around to drive the 736 miles back—and because I was still a little angry by proxy for Chuck's former partner, another "nice and proper" woman who had been left behind. Mostly, though, I was probably just feeling ashamed that I'd let so much time elapse since the last time I'd enjoyed "Bowden ear."

Scott did go see Chuck, on assignment from *High Country News* to write a profile of him. And so Molly Molloy, Chuck's current partner—a journalist behind the border news site *Frontera List* who had helped Chuck (and our fact-checkers) with the story of Emilio—called Scott within a few hours of finding Chuck's body.

There was an autopsy, but does it matter exactly what killed him? There was a lot of hard living, though less of late, Molly says. But Scott believes and I believe that it was the toxic residue of what he saw and reported—which he sometimes claimed he'd quit trying to do, before going on another binge of reporting and writing— that was the underlying cause. "A literary career should be not a career but a passion. A life. Fueled in equal parts by anger and love." So wrote Edward Abbey in "A Writer's Credo," one of Chuck's touchstones. Chuck kept going because he loved to write. And because he kept hoping his work would lead to change, but it never did, not really, not in a big way, not enough. He'd write about how the migration, the globalization, the forces of addiction and lucre and deviance were as unstoppable as hurricanes. But part of him needed to believe that he'd stop at least some of it. If not him, who?

"He wanted me to do it, he wanted other people to do it, because he didn't want to be alone out there," says Scott. "I'd ask: 'Why do you do this?' And he was like, 'Why the fuck don't you?' He didn't say that out loud. He never did. To me or to anyone. But I think he thought that all the time."

Reprinted from Mother Jones, *September 3, 2014.*
motherjones.com/politics/2014/09/remembrance-charles-bowden-writer.

CLARA JEFFERY is the editor-in-chief of *Mother Jones*, which was named "Magazine of the Year" by the American Society of Magazine Editors in 2018. During her tenure, *Mother Jones* has won other National Magazine Awards for general excellence, reporting, and video.

COLLABORATORS

Interviewing a Tire

JACK DYKINGA

On one assignment Chuck Bowden and I were doing a story out in the Cabeza Prieta wildlife refuge, and we ran across an old wreck of a car, probably abandoned by a smuggler. Chuck hunched down, almost on his stomach, doing an interview with a tire, carefully writing down "Lifesaver Radial" and its size. I thought, "It's so rare that you find a writer who can actually see, and is visual." In that regard, he had a terrific sensibility to what's visual and what's the truth. The worst thing is to be a photographer working with a writer who uses hyperbole—they pile exaggeration atop imagination until it doesn't resemble anything you actually saw. Chuck was very meticulous about being literal, and frequently he came back to me, after we had done a story, and looked at the images to make sure he got the descriptive details right. A huge, huge source of my respect was his commitment to the truth.

Chuck had written for *Aperture*. How does a writer get an article in a photographer's magazine like *Aperture*? He'd never admit this, but I think Chuck was a closet photographer. He thought visually, so it was a natural transition. I think visually, and I don't necessarily have to take pictures—I can just see it sometimes. And in a writer, that ability gives him an extra leg up on everybody else. Because he is so good at observing, he's not only seeing the obvious—the patterns and the visual compositions out there, but he's also sensing the feeling of the subjects when there are people involved. Chuck was really careful about that. One time when I was talking to him about interviewing somebody, we both mentioned about how our tallness could intimidate people. And Chuck said, "I'll tell you a secret. Whenever I'm interviewing a little old lady, I always make sure that I'm sitting lower than she is, and I talk very softly." He would always be very cognizant of the situation and try to find the best way to be the observer, the fly on the wall, even though he was gangly and tall.

Chuck and I both played well with others and have an ability to mingle with a wide strata of people, economic and intellectual. Chuck was intellectual, and I'm funny. I can be endearing, and I try to charm people. Chuck charmed people in a different way. My wife, Margaret, would say that it's because we both were the youngest in our families. We both could put people at ease, and that's always good. Somebody once told me that they thought that Chuck came from a lot of money because he had this sort of entitled feeling. He didn't come from money, but that's how they perceived him. And, they said he had no fear.

I'm amazed when I hear stuff like this. What are you going to be afraid of? What could they do to you? Chuck failed at times and quit jobs. It may be difficult for people who have never quit jobs or been fired to see how they could make it. I don't understand that lack of confidence, and Chuck was not encumbered by that at all—he was very confident in his own abilities.

And he was always ready and able to carry on a conversation. I just loved it when he lectured me on photography. I got a kick out of it. One time I had to say, "Look, you really don't know what you're talking about." He understood the visual concepts, but he tripped over the technical parts. Yet, he never let that get in his way of delivering a good sermon: "You people need to know this!" And when he preceded it with "you people," you knew you were in trouble.

I don't know if his memory was photographic, but he certainly had one of those garbage-can minds—whatever goes in, stays in. And he liked to mentally joust with people. He was like a gunfighter saying, "Ya' feel lucky, kid?"

Sometimes he'd ask people, "Oh, have you read this book or that book?" But he was the real deal, because he had read them.

Charles Bowden fording Paria River in winter, 1986

I think what made Chuck so good was his background research. Probably the number one failing among journalists today is that they just read a press release and write the story, instead of questioning things. Chuck questioned everything. Not only questioned it, but knew the background and where to find the rest of the story.

Charles Bowden and Jack Dykinga retracing John Lee's winter trip down the Paria River, 1986

Which other reporter would have known that some friar in Baja wrote about Indians picking seeds out of their excrement and eating them? Chuck did, and he wrote about this.

Chuck had a deep, deep appreciation of knowledge. Once I went over to his house and he was reading E. O. Wilson's book on ants. He acted like he had found nirvana. He said, "Can you believe this?! That this guy is this nutty about ants?!" Wilson is now famous, but Chuck knew about him a long time ago. Chuck was very eclectic, sort of like a black hole for information, from the carrier pigeon's demise to the geology of the Grand Canyon, and he sucked it all in. His reading list was off the charts in diversity. He not only swallowed what he read, but he could regurgitate passages at will.

My initial respect for him was as a journalist and his basics: tell the truth and confirm. But that, combined with his sense of seeing, made him extraordinary. I don't know any other writers who saw as well as he did, and as clearly.

In May 2010, I was diagnosed with idiopathic pulmonary fibrosis and was told I needed a double lung transplant and double heart bypass. Without surgery, in 2014 I was dying, so I tried to reach Chuck to write my obituary. A friend found him, and within ten minutes Chuck e-mailed me.

jack
   i talked to bill. consider it done if need be—i just got a new box of crayons. your apparently too lazy to answer your cell phone.
   now lay off that whiskey and let that cocaine go.
   oh, and in minnesota i recommend the walleyed pike considering bleak, lake woebegone local fare. for god's sake dodge the lutefisk.

chuck

Then a few days later, as I lay in the intensive care unit listening to a specialist describe the operation procedure, Chuck walked in, surprising me and astounding the staff. I don't remember much of his visit or what the doctor told me, but sometime after midnight three weeks later I texted Chuck on my phone and gave him a detailed update on my condition.
   Chuck replied around sunrise,

jack
   i understand. sorry about the mask and glove moment—the staff who led me to the door said nothing and i managed to miss the billboard sign. and what the hell, since you have to bother with this you might as well be the first double double and get in the Guinness book of records.

i don't know anything about transplants but i do know that given such invasive chopping on you there will be a sense of depression to battle. being caged in Phoenix in the summer is probably better than being outside. on the way back from Los Angeles i came by again but your ward was having a moment of solitude it seems with no visiting. so i went over to the Heard Museum to see a friend. the people there wandering the courtyard in the summer blaze had all the zip of zombies.

given my little jaunts into the world, i notice there is not a lot of fair out there. so i am glad you caught a break. and of course St. Joseph seems to be the place for such treatment. i suspect the therapy will become addictive for you because you will finally feel that major American drug, a sense of progress, the same sensation as when training for a marathon where week by week one savors glimmers of change.

i'll be in and out of Phoenix and check in with you if that is possible. i'm down nogales at the moment where they are warehousing a thousand or so kids from Central America. they're not likely to have a St. Joe's as option in their lives. We do which is a piece of luck for us.

as Johnny Cash advises lay off the whiskey and let the cocaine go.

You caught a break. And all the canyons will be there when you trot out of the medical caves.

as Randy Newman, our national poet laureate, explained:

In America you'll get food to eat
Won't have to run through the jungle
And scuff up your feet
You'll just sing about Jesus and drink wine all day
It's great to be an American

Chuck

Charles Bowden, hiker, 1986

That was my friend Chuck. I survived my surgery, but two and a half months later he died of a heart attack.

Photographer JACK DYKINGA was born in Chicago, where he also earned a Pulitzer Prize for feature photography. He has written numerous books, including *A Photographer's Life* and, with Charles Bowden, *The Sonoran Desert* and *Stone Canyons of the Colorado Plateau*. He is a cofounder of the League of Conservation Photographers.

Dickens, Melville, and Bowden

MICHAEL P. BERMAN

If Charles Dickens wrote a novel set in the twenty-first century about the border between Mexico and the United States, and if the story had a character who spent his life on the currency of words dedicated to this land and its people—a tall man, with long fingers, and an angular body, coiled and quick to spit venom at any injustice, a man with a resonant growl in his voice, equally well timbered to cast aspersions on the corrupt and powerful as to welcome a young, stray, nameless pup of an artist to a finely cooked meal, glasses of red wine, and ten-hour conversations that put the work and his talking at the center of the universe—then Dickens would have modeled the character on Chuck Bowden.

Our conversation always led us to one unfathomable place: how to get people to see what is there. We both wander the wildlands along the border. I once told him I felt safer on the Mexican side, and, with the more macabre realm of Juárez, death, and drugs seething in his mind, he spent most of the night trying to convince me of my error. Just about sunrise, he got tired of trying to make a beautiful world seem dangerous. He told me he had just got back from the Big Bend country and how each night he would walk off with his sleeping bag and throw it down, and he gave me the admonition that there was nothing to worry about as long as you slept a couple of hundred feet from the car—and we went to bed.

Chuck had a voice that could make you believe. A voice that would excoriate both the good and the bad among us for our hypocrisies. Prophetic, he wrote with the beautiful poetic prose of an American, a language that spoke to our future.

"Predator's View," Chuck's favorite photograph by Michael Berman

I'll admit here that I had never read more than ten consecutive pages of nature writing before I met Chuck. Yet I love to read. I spent a year of graduate school, during which I was supposed to study photography, reading the complete works of Melville— *Typee, Omoo, Mardi,* and *Moby-Dick.* I read Francis Parkman and James Fenimore Cooper, searching for a sense of the American frontier, and W. E. B. Du Bois and Willa Cather for things I did not know; Henry James to explore the American mind and his brother and a half-dozen other writers because there is something about

Americans, a bastard mix of every race, creed, and vision, for what might be that has allowed us to conceive of both a marketplace and the wilderness as the realm of the sacred.

And at the end of one of those ten-hour conversations—Chuck threw a thick manuscript at my feet and said, "I want to do a book with you." I thought, "Shit … with me … the famous Mr. Bowden. Damn, I'll actually have to read a nature book." And, like any American fool who has considered the exigencies of his career with an empty bank account and no firm prospects, I thought, "What the hell. Yeah, I'll do it."

So I took that manuscript home. Sat in a chair. Read it cover to cover and was converted. We joined the brilliant Mexican photographer Julián Cardona and, together, composed and published a trilogy titled The History of the Future. And I now realize that I stand in the shadow of one of the finest pieces of contemporary American writing, that Bowden's three books achieved a judder for the American mind that is so profound that it breaches that same dimension into which Melville chased his whale and got lost. For this is the true territory of Wilderness—a realm that is not bounded by maps, prescriptions, or humanity, but rather by the unfathomable darkness of our human desire to bring the white whale under our dominion.

Melville could not sell five hundred copies of the first edition of *Moby-Dick*, because he so disturbed people who feared a good writer had become an obsessed man and shied away from his beautiful story. If there is a future, as with Melville, people will find and read Charles Bowden.

Contemporary American landscape photographer and painter MICHAEL P. BERMAN lives in New Mexico. His photographs can be found in *Gila*, *Sunshot*, and two volumes of Charles Bowden's History of the Future trilogy, *Inferno* and *Trinity*.

Over the Line

ALICE LEORA BRIGGS

> *This is the skin of the world and this
> skin covers whatever the world is or
> will be. This is the face of murder and
> torture and of love and dreams.*
>
> CHARLES BOWDEN, *Dreamland:
> The Way Out of Juárez*

Years ago Chuck Bowden gave me a close-up view of extinction at
the now defunct Minutemen outpost on the King's Anvil Ranch,
just south of Tucson. As we drove through the gate, banners
flapped in the breeze and proclaimed WELCOME MINUTEMEN
in scarlet letters, but the self-appointed border guards had gone
home. A lone caretaker loped across the yard to greet us and to
share the biology of hundreds of rusting bicycles heaped against a
nearby stucco building. He unfurled a tale about foiling alien bike
riders while raising funds for Minutemen barbeques and beers.
It went like this:

> *Coyotes* led groups of Mexican immigrants to caches of bicycles
> in Arizona's Buenos Aires National Wildlife Refuge and pointed
> their *pollos* toward Tucson for the final leg of their journey.
> Riding over cactus thorns on patched tires, few if any Mexicans
> peddled all the way to the Old Pueblo. Minutemen gathered the
> wreckage of failed attempts and set to work painting and polish-
> ing frames, oiling chains and re-patching tires. The overhauled
> bikes were auctioned and the beer and beef budget restored.
> But, after a time, the Minutemen began to notice certain flaws
> in their fundraising scheme. A few Mexicans came to the auc-
> tions to successfully bid on the bikes and the bikes reappeared

Charles Bowden in "Reasons for Leaving"

in the semi-desert grasslands of the wildlife refuge. They were repeatedly gathered, restored, auctioned, cached, briefly ridden, and discarded. Finally, the machinery of this enterprise died in a massive tangle against the walls of an out building.

Chuck was partial to ecosystems, and one of his main interests was the ceaseless industry of creatures feeding themselves and each other. He was a gleeful participant in human, as well as intra-species, feasting. He dropped tepid hunks of tripe in the yard behind Jim Harrison's house in Patagonia and enjoyed early morning feuds between vultures and ravens. Hummingbirds strained his budget with the sacks of sugar he bought and boiled into gallons of nectar, just so he could sit in the storm of birds that came to suck dry nearly a dozen feeders.

Working with Chuck on *Dreamland: The Way Out of Juárez* was another sort of feeding frenzy. When I got home from a 2005 exhibition in Chicago, my husband was reading *Blood Orchid: An Unnatural History of America*. He remarked that my drawings and Chuck's words were pulled by the same undercurrents and suggested that I send some images to Chuck. I burned a CD and wrote a quick postcard, but doubted that Chuck would reply. He e-mailed me several days later and asked me what I'd like to work on with him. I replied that the seven deadly sins were always available. That same night he sent five unpublished manuscripts. *Dreamland* was not among them, but I read them and searched for an entry into Chuck's writing. I never found the front door, so I just walked in the back. By the time the *Dreamland* manuscript came my way, I understood that I could always find a place where any drawing would dovetail with Chuck's writing.

Dreamland was born out of Chuck's generosity. He handed me words and indicated that I could respond to them however I liked, that their primary purpose was to keep the drawings from bumping into each other as the pages were turned. I am pretty sure that Chuck extended this same bigheartedness to other people he worked with, but at the time I attributed his trust to the hail of e-mails that shot between Texas and Arizona for two years before our initial face-to-face meeting. We discussed a lot of books, but rarely *Dreamland*, though Juárez was an enduring topic. We talked about the *Songs of Solomon*, Somerset Maugham's *Of Human Bondage*, Sherwood Anderson's *Winesburg, Ohio* and his letters to a woman he loved, *Confessions of Saint Augustine*, Rick Atkinson's *The Guns at Last Light: The War in Western Europe, 1944–1945*—to name a few.

Charles Bowden in "Shoal" (detail)

Charles Bowden in *"Tocino Fresco"*

"Smoke + Gun"

We rarely spoke directly about how we might each contribute to our record of the bloodbath in Juárez. We just opened the floodgates and fed the pond we'd both been drinking from for years. Chuck once shared with me a prod from a friend who wrote to ask him when he planned to take off his "shit-stained glasses." Since my work was, and still is, tightly fastened to wars, famines, plagues, and various other disasters that decorate human history, I was familiar with such remarks.

Chuck wrote most of the words that became *Dreamland* years before we met. And, though I lived on the border for ten months in 2008–2009 to complete the drawings for *Dreamland*, I also had created much of the work that appears in the book before meeting Chuck.

Most often, Chuck and I worked independently, but we occasionally met up on a two-way street. I mentioned that I was planning to draw one of the elaborate arrangements of confiscated guns, ammunition, and drugs that soldiers and police staged in Juárez. These ongoing displays that celebrated arrests resembled the illustrated lists of tribute payments in Aztec codices. Chuck responded by adding a passage to *Dreamland* that pulled this centuries-old tax system into the light of contemporary Juárez. I had no training as an illustrator, so it took me a while to create images that reached into Chuck's narrative. I remember waking one morning to realize that I would draw a caged canary vomiting an ornate pattern in response to Chuck's repeated references to "Lalo's Song," the testimony of a US government informant employed by drug traffickers. From these exchanges, I learned to pass the same regard to the book's designer, Kelly Leslie. When she indicated that drawings of a shovel or a stack of pesos would be helpful, I made them.

To correspond with Chuck was a career move. That is, it had the capacity to become a career. He reeled off paragraphs faster than I could muster partial sentences. I cobbled replies to his storm of e-mails and sent jpegs of drawings in reply to his thousands of words. In the early years of our friendship, I admitted defeat and backed away from the keyboard on a regular basis, but my absences were most often measured in hours rather than days.

Chuck introduced me to Juárez. Walking into a city that resembled the tsunami on the backside of my brain was a revelation. We traveled to restaurants and bars; execution sites; a death house; and an asylum for the insane, shell-shocked, and drug-addled, but we never went to any of these places together. Usually, I went with a friend or two. When I went alone, Chuck's words kept me afloat in various tempests, cesspools, and bottomless lakes.

Chuck was no stranger to dirt and neither am I, but his talent for joyful squalor exceeded my meager bedlam. I know of two women who devoted themselves to tidying up his chaos in the kitchen, on the page, and elsewhere. When it came to writing, Chuck whipped up vats of *prima materia* until they coagulated, but had little interest in polishing off sprues or cleaning cooking pots. Passages from previous texts were sometimes stirred directly into the next batch.

Chuck looked at the world through broken and darkened windows. He read books on a Kindle with cracks chattering through the glass. Half of his laptop screen was obliterated by the blue-black flickering of a failing LED backlit display. He knew how to use things up completely. When it came to encounters with the material world, Chuck was what poet Mark Strand called a "blizzard of one."

He loved the outdoors, and so long as I knew him, Chuck had a chair to sit in just beyond a back door, a seat he would occupy until he became the furniture and earned the regard of any animals wandering nearby. In Patagonia, he lived alone much of the time and invited the outdoors right into the house. Spiders dangled from kitchen cabinets, and a dark crust encased the buttons on the phone.

I watched the slow erosion of Chuck's teeth in concert with his ditty bag as he moved between Las Cruces and Patagonia. The days of bright enamel and fine leather were over. His ditty bag slouched on the countertops of bathrooms—an open, dirt-filled maw that stared up at me whenever I washed my hands. In 2008, one of my front teeth dropped out, a badly rigged repair from a Chicago pistol-whipping. I tried not to smile when I visited Chuck and Mary Martha Miles in Tucson, but when I saw them, I smiled anyway, of course, and later grew ashamed of my vanity as I watched Chuck's teeth fall out one by one.

Any words I manage to wrangle onto a page won't capture the gravelly voice, curiosity, mischief, and steely eyed kindness that Chuck Bowden spilled all over my life. His parting gift to me, as well as to journalist Julián Cardona, was to invite us to dinner, sit us down, and inform us that we had been working on separate aspects of the same project and that the outcome would be far more effective if we joined forces. Four years later, as Julián and I are finishing this project, we fully appreciate Chuck's insight.

Chuck's lifework was a chronicle of leave taking. During his final decade, he spent most days on the road. He never seemed comfortable staying in one place for very long, and I guess that included his own skin. I was shocked when his final partner, Molly Molloy, called to say Chuck was gone for good. I went through the motions of life as usual for a few hours, but when I stepped out the back door, I was brought to my knees. A dead hummingbird lay at my feet.

ALICE LEORA BRIGGS has exhibited her drawings and architectural installations in museums, galleries, and nonprofit spaces across the United States and in Europe. She lives in Lubbock, Texas.

Heart's Desire

MOLLY MOLLOY

A flurry of e-mails from Chuck ... and so I drive. Rearranging the work schedule, bargaining with colleagues to take my shifts so that I can drive three hours before daylight or into the dark. To be in a new place with Chuck, to sleep out. Never a tent. Never a campfire. Nothing to cook. Tiny backpacking stove for black coffee at dawn. Ham, cheese, a loaf of bread. A bottle or two of red wine. Cold desert dark, the ground, sleeping bags, two pillows, canvas chairs, and a hat.

There are many things to learn. This time, in March 2007, we would meet near the eastern entrance to Aravaipa Canyon, the way less known to Tucson hikers. The canyon had been scoured by flash floods during summer and winter storms in 2006, uprooting stands of cottonwoods, obliterating trails, and changing the wandering course of the creek. Chuck wanted to see how it looked, the first spring since the destruction. Aravaipa lay at an intersection of the Sonoran and Chihuahuan Deserts—a rich ecotone between these distinct biological and geographic zones in the southwestern world. I had not been there before, so all was new to me.

The way toward the canyon from the fork in the road at Klondyke was rock and dust with confusing turns, at least as I remember it now. We claimed a spot at the Fourmile Campground and drove north to the wilderness entrance. Then we walked. Once near the creek, the opening spread out into silver, blue, and shades of green. Stands of cottonwood saplings seeded in the flood, pencil-thin, all the same height, straight silver trunks topped by clouds of bright yellow-green leaves. The water shone silver, bronze, or polished steel—depending on the angle—reflecting in a darker shade the intense celeste of the sky. Along the wide flat stretches of gravel at the water's edge, an even more intense chartreuse bloom of algae and darker green of watercress in the shallows.

I am a terrible navigator, and Chuck was righteously incredulous of my inability to find my way in a new place. On this first walk along the creek through Aravaipa Canyon, I asked without thinking, "Which direction is the water running?" Perhaps I meant east or west, but he turned and said with a kind of scorn, really disbelief: "Downhill."

I chalk up my lack of any sense of direction to being left-handed. While driving, I would turn a map upside down if we were headed south. "What in the hell are you doing?" Chuck would ask. I had to hold the map in the direction we were going, else I could not tell which way we should turn. Chuck considered it a true disability to lack a normal sense of direction, something he had as a birthright in his head. And perhaps that explains his skill at walking long wilderness distances for all the years of his life.

As we walked into the canyon, the walls stretched up in a curving embrace to the wide gravel path. In the few pictures I have from these trips, Chuck is a tall figure in shorts and a loose cotton shirt, shoes wet from wading the creek, carrying only a small water bottle, walking many yards ahead of me, framed by stone cliffs and tall trees bending over the trail above the floodplain.

We also took a hike into the Galiuro Wilderness, uphill from Aravaipa. I remember the heat surprising me and nearly overtaking Chuck. He was still a heavy smoker then, and at a steep place on the trail, his face turned beet red, sweat poured down his neck, and he had to sit down for some minutes to recover. I remember my own panic as I tried to imagine what I would do if he could not walk out (Chuck was six foot four and weighed perhaps

180 pounds, there was no cell phone reception, and I might not be able to navigate the road back to Klondyke, where there might or might not be people).

We had carried some jugs of water in the truck, but when we finally got back to the campground, as if from God and the angels, we discovered the iron pump and spigot that gushed crystal cold water at high pressure from artesian springs. After the hot dry walk through the uplands, the abundance of springwater tasted like a banana split, or perhaps the coldest cold beer I was dreaming of. The water was excess—as over the top as Mardi Gras—and we drank as much as we could hold, and poured bottles of it over our heads, instantly going from sweaty, dusty, and overheated to shivering in the March wind.

Nearing dusk, we noticed that the campground was situated in open range. A huge red bull and several cows browsed nearby, nibbling green grass nurtured by seepage from the spring. They didn't seem too interested in us, but they did stare. We slept like logs on the hard ground. I don't remember who woke up first, but I remember raising my head around dawn and seeing the giant bull perhaps no more than thirty feet away from our sleeping bags. Chuck whispered: "Don't move." The cows had wandered to the other side of the campground, and we were now lying flat on the ground between the bull and his harem. Chuck stood up and charged at the bull, waving his long arms and yelling something like "*Raus! Raus!*"—a German command his mother had used on the farm when he was a toddler.

We walked for miles along the creek and up a side canyon. I would stop in the stream to pick up rocks, a habit Chuck found absurd—he thought rocks should be left in place, every single one of them. But, for some reason, I had to keep a chunk of white milky quartz from that walk. I searched hours for it on another day in March, eleven years later, when I meant to start writing this essay, determined that I could not write a word until I could hold that rock in my hand. I looked where I thought I had put it, on shelves where it might be working as a bookend. I finally found it in the garden, catching storm runoff from the roof.

Perhaps I had put it there where it might not feel so out of place, since I had robbed it from the creek where it belonged. It is a reminder, as well as a talisman against my fear. I need cold, hard reminders. Likewise, the photographs of Chuck walking far ahead of me, never looking back. My fear that he would walk away forever.

Neurosis is thwarted nature. Name your most basic need, your most cherished desire, the very closest thing to who you are. Then, make it impossible to get. Chuck was better than most of us at satisfying his needs, at getting what he desired. He could also untangle that desire and channel it ferociously into his work. What is "Torch Song" anyway,[1] if not a terrifying unraveling and a paean to desire, appetites, and the realization of deeper yearnings that remain submerged and unfulfilled? Chuck hungered for freedom—a desire that often crashed against his own knowledge of what humans need from each other, and what we are capable of doing to each other in the quest to get what we desire.

I loved Chuck intensely, and that love fulfilled my most basic need. But because of who he was, that same love thwarted my other desire, the shameful one, the antifreedom one, the one he despised: a yearning for safety and security. In my mind I knew (and now know more than ever) that feeling safe and secure is an illusion. But my heart is more bloody and basic. So I obtained my heart's desire for that wild great love by sacrificing my need for safety and security.

A trip with Chuck would begin with cryptic e-mails, a date and time, the semblance of an itinerary with directions he figured even I could follow, and some reason he had to get away from a constant stream of people at his house—parties and wine with people he seldom named. When we first met he had called his house a salon where he was the attraction. But when he was not writing, his desire was to be driving to a place to get notes for more writing. The work was everything. I wrote back offering to turn myself into a glass so that his fingers would be wrapped around me.

In December 2006, I looked up the unclassified secrets concerning Félix Rodríguez and sent Chuck an e-mail with details.[2] We met the next day in a Lordsburg café along I-10. I remember it as cold and bleak, the sun low and bright, as on many a midwinter day in the high desert. In this case, Chuck was pursuing a source from inside the US Drug Enforcement Administration, a man who had investigated the murder of Enrique Camarena and discovered that men deep inside his own country's secret agencies had participated in the kidnapping, torture, and murder of a fellow agent.

Chuck said that his source had promised him a "suitcase full of documents" that would verify his story—that Cuban CIA operatives, including Félix Rodríguez (later exposed in the Iran-Contra affair), had also been in Mexico in 1985, working with Mexican security police, drug traffickers, and government officials. All for the purpose of funneling drug money to right-wing "contra" insurgents against the Sandinista government in Nicaragua.

Apparently, there was no suitcase of documents. At least the source had long since lost possession of them. Still, the source had told Chuck what he remembered, then remained in the shadows with his story for another eight years.[3]

We burned through a few hours available to us in Lordsburg on that bleak midwinter day, just as we spent such stolen time in past and future years, and then rushed back to separate obligations. On the drive home to the east and across the Continental Divide, my heart would split open, part of it beating inside my chest, while the other half lay bleeding along the highway where the rains run off to the west.

I don't know when exactly Chuck decided he was going to leave Tucson and come to Las Cruces to stay, but it was sometime between late November 2008—soon after our first interviews with the man we called "El Sicario"—and September 2009. When Chuck got to my house that afternoon, he had only his computer, a few books, and some clothes. And this big piece of Le Creuset cookware in a bag from a fancy kitchen store in Tucson—a big iron pot covered in yellow-green porcelain, almost the color of the cottonwood trees in early spring. He asked if I liked the color. It's a hard moment to remember clearly. He said, "I'm not easy." I said, "I know that." And he stayed until the day he died.

My little house filled up with people when word of his death got out. And many phone calls. People I had never known calling for Chuck. And people writing for newspapers. One call I remember came from a young woman at a big city newspaper. I went into a back room to talk because people were filling all the other spaces. She asked perfunctory obituary questions, and I tried to answer. Then she asked something like "Can you tell me something about what it was like to be with him?" And I looked up at a shelf where there was a stack of old notebooks. For some reason, I grabbed the one from March 2007 because I remembered the map I drew late that evening at the Fourmile Campground near Aravaipa Canyon.

Chuck and I were sitting in the canvas chairs, drinking wine, and wrapped in sleeping bags as the night got very cold after our day of walking in the hot sun high up in the Galiuros. And Chuck started talking about his idea for *Trinity*, a book that would trace the arc of power that made a big circle on the map, with the Trinity test site at the top; the Comanches to the east; down to the Big Bend, Ojinaga, and Juárez, and up to the mountains of Lincoln County; then west and south again to Palomas, Chihuahua, and Columbus, New Mexico, where Pancho Villa invaded the United States in 1916; then west to the New Mexico bootheel, the Gila River, the high grasslands of the San Rafael Valley, and the

Charles Bowden at Sycamore Canyon, 2012

near-tropical Sycamore Canyon in southeastern Arizona. And as
he talked in the dark that night in Aravaipa, I tried to sketch on a
map in my notebook the grand circle of place-names and to understand what he meant about dreams of power and failures of power
rooted in this contested place. I wanted to remember how it was
that night, in that place, where I learned, and felt in my bones, the
depth of his knowledge of this ground where, as he later wrote,

"our ultimate dreams of power erupt and here these dreams turn to nightmares that still haunt our lives." Chuck observed that "the ground remains" and concluded that "my life is as broken as the ground that made me."[4]

Less than a month after that night, he wrote on a manuscript that became *Trinity*: "Begun April 30, 2007." I tried to explain this to the woman on the phone from the newspaper, because in my mind, it perfectly answered her question. I failed of course. But I keep trying. To be with Chuck was to inhabit a huge territory, to breathe the same wind, sun, dust, and darkness—to be present when the ideas became the words on the page.

A few days ago, I drove through the Bosque del Apache Wildlife Refuge on my way home to Las Cruces from a trip to Albuquerque. It is late, after 6 pm. I see only a few Canada geese, a lot of ducks I can't identify, clouds of swallows, and one brilliant vermillion flycatcher. Wind roars through the cattails by the big pond. It is so lonely. But I can't drive by here without stopping. I think Chuck wants me to stop. I want to stop. This is a place in the geography of our lives where Chuck is still present. The animals, the birds, the sky, the clouds, the mountains, the sunset, and the distance all became part of him and remain with us in his words. It is hard for me to be alone in these places. He is so present and, at the same time, gone.

Look, walking way up the trail. I can barely see him—a tall figure, long arms swinging. There's that stand of silver cottonwoods, glowing gold and green along Aravaipa Creek. The canyon walls tower around him, the trail narrows as the canyon closes in. The creek tumbles along, cold, clear, and rimmed with watercress. I stop to pick up another beautiful rock. It's too heavy. I'll never be able to carry it home. This trail washed away months and years ago. I'll get lost if Chuck gets out of my sight. I call out, but he can't hear because he's too far ahead. But I know absolutely, he's still walking.

MOLLY MOLLOY is a border and Latin American studies research librarian at New Mexico State University in Las Cruces. She also works with detained immigrants seeking asylum.

NOTES

1. Charles Bowden, "Torch Song: At the Peripheries of Violence and Desire," *Harper's Magazine* (August 1998): 43–54. harpers.org/archive/1998/08/torch-song-2.

2. "CIA Debriefing of Félix Rodríguez, June 3, 1975," nsarchive2.gwu.edu//NSAEBB/NSAEBB5/index.html.

3. The agency files remained cloistered, except for a few that became evidence in federal court, and ended up on the internet years later. Eventually, in 2013, Chuck's source decided to go on the record. By that time, Chuck was living in Las Cruces. We made several trips to interview sources for the story that finally came to light after Chuck died. Charles Bowden and Molly Molloy, "Blood on the Corn," November 19, 2014, medium.com/@readmatter/blood-on-the-corn-the-complete-story-488f55d4f9ea.

4. Charles Bowden, *Trinity* (Austin: University of Texas Press, 2009), 4.

White, Red, and Black

JULIÁN CARDONA

Juárez was the book that Chuck never completed. He tried over and over again. Its pages remain unfinished to this day.

He published five books on this section of the border, though it could be said Ciudad Juárez appeared heavily in his work *Killing the Hidden Waters*. Of those five books, I participated in three and I came to understand the rest closely.

I am often asked how we worked together. Our dynamic was not work meetings, mulling over topics to try for the next book, or even to assess the status of the project in progress. Instead, our duties required grill-outs, good wine, and books. I would visit Chuck in Tucson, and the conversation on any kind of topic could last for days. We went out to the surrounding desert areas in search of the traces of illegal immigration, though Chuck might take off to Juárez when it was pertinent. That's how it happened in 2008, after Mexican president Felipe Calderón sent thousands of soldiers and federal police to Juárez. Even if we did not have a contract with a magazine, we would go wherever it was necessary to go.

Charles Bowden arrived in Juárez in 1995, when we were feeling the hangover left by the presidency of Carlos Salinas de Gortari. During his term, Mexico became the country that exemplified the triumph of neoliberalism in the world. History was over, the Soviet Union had collapsed, an era of wonders that humanity had never known was coming, and Mexico, of course, was on a hasty road to proudly claiming its place among the countries of the first world.

Juárez: The Laboratory of Our Future was an accidental project. Chuck came to the border to investigate the murder of Bruno Jordan and ended up publishing our book on Juárez before his own *Down by the River* appeared in print. Unlike the years when we worked on *Exodus/Éxodo* and *Murder City* (collaborations solely between him and me), I appear in *Juárez* as one of many photojournalists who show him what happens in the city.

He and I referred to this as "the Juárez book," as if the rest originated from it, while, at the same time, it contained and explained everything that Juárez represents. The dedication that I wrote (I did it because, before I met Chuck, I had conceived and organized *Nada que ver*, the exhibition that was the basis for the book) delineates the main impetus that compelled us both to complete our work in the following years: "For all the children, teenagers, women, and men who have been victims of physical and economic violence in Ciudad Juárez." This dedication perished at the hands of Carlos Vigueras, who accompanied Chuck to Juárez before meeting us, and had become the leader of one side in the war for fame among photographers. At his request, Aperture substituted "economic violence" for the word "poverty"—a very poor connotation. Poverty exists everywhere; that is not the point. In Ciudad Juárez, the forces of globalization had been unleashed three decades earlier and the effects remained visible, though most people preferred to ignore them—the growing violence, the drug trafficking, the increase in addiction, the informal economy, uncontained urban sprawl, the lack of educational and social infrastructure. This is what Chuck called our future.

The past is a recurring theme in Chuck's work. He quotes a phrase from Carl Sandburg: "I tell you the past is a bucket of ashes." And Chuck notes, "I love this line and do not believe it." Chuck tells us that the future must be sought in the vein of the past. In this sense, the Juárez book is an exercise in memory. The violence

Charles Bowden in front of a notorious death house in Ciudad Juárez

that exploded in the city in 2008 would have seemed spontaneous without this work, published ten years earlier.

Chuck and I differed over what made Ciudad Juárez the most violent city in the world. Chuck placed greater weight on the factors portrayed in the Juárez book. Without denying that these factors contributed, in my opinion Felipe Calderón carries the most responsibility.

In any event, in *Murder City* (our last collaboration), Chuck anticipated what would later turn into evident truth with the disappearance of forty-three students from Ayotzinapa, Guerrero:

"It was the state." As in Juárez, militarization has been the driving force behind violence in the country that, before Calderón, had been on the decline for two decades, and then, with Enrique Peña Nieto in 2017, reached record numbers. With the recently approved Internal Security Law, the deadly legacy of Felipe Calderón has been legalized and what Chuck portrays, not as a war against drugs but as a war *for* drugs, is official government policy.

Chuck points out the low wages paid to assembly workers and records the effects this produces in Ciudad Juárez. Paradoxically, the movement led by Trump has condemned the "Davos party" government and, in calling for renegotiation of NAFTA, refers to Mexico's low-wage policy as an unfair trade practice (a criticism also leveled by American and Canadian labor unions). Trump's rhetoric portrays the United States as the loser in globalization, but Chuck demonstrates—along with our photographs—that Juárez workers are not the victors to the detriment of US workers now displaced from their manufacturing jobs. And it is mostly US—not Mexican—companies and capital that take advantage of low wages in Mexico to export to the United States through NAFTA.

There is no nationalistic vein behind Chuck's arguments. *All the milk is white, all the blood is red. And all the power is black.*

In the reality that he finds in the streets of Ciudad Juárez, Chuck tries to present images to his readers and then asks them to look at themselves in the mirror.

Initially, Chuck e-mailed other photojournalists of *Diario de Juárez* (now renamed *El Diario*), but for some reason, he only maintained constant communication with me. It was during this time that our relationship solidified.

We began working on what would be *Exodus/Éxodo* six years after NAFTA went into effect, when we received news that thousands of migrants were moving daily to border towns in Sonora. The Juárez book had been published two years before, and we both anticipated how NAFTA would affect the Mexican countryside.

The cause of the migration of millions of Mexicans at the end of the nineties has been much discussed, and it could continue to be discussed. Many farmworkers told us that they were displaced from the market by free trade and forced to migrate.

Chuck and I concluded our project several years later. I had titled the volume on immigration *The New Americans*. However, I accepted *Exodus/Éxodo*, the title Chuck proposed so that it would better fit other titles in his trilogy with University of Texas Press, which started with *Inferno* and concluded with *Trinity*.

One afternoon in Las Cruces, Chuck asked me to suggest an image that would finalize the book. The photograph of a house, with "Baghdad" written on the wall, and cars destroyed by Hurricane Katrina, led to a long conversation about the East, the West, the decline of empires, and, ultimately, power. This during the George W. Bush administration. And, although the image of the United States would soon collapse, US power was still unquestioned at the time Chuck and I began our collaboration. Now, the Trump presidency has revealed deep internal divisions that have sent repercussions throughout the world.

Chuck emphasized leaving a record of his work. Although the three books we collaborated on may not have had profound influence, they maintain active links with the present—two with Trumpism and one with Calderonism.

Take *Murder City* as an example. Chuck did his job, yes. I did mine. The international human rights organizations and the United Nations, itself, documented in their reports the systematic violations of human rights committed over more than a decade by Mexican federal forces, including the military. But power, of any size, is black, and militarization in Mexico is healthier than ever.

The spirit of Chuck's writing lies in the battle for life, not in the battle for power, and this one oozes milk and blood.

Photojournalist JULIÁN CARDONA may be best known for his images in Charles Bowden's books *Juárez: The Laboratory of Our Future* and *Exodus/ Éxodo*, but his photographs of life along the US-Mexico border appear in a number of publications and have been exhibited in the United States, Mexico, and Europe. He is based in Ciudad Juárez, Chihuahua, and has won a number of awards, including the Lannan Foundation Cultural Freedom Fellowship.

Traveling and Not Traveling with Chuck

EUGENE RICHARDS

A freak thunderstorm hit Brooklyn early this morning, things banging and whizzing around. I awoke at 3 am. When I looked out, all I could do was stare. To begin with I'd forgotten that the old maple tree out back was so fucking big, over three times the height of our house, its limbs brittle and bruised looking, creaking, groaning. The sixty- to seventy-mile-per-hour gusts were pushing at it, threatening to overwhelm it, causing it to sway, sickeningly, half a foot one way, half a foot the other.

I sat at that window, in the dark, for something like an hour, then swallowed another half of a sleeping pill, enough to slow the thoughts I've been having about getting old, hoping to maybe sleep until 8 o'clock. I awoke at 6, hearing what I believed were schoolchildren screeching, thinking that dawn had happened. The tree and the rain and the wind were still at it. A large branch had broken off, but the tree was still standing. I thought about waking Janine; this was a reason to feel good.

It's been four years since Chuck died. It's been that long, but I'm still thinking that I can call him up whenever I want. Today if I want.

"Chuck."

"Yeah," he'd answer, puffing on a cigarette. "Is this Gene?"

"It's Gene."

"Gene!"

He'd say my name in a way that lets me know that this is a good time to talk.

Chuck Bowden in his truck, Plano, Texas, 1998

If I were to call him today, I'd tell him that a publishing house down in Texas has asked me to write a little something about him for a kind of remembrance. He'd be pleased hearing that. He always said I ought to write more. But then I'd have to tell him that I'd been having an awful time doing it. I mean, what do they expect? My first wife, Dorrie, died thirty-five years ago and I'm still struggling to come to terms with my memories of her. Hidden amongst the good times—being smitten, the love—are regrets for things I did to her and didn't do for her. Once I'd thought they'd go away.

I'm seventy-four this year, older than I ever thought I'd be. I met Chuck in 1995, having been assigned by *Esquire* magazine to join him in Plano, Texas, to report on the then new-to-the-headlines tragedy of rich white kids OD'ing on heroin. As it turned out, Chuck and I were close to a perfect match for this job—he a guy who wrote in a graphic but poetic way about drug dealing, murder, and poverty across the Mexican American border, and me a guy who made pictures too gritty and close-up for most people's taste, of drug dealing, murder, and poverty in America's inner cities.

So we were attuned to one another. But even with all the knowing between us, our time in Plano was painful—going face-to-face with parents who were still in shock and mourning for their kids. Best as I can recall, when we slumped down on the stools at the hotel bar that first night, Chuck, who had a way of never not talking, said very little. I just sat there. What I came to notice that night was just how much Chuck would drink, which was really none of my business, except that I so suddenly cared for him. And he took notice of the fact that though I wasn't much of a drinker, I was the one who couldn't find his way back to my room, couldn't recall the room number or even what floor it was on. Stress, an old head injury, or whatever, I was losing my mind.

After Plano, Chuck and I hoped to work a lot more together. But no, we were teamed up on a total of only three magazine stories over all the years, the one for *Esquire* and two for *National Geographic*. The one we did for *National Geographic* on North Dakota provided a kind of slowing down for Chuck, no machine-gunning, no funerals to attend. We had a lot of fun out where probably a lot of people wouldn't have, in a place that's so cold in winter the locals consider the forty-below weather a kind of God-given electrified fence that "keeps the riffraff out."

What a great job. We searched through abandoned farmhouses, wondering who had lived there and why they left, walked in fields strewn with sculpture-like plows and derelict cars, hurried in and out of what turned out to be meth houses, imagining people creeping up on us. We ached from the cold. Then one morning we saw wolves (said to have been eradicated in this state) crossing a field in Corinth. There were two of them, probably a male and a female, both gorgeous in the gnarly, bristling way bears are, larger than I would have imagined, moving as if in slow motion in the direction of the town of Crosby and the Canadian border.

A couple of years later, I met up with Chuck in eastern Arkansas to work on what would be a different kind of story for *Geographic*, one that would interweave this photographer's remembrances and pictures of life in the delta in the early '70s with reporting on what the region's like today. Because Chuck had a traveling companion, Molly Molloy, with him on this trip, we opted for each of us to go his own way—a couple of interlopers ("You're snooping," one old boy yelled out) wandering about the flat and emptied-out counties bordering the Mississippi. Then, on a day that Chuck was without Molly, we drove some fifty miles south of the town we were staying in down to Elaine, Arkansas (pop. 538), where on September 30, 1919—not quite a hundred years ago—mobs of white men armed with rifles, shotguns, and axes took to slaughtering black men, women, and children. People out picking cotton, who hid inside their homes, who fled into the canebrakes, were killed. Two hundred thirty-seven black people were killed. May well have been more. But since no white eyewitnesses came forward, it's said that nobody at all knows.

We drove around the tiny town for twenty minutes, with my imagining that we were in a time capsule and that the people who had been killed would appear to us tumbled over in the fields. Toward evening Chuck interviewed a handful of Elaine cotton farmers. They invited us in, trusted him. The one who was the friendliest declared that his great uncle had done a share of the killing. "I have the .30 caliber he used," he said. He offered to show us the weapon next time we passed this way. But we said, "No need."

Then, explaining that we had a ways more to travel before dark, we headed back.

What do I remember about the drive back to Forrest City? I felt awful, but kept quiet. The times that Chuck and I traveled any kind of distance together, whatever I wanted to say to him I mostly kept to myself. He did the talking. It was as if he couldn't help himself; anything he'd have on his mind at any moment would pour out of him like steam from a kettle. Bang, the lumpish bodies and streaming blood of murders in Juárez would smack up against sightings of the desert flowers and hummingbirds he loved. I'd listen to him spinning and soaring; he was the best storyteller I'd ever heard. But by the time we were most of the way to where we were going, I'd have grown anxious. I'd get this feeling that I didn't exist. Do you know what I'm saying? Traveling with Chuck could be rough. But the truth is, not traveling with him is something that I can't think too much about.

Photographer, writer, and filmmaker EUGENE RICHARDS has visually chronicled some of America's most difficult problems: racism, drug addiction, incarceration, terminal illness, war, and poverty in powerful books such as *Comforts or Surprises: The Arkansas Delta*; *Exploding into Life*; *Below the Line: Living Poor in America*; *The Knife and Gun Club*; and *Americans We*. His films include *Cocaine True, Cocaine Blue*.

TRAILING BOWDEN

Bowden's Need to Walk

JUDY NOLTE TEMPLE

> *The earth is no wanton to give up all*
> *her best to every comer, but keeps a*
> *sweet, separate intimacy for each.*
>
> MARY AUSTIN, *The Land of*
> *Little Rain*

Chuck Bowden loved the land and he loved the female body. Perhaps he loved both too much. Chuck was a passionate writer about his love affair with the natural landscape and how it was being raped by mankind. He was also a man who admired women's bodies from afar, while trying to cope with the women in his life. I learned this as our lives intersected in the mid-1980s, when I directed a southwestern literature program to which Bowden contributed. We were an intellectual odd couple.[1]

What could I, a women's history scholar, and Bowden, tough journalist and Ed Abbey devotee, have in common? I discovered that Chuck had been intrigued by Victorian women's bodies, which they used for hysterical rebellion against the physical and mental corsets of their era. To learn that Chuck had written an entire thesis on unhappy women was a godsend for me. I, too, was writing about Victorian women. My American Studies PhD topic was the thirty-year-long diary of a most unhappy nineteenth-century woman. I was bogged down because the diarist was a chronic complainer. Chuck loaned me a heavy box containing his dissertation with its tough Chuckesque title: "Broke Bodies: A Look at Nineteenth-Century Notions of Health." And it was Chuck who gave me the final, much-needed push to complete my dissertation on diarist Emily Gillespie, whom I'd grown to dislike because she was so critical and querulous about everything. He said,

"God damnit, of course she was a shrew. Any truly alive woman in the nineteenth century would be. Find out what made her that way." Although Chuck's thesis would never find the light of day, thanks to him mine did.[2]

By the time I met him, Chuck Bowden had turned his gaze toward the body of the natural world and the lush bodies of living women. Feminist scholars in the 1970s explored this conflation of nature and woman, demonstrating how both were desired and ravaged by men. Susan Griffin's *Woman and Nature: The Roaring Inside Her* showed how everything from fairy tales to pornography depicted women as fair game for men's exploitation. Annette Kolodny's *The Lay of the Land* analyzed the complex American "pastoral impulse" that envisioned this new virgin land as both nurturing and awaiting to service man. How apt that the first chapter in westerner Bowden's 1977 book, *Killing the Hidden Waters*, was titled "The Lay of the Land."[3]

Chuck Bowden spoke at the 1985 Tucson conference I organized, "Old Southwest/New Southwest." Building on the nature-as-female theme, he condemned those environmental writers who perpetuated the image of the untouched virginal Southwest, while ignoring its endangerment by development, mining, and water overuse. In the collection of essays based on the conference, he warned, "We have created a kind of pornography that fantasizes a natural world that barely exists any longer and that we do not live in. And this is dangerous for us and dangerous for the tiny islands of wild ground that survive."[4]

Like his predecessors Mary Austin and Edward Abbey, Chuck Bowden sought anew the intimacy of walking wild ground in his 1987 book *Frog Mountain Blues*. And like Austin, Bowden acknowledged the footprints of other humans on the Santa Catalina Mountains that frame Tucson on two sides. He honored the original indigenous name, "Frog Mountain," then traced the subsequent layers of names and claims on the land. His walking companion was photographer Jack Dykinga, who captured the debris that defaced the mountain—earthmovers at its base, town homes crawling up its side like skin cancer.[5]

Then Bowden walked: "I shoulder a pack and start walking and looking for those things that are hard to name but easy to feel. And I know where to go. I go to the deserts, the forests, the plains, and the peaks. I go to the mountain." He realizes that the wilderness he loves is vulnerable to others' less-loving touch. "All the way up, we have the city at our backs, a living, crawling thing probing the desert with subdivisions, roads, and machines." Bowden is seduced by the unconquerable female power of nature he is dedicated to salvaging: "Whenever I return to my city, the range snaps against the horizon and bristles with promise, a generous green mound beckoning me to come back and try my hand again."[6]

Chuck's conflicted obsession with women's voluptuous bodies and real-life women's needs was more explicit in *Blue Desert* (1986). This first book in Chuck's "blue period" oscillates between his need to walk in order to observe cancerous development of wild lands, and the needs of his wife Kathy as cancer ravages her body. "She has large breasts hanging from a thin body. She finds a lump." With classic Bowden self-irony, he confesses, "I have had her schedule the operation so that it will not interfere with my walk, with this story. I am inflexible on this point and cannot be budged. My work has become my religion and I use it to keep at bay all demands and duties."[7]

He weaves together nature and Kathleen in a heroic promise: "The moon—I draw power from the moon. I think—no, I do not think, I know with certainty—that I will make it and she will make it and that we are both looking at the moon and I will pull her though the dark cave of anesthesia and the knife and the pain and the huge bandage wrapped across where her breast once spread as generous." Kathy Dannreuther, Chuck's wife, was my friend and colleague when *Blue Desert* came out. I was outraged on her behalf when I read its depiction of her breast cancer and of their marital tension juxtaposed with Chuck's ever-present admiration of other women's ample breasts. Kathy felt the book's exposure of her breast cancer and their dissolving marriage invaded her privacy. However, I recall her then saying something like, "It hurts now, but I'm immortalized in literature. I'm in Chuck's book." *Blue Desert* opens, "For Kathy, who crossed blue desert with me.[8]

The second conference on southwestern literature was held in 1987, the same year that *Frog Mountain Blues* came out. The conference theme, addressing the edgy disconnect between loving open ground and then filling it with cities, was "Open Spaces, City Places: Contemporary Literature in the Changing Southwest." Bowden's contribution to that conference and essay collection was "Dead Minds from Live Places." He explicitly linked the exploitation of the West with the exploitation of the female body: "As a young boy I was fascinated with William Cody, and as a man I continue to be. Buffalo Bill represents the best and worst elements of Americans confronting the West. Cody is the lover who rapes the object of his love and then lives by selling pornographic movies of his lustier moments. We can find his face anytime we care to look in the mirror." In classic Bowden style, he confessed his own occupation of—and occupation with—urban spaces that were devouring the land like a tumor.[9]

By the 1990s, our paths had diverged. I entered the quiet world of academia, while Bowden moved into a much less tidy and safe world—the narco borderlands. University presses had been the venue for Chuck's early books and for my collections of essays, to which he contributed. But his creative and journalistic instincts led him to more immediate outlets, to stories set in dangerous urban places.

Again a woman's body drew him deeper into the world of drugs, rape, and death. In an unforgettable *Harper's* article, Chuck's prose and the accompanying graphic photos of corpses forced comfortable readers to see the unseeable. "I am here because of a seventeen-year-old girl named Adriana Avila Gress. The whole thing started very simply. I was drinking coffee and reading a Juárez newspaper, and there, tucked away in the back pages, where the small crimes of the city bleed for a few inches, I saw her face. She was smiling at me and wore a strapless gown riding on breasts powered by an uplift bra, and a pair of fancy gloves reached above her arms almost to her armpits. The story said she'd disappeared." Bowden continued, "That's when it started," as he began the journey toward "understanding the world in which beaming seventeen-year-old girls suddenly vanish."[10]

I leave the later part of Chuck's body of work to others, for I remember him in those *Blue Desert* days. I think of him as a perplexed man writing revelatory prose about his quest to understand the women in his life—the ones he lusted after, the one he lived with. No wonder he sought respite in deserts, "the breathing-spaces of the west," as earlier walker John C. Van Dyke called them. Chuck Bowden needed to walk.

JUDY NOLTE TEMPLE is professor emerita of Gender and Women's Studies at the University of Arizona. She edited two volumes of essays from the "Writers of the Purple Sage" project, *Old Southwest/New Southwest: Essays on a Region and Its Literature* (1987) and *Open Spaces, City Places: Contemporary Writers on the Changing Southwest* (1994).

NOTES

1. The 1985 conference was part of an NEH-funded grant to Tucson Public Library called "Writers of the Purple Sage." The project produced a cassette recording and scholarly portfolios about southwestern literature. They are available in digital form from the Tucson Public Library catalog. The project also produced a program on National Public Radio, "The Wilderness Still Lingers," which includes Chuck Bowden's voice.

2. Bowden's 346-page dissertation is held at the Charles Bowden Papers (SWWC 112), The Wittliff Collections, Texas State University, San Marcos. My

diary research resulted in a book published under my previous married name, Judy Nolte Lensink, *"A Secret to be Buried": The Diary and Life of Emily Hawley Gillespie, 1858–1888* (Iowa City: University of Iowa Press, 1989).

3. Susan Griffin, *Woman and Nature: The Roaring Inside Her* (New York: Harper and Row, 1978; repr., Sierra Club Books, 2000). Annette Kolodny, *The Lay of the Land: Metaphor as Experience and History in American Life and Letters* (Chapel Hill: University of North Carolina Press, 1975), 88. Charles Bowden, *Killing the Hidden Waters* (Austin: University of Texas Press, 1977).

4. Charles Bowden, "Useless Deserts & Other Goals," in Judy Nolte Lensink, ed., *Old Southwest/New Southwest: Essays on a Region and its Literature* (Tucson: Tucson Public Library, 1987), 139.

5. My pairing of Austin with Abbey is purposely ironic, for Edward Abbey's arrogant introduction to a 1988 edition of Austin's *Land of Little Rain* displaced her own prologue, which I quote as the epigraph to this essay. Frog Mountain was the name that the O'odham people—still called Papago when Chuck wrote his book—gave to what came to be called Mount Lemmon.

6. Charles Bowden, *Frog Mountain Blues* (Tucson: University of Arizona Press, 1987, 1994), 11, 101, 119.

7. Charles Bowden, *Blue Desert* (Tucson: University of Arizona Press, 1986), 166.

8. Bowden, *Blue Desert*, 167.

9. Charles Bowden, "Dead Minds from Live Places," in Judy Nolte Temple, ed., *Open Spaces, City Places: Contemporary Writers on the Changing Southwest* (Tucson: University of Arizona Press, 1994), 23.

10. Charles Bowden, "While You Were Sleeping," *Harper's Magazine* (December 1996): 44.

Bowden Nails the Door Shut behind Us

TODD SCHACK

I never knew Charles Bowden. But twice a year, like clockwork, I watch as he grabs a classroom of students by the gullet, and in his rhythmic, cotton-soft southwestern rasp says to them: "You will *not* look away from this. You *will* listen. Now forget everything you think you know about the *Border*." He says this last word with contempt, "Now forget everything you *think you know* about drugs, about drug habits, and things like rational explanations for all of this ... that's right, forget it, forget it all, and just listen to me tell you a story for awhile." And I watch, even now, four years after his death, as his words seep into the very marrow of these students, as his voice beckons them to look for the first time at darkness they are conditioned to deny, how within days of hearing him, reading and listening to him, they are never again comfortable with their own ignorance.

You see, I'm a professor of journalism. And it is my conceit that rather than churning out more mediocre journalists to the world (we have something of a glut, Bowden would agree), I play a small role in introducing them to those journalists who do it not for career or something as stupid as money, but rather because it is a *necessary* work—because it can't *not* be done—those who would gladly walk away from it if they could, but they can't.

And Bowden is the ace in the hole.

I believe it's his voice that gets them every time. Yes, his tone, his prose style, the authority of his voice in print, sure, it's all there, but I'm talking about his literal, spoken voice. His cadence, the rhythm of speech, the way in which his pronunciation and expression betray a fatigue of the ignorance of our times, a hard-earned impatience for imbecility and a contempt for what passes as common sense.

I've taught *Murder City* and *Dreamland* now since they were both published in 2010. Thirty students per semester, going on eight years now, that's almost five hundred students who have bought these books and read something like they've never encountered before.

Early on there was confusion, "What *is* this?" they'd ask, mystified. "Is it journalism, is it even *non*-fiction? Is it poetry; is it some sort of fever-dream?" I settled on an experiment because I had a hunch about the key to unlocking his work for them would be … his voice. The literal, spoken voice I just mentioned.

So I split my next class in two: First group, I required they listen to a radio interview of Bowden discussing *Murder City*, before they read the first pages. Second group, just read. Sure enough, next class I get all the bewildered expressions and predictable questions from the second group: "What *is* this?" First group, their expressions were different: they wore a look that is described only by the original definition of the word "awesome." Like they just witnessed something that is at once beautiful and terrifying. And they *got* it.

I don't bother with this exercise anymore. Once was enough. I just require all students to listen to his voice, let that rhythmic, cotton-soft southwestern rasp and the fatigue of the ignorance of our times saturate their consciousness, and then, just read. When we meet again, after they have let Bowden grab 'em by the gullet and say: "You will *not* look away." Something beautiful and terrifying. He's one of the few journalists, and certainly the only *American* journalist, who can do this to them. What he does to them is significant, and bears discussing.

Bowden said in a June 4, 2010, interview with Brooke Gladstone on NPR's *On the Media* what he wanted to do with his audience:

> My dream is to invite a reader into a room and pour a nice cup of tea . . . and then nail the door shut. I want them to look at a forty-year war on drugs that has created a police state in the United States, the largest prison population per capita on Earth, and slaughtered tens of thousands of Mexicans. I want them to taste it, not just read some policy statement. And that's why it's disturbing—'cause I want people to be disturbed, it seems to me that's the only way things are ever going to change.

This, to my mind, is his literary legacy. The way he invites us into his space with the smooth cadence of his voice, then nails the door shut behind us and forces us to reckon with that which we'd sooner deny. For students, the impact of this forced reckoning is epic, its scale that of an existential crisis. It is precisely in the way in which he strips away layer after layer of unexamined assumptions; the way he excavates meanings long buried and forgotten; the way he exposes useful lies and what he calls the "failure of language" that quakes these students to the core of everything they've ever believed to be real, true, and just.

When Bowden says to them—"These illusions are teddy bears we clutch in the dark hours, comforts that enable us to sleep"— and then, in a locked room he one-by-one strips away those soft, comforting teddy bears, I watch as my students reluctantly give up the remaining shreds of innocence begat by ignorance. And his real literary legacy—to my mind—is watching them walk out of that room awake, in new-hatched skin, free of the illusions that enabled them to sleep.

I never met Charles Bowden. But at least I know I have a date, one in the spring and one in the fall, where I get to watch him invite my students into a room, pour them a nice cup of tea, and then nail the door shut, and say: "You will *not* look away from this. You *will* listen, and you will never look at this subject again with the same eyes."

TODD SCHACK is associate professor of Journalism and Media Studies at Ithaca College, New York. He specializes in literary journalism, and his research areas revolve around the wars on drugs, terror, and what he calls the "dark side of globalization."

Muir, Abbey, Bowden

MIKE EVANS

Muir, Abbey, Bowden. These three, in that order. Three shelves in my library and three authors whose work came severally rushing at me as if in a single thought. Forty years of reading and I am hiking up a wild canyon, all the switchbacks negotiating the same creek, treading upstream, refreshed and renewed at every ford, struggling to not lose my footing. I encountered each author in sequence, and thus fixed three distinct eras in my life. Each stream crossing proved more challenging as the terrain grew steeper at higher elevations. Unbeknownst to me, I had been formulating my very own environmental policy. Through reading Muir, Abbey, and Bowden, my livelihood growing native plants, and lots of camping and hiking, I was laying a foundation and building an ethic. I feel as though those guys have been walking with me, and I know that on the trail ahead we will run into sections more precipitous and dangerous.

Neither John Muir, Edward Abbey, nor Charles Bowden ever desired to be classified as "nature writers." Each worked hard to change their culture, influence at least a generation or two, more if possible. Each wrote about the beauty and virtue of the natural world, showcasing the magnificence of untouched wilderness on one hand, while holding a mirror in the other to reflect the confusion of our basic human state. Muir engendered a conservation philosophy and helped establish a system of national parks. Abbey sounded an urgent alarm that modern industrialism and "progress" could take out irreplaceable nature faster than we thought. Bowden showed us that we all own a piece of this, and he did so by exposing the uncomfortable truth that in order to save wild places, we need to have as insatiable an appetite for dark quiet nights as we have for bright lights, frenzy, fury, fame, and fortune.

John Muir spoke over a century ago, and his biographies are abundant, his stature international. We study him in our institutions of higher learning, and, a few years back, he even got his own postage stamp. His style might appear antiquated, but Muir's message is current: nature heals the soul. One hundred years later, though he did not live through the entire twentieth century, "Cactus Ed" Abbey spoke as though he could see into the twenty-first. Abbey's timing was either perfect or subversive, depending on your point of view. There is no denying that his stuff bears as much relevance today as it did when it was written thirty years ago, maybe more. Ed's biographies are still trickling in, and folks are in agreement—like John Muir, he really was a voice crying in the wilderness; but I don't believe he will be getting his own stamp. His message definitely rubbed a few higher-ups the wrong way.

Charles Bowden has only recently passed, and we are suddenly waking up to the realization that nothing new will come from his pen. This is a harsh fact for those of us who grew to appreciate a good punch to the gut when dabbling in "environmental issues." From an unforgettable day thirty years ago when a friend handed me a copy of *Blue Desert*, I knew Bowden's books would be easy to recommend but hard to comprehend ... why does it feel so good to be so blue? Is this poetry, prose, or unimpeded train of thought? Next came *Desierto* and *Mezcal*, and since I had spent some time kicking around Mexico during a few vigorous years—exploring, camping, surfing ... absorbing its very old culture—I felt as if Chuck had been my traveling compadre.

Whereas I felt safe with Muir, and unsure with Abbey, I was at times downright scared to be with Bowden. Maybe he would not be so easy to recommend after all. I share his intense focus on the region of our southern border, a country unto itself, a belt of land with no definite boundaries but oh such an identity, a state of

Charles Bowden, Ed Abbey, and Dave Foreman (left to right), with Ed's wife, Clarke Abbey, and children Ben and Rebecca, Tucson, Arizona, about 1985

mind as much as a plat of land, a place where I live. And he could see, and cause to be seen, the virtually unseen world of this timeless land where everything is constantly changing and yet everything remains the same. Migrations, civilizations, economies, natives, pioneers, stewards, wayfarers, "other" creatures, wind and weather, basin and range, vegetation, the throbbing heart ... the pulse of our dry thorny landscape that shouts "Keep Out!" while salaciously luring you in.

The desert has fascinated philosophers, thinkers, writers, and mystics from time immemorial. Add in your occasional storyteller, desert rat, rock hound, botanist, lion tracker, cowboy, woman of the night, herpetologist, *narcotraficante*, javelina, walker in the night, rattlesnake, border agent, goat herder, truck driver, rancher, saguaro, creosote, ocotillo, hummingbird, elephant tree, calendar stick, baked rock, shifting sand, full moon, and howling coyote. Now you have a desert diorama, but not the one you would find at a natural history museum. Bowden's desert includes the whole package—the sunrise of an Arizona picture book next to the gravesites of the hopefuls who never made it; a pristine spring in the driest of dry lands, adjacent to a sea of discards including backpacks, clothing, empty bottles, and personal items left behind by hundreds of frightened pilgrims scurrying in the dark to a new life across the line. And, of course, the turkey vultures. Ed had warned of the turkey vultures—they will always be watching.

Charles Bowden's books on life and death in the world of our desert borders are so honest and severe that, quite simply put, they are not for everybody. But everybody should read them, if for no other reason than to experience his exemplary skill. People say good things come in threes—*Blood Orchid, Blues for Cannibals, Some of the Dead Are Still Breathing*. Then we got a batch on all that business in and around Juárez—*Down by the River, A Shadow in the City*, and *Murder City*. And finally, those big books about that line we have drawn in the sand— *Inferno, Exodus/Éxodo*, and *Trinity*. All interspersed with a dozen or so closely related gems.

The author's style was unmatchable and his versatility astounding. Over the years, I have also followed Bowden when he occasionally wrote for popular magazines. He possessed an amazing ability to tone it down, his readability and relevance uncompromised, message consistent, but presented in a language more digestible to the masses.

I think John Muir probably would have liked Ed Abbey and Charles Bowden. Each wrote from the heart and to the heart. Muir told us to get outdoors for our own good: "Everybody needs beauty as well as bread, places to play in and pray in, where nature may heal and give strength to body and soul."[1]

Abbey warned us to temper our activism with pure fun: "It is not enough to fight for the land; it is even more important to enjoy it. While you can. While it is still there. So get out there and mess around with your friends, ramble out yonder and explore the forests, encounter the grizz, climb the mountains. Run the rivers, breathe deep of that yet sweet and lucid air, sit quietly for a while and contemplate the precious stillness, that lovely, mysterious and awesome space."[2]

I followed their advice, my life took on a discernible form, and I kept reading.

Charles Bowden reminded us: "The forest is that essential fact that confronts all human beings at the end of the twentieth century, an image of the promise we have betrayed and a chance to redeem ourselves from our folly.... We are not gods by a long shot, but, by chance, we live at a time when we can make godlike mistakes."[3]

Anyone can tramp up this canyon with me. When my kids were young, they got unforgettable sunrises and sunsets, cold water camp baths, and exposure to great writers. Now they have their own canyons to hike. It's a long trail. Sometimes these days I sit by the fire with my young grandsons, and we read John Muir aloud. We like "Stickeen," Muir's short memoir of his dog bravely crossing a glacier, and they have heard the story many times. We can reenact it on some fantastic hike someday. That's when I'll point them upstream toward Abbey and Bowden, helping them to build their own environmental ethic.

MIKE EVANS is founder and president of Tree of Life Nursery in San Juan Capistrano, California.

NOTES

1. John Muir, *The Yosemite* (New York: The Century Company, 1912), 256; and John Muir, *Nature Writings: The Story of My Boyhood and Youth, My First*

Summer in the Sierra, the Mountains of California, Stickeen, Selected Essays (New York: Library of America, 1997), 814.

2. Edward Abbey, speech to environmentalists in Missoula, Montana, and Colorado, ca. 1976, in Reed F. Noss, Allen Y. Cooperrider, and Rodger Schlickeisen, eds., *Saving Nature's Legacy: Protecting and Restoring Biodiversity* (Washington, DC: Island Press, 1994), 338.

3. Charles Bowden, *The Secret Forest* (Tucson: University of Arizona Press, 1993), 51.

A Desert Evening with Chuck

MICHAEL LUNDGREN

I found the house before dark. The air smelled of rain, but there wasn't a cloud in the sky. Chuck was sitting on the front porch amid what appeared to be a thousand hummingbirds.

"They drink a gallon of sugar water a day," he said. "Not for their sustenance, but for the energy they need to catch insects … and to fight each other. They might be the most violent of birds. Go figure. I wonder why there are so many embroideries of them?"

Tucked up against the edge of a creek in what some might call the highlands of the Sonoran Desert, this was his summer getaway from the heat of Tucson. We sat there for hours, chatting and sipping red wine. The sphinx moths replaced the hummingbirds as the day paled, their velvet wings brushing up against each other at the dozen or so feeders. I was there to learn something from Bowden—about the desert, about his own time, about the world through his eyes. In the gathering darkness he spoke urgently of the mesquites around us that were dying, of deep desert washes where the water used to flow year-round, of *sicarios* (hitmen) and factories across the border, about how his travels and research had made it easy to believe in an unkind world.

A few years earlier, I had met Chuck in the back room of a cool used bookstore in an uncool suburb on the outskirts of a desert city. He was reading about the blacktail rattlesnake, from *Some of the Dead Are Still Breathing*: "Each individual eats one or two wood rats a year. In hard times, they can skip eating for a year or more. Given a lifespan of twenty-plus years and the speed of a strike, this suggests that the strike—that image burned into human consciousness—is a minor part of a blacktail's life, adding up to a minute at most."

Chuck peered over his glasses: "They use their venom once a year. What's your track record?"

He wrote about snakes because of our fear, because our misperception of them can be transformed into a metaphor for the larger discrepancy—between the world and our understanding of it.

Chuck was drawn to landscapes that are multivalent. Richly storied, they are simultaneously primitive and occupied—by the tension of the present and the ghosts of history. His unapologetic-yet-humble writing reflects this complexity back at us, becoming over time a mythology of what it is to be a human in this particular place and time.

When Chuck writes about the sucking sound a mesquite makes when it drinks, he's not writing about biology (or is he?). He's writing about what we can't hear, to unearth what we don't want to know. His work has always been about borders, not just the one that lay a dozen miles south of where we sat that September evening, but also the ones that haunt our dreams. He channeled the darkness of his own experience as a parallel for the world's, and, consequently, his writing often feels like it's on the edge of a psychic collapse—a fitting form for much of his subject matter. To write the things he wrote, he had to find a corollary within himself—to enter into and almost become his subjects, whether it was a prison, a politician, a murderer, or the apathy of nature. His narratives are sweeping but metered, the plot and conceit of the piece often only apparent at the end. To appreciate his writing you may have to enter into this vision, however obscure.

Our own evening had grown dark, the way it does in the desert before the firmament comes alive. The sphinx moths exited the performance just before the bats arrived. They dipped out of the sky to sip the artificial nectar, rose back up in an arc, their paper wings black on black against the night. We drank more wine and grew silent for what felt like a few moments, and also an eternity. Stars began to emerge, only to be consumed by fast-moving clouds, dark in their passing.

Out of the charcoal light, Chuck turned to me in a gravelly voice: "So what's the solution to the whole damn mess? In one sentence."

"Well, human beings had better start seeing themselves as part of nature."

"That'd help, wouldn't it. Oh, by the way. I thawed some more tripe and beef hooves for the ravens today. They've been largely absent devouring a roadkill doe about a hundred yards from here. But apparently, they're ready for a change of diet, since they came to the French door and squawked at me. Hell, I have to go to Nogales tomorrow to get another bag of guts."

And, with that, an epic monsoon storm descended on our little patch of Sonoran Desert. It came down in waves. Blasts of thunder followed beams of lightning so bright they could irradiate you. Chuck was lounging on a folding plastic lawn chair. A lengthy man, his legs stretched straight off the end of the chair and out from the rain shadow of the porch. With each flash I could see him grinning at the *whole damn mess*, while his pants darkened with the summer rain. We stumbled inside to our beds, using the wall as both guide and support. He closed his door and glanced back: "Next time will be better."

I awoke at 4 in the morning to the smell of black coffee and the staccato of fingers on a keyboard. I stumbled out into the darkened living room where Chuck sat, underlit by the glow of his laptop, *swatting away*, as he might say, at his next book.

Artist MICHAEL LUNDGREN's published works include *Transfigurations* and *Matter*. He also collaborated on *After the Ruins, 1906 and 2006*, with Mark Klett, Philip L. Fradkin, and Rebecca Solnit.

The Mesquite Tree and the Endless Loop

TOM SHERIDAN

Reading Charles Bowden over the years is like an endless loop of hunger and appetite and soul sickness that can never be cured. There are iconic works such as *Killing the Hidden Waters* and *Down by the River* that impose real discipline on his narrative and his prose. But then there are *Blood Orchid* and *Blues for Cannibals*, which erupt like lava and flow with no beginning or end and can be read interchangeably, the message always the same. We live in a Culture of Death. We kill, but we do not love. As he puts it in *Blues for Cannibals*: "The last common feeling we have is depression, and it is so common, we only notice it when we cannot bear any longer to go on." Bleakness broken only by the feel of a woman's body or the taste of red wine or an obsession with cooking and gardening to pull us back from the abyss, if only for a moment. *Blue Desert* was the first of these meditations, and it was a revelation: a dark night of the soul that ranks with Edward Abbey's *Desert Solitaire* as essential reading about the modern Southwest. But then came *Mezcal* and *Red Line* and *Desierto*, like Hollywood sequels, covering the same ground over and over again, spewing lava as it inched its way to sea. Dip into any of these books for the first time, and you will be struck by their power. Try reading them consecutively and you feel like you're trapped in the same nightmare that rises up and grabs you by the throat, again and again.

Bowden loved to set up straw men and let the lava grind them down: I'm not an intellectual. I despise academia. I carried a thousand-page book about Stalinist Russia into the desert and did not read it. And yet Bowden was an intellectual, almost a PhD, his abandonment of his degree in history a ritual killing of a part of himself that never quite died. The books that stick with me—other than *Blue Desert*—are the ones that channel his prose and take-no-prisoners intellect into the framework of a subject outside himself. I wish there were more of them.

Killing the Hidden Waters was the first. I read it as a graduate student and was stunned by its terse poetry and how it made connections nobody else was making at the time. Legend has it that Bowden wrote it as a report for the University of Arizona Office of Arid Lands. No one there knew what to do with it, so they fired him. Luckily, the University of Texas Press recognized a new and important voice, and Bowden's career as an author was launched.

Bowden then became a reporter for the *Tucson Citizen* under editor Dick Vonier. One line of stories on migrants crossing the western deserts led him to mentors such as archaeologist Julian Hayden and desert rat Bill Broyles. Other stories, especially the sex crimes, set him on a journey that started with *Blue Desert*. Read that book's final "coordinate"—"Bone"—and you see the author of *Down by the River* and *Murder City* being born into a world where pure evil hovers in the darkness, beyond ken, a missing seven-year-old girl in Tucson leading like a fever dream to all the dead women in Juárez with their arms sticking out of their graves. Booze couldn't soften the journey. In *Blue Desert*, he writes, "My guts felt like hot stones and the booze just steamed off with little effect except the moral slap of a promised hangover."

Before that odyssey brought him to the border, however, he and Dick Vonier started the late, lamented *City Magazine*. For a time, Bowden pursued another cancer in the Southwest, one that ate away at people's savings and the desert he loved. *Trust Me: Charles Keating and the Missing Billions*, which Bowden cowrote with investigative reporter Michael Binstein, explored the real estate boom and bust of the 1980s and the man who came to epitomize

Unidentified man (left), Charles Bowden, Charles Keating, and Richard S. Vonier

its greed. Would-be "merchant prince" Charlie Keating plundered Lincoln Savings to create a baroque resort beneath Camelback Mountain in Phoenix and his vision of a shining city on the hill in the foothills of the Estrella Mountains, where pornography would not be permitted. By then I felt there was a little bit of the Nietzschean in Bowden, that Keating captured his imagination by the sheer force of his will, even though Bowden despised everything Keating stood for.

But financial shenanigans were not the all-consuming storyline Bowden was searching for. He toyed with radical environmentalism beginning with his essay on Dave Foreman in *Blue Desert*, but

the rather tame monkey-wrenching of Earth First! could not compete with the world Art Carrillo Strong exposed him to. Author of
his own book, *Corrido de Cocaine*, Art was another of Bowden's
mentors, an ex-cop who knew Tucson's underbelly and watched
the city's drug scene change from a few downtown heroin dealers
to cocaine central. After Art died, Bowden made his own contacts
with the DEA and some Mexican reporters and photographers,
especially in Juárez. He didn't speak enough Spanish to go much
deeper, but going much deeper probably would have gotten him
killed.

One result was Bowden's masterpiece. *Down by the River*
weaves the tale of Amado Carrillo Fuentes's Juárez cartel in the
1990s with a family nightmare that tallies the cost of the "War on
Drugs" on DEA agent Phil Jordan and his extended clan. The book
moves back and forth between the people who pay the price of a
multibillion industry run by sadists and sociopaths, and the pow-
ers that be in Mexico City and Washington, DC, who maintain
the fiction that Mexico and the United States are partners in the
War on Drugs. Time and again, DEA agents uncover evidence
of corruption and collusion at the highest levels of the Mexican
government, and time and again, their evidence is denied and
suppressed. Corruption in Mexico entrenched itself during the
Spanish colonial period. But flushing $20, $30, $60 billion in drug
money through its political system fuels levels of graft, intimida-
tion, and denial more baroque than any colonial cathedral.

The first time I read *Down by the River*, I wanted more: More information on the workings of the cartels. More reporting on how
the drug trade was poisoning a Mexico I had fallen in love with in
the early 1970s. I thought the book painted a DEA vision of Mexico, one full of slaughter and corruption with none of the warmth
or joy of the Mexico I knew. But when I read it again in preparation
for this essay, I better appreciated what Bowden was trying to do.

As he free-falls into the nightmare of the Jordan family and the blood-drenched terror of the drug trade, facts swirl away in a fog of denial and bureaucratic double-speak, and no one in power is ever held accountable. Nothing changes except for the corpses.

After *Down by the River*, there was really nowhere else Bowden could go with the narrative. *Murder City* chronicles the violence in Juárez with mind-numbing detail, Bowden waxing almost nostalgic for the days of Amado Carrillo Fuentes, "the golden age of peace in Juárez, when murders ran two or three hundred a year." But since Carrillo Fuentes's death in 1997, things only got worse. Cartels splintered and reformed, new and more barbaric organizations rising from the ashes of the old ones.[1]

Nothing changes, and the reason is simple. Corruption in Mexico may facilitate the trade, but in the final analysis, the illegal drug business is the essence of capitalism at its amoral best. To call the market for drugs in the United States insatiable is an understatement that demands a stronger synonym. As long as our appetite for cocaine, methamphetamine, and that oldie but goodie, heroin, remains unslaked, ambitious entrepreneurs are going to meet market demand. When you throw in a two-thousand-mile border with the greatest wealth disparity in the world, you begin to understand why the War on Drugs is a tragicomic charade.

Bowden knew that, and like the DEA agents he chronicled, he couldn't get anyone in power to pay attention. He saw the carnage and wrote about it with savage eloquence. But nothing changed. By *Murder City*, even he admitted the toll it had taken on him. "And something has changed inside, something in a deep part, near that place we can never locate but often claim is the core of our being," he wrote. "In the past, I have covered kidnappings, murders, financial debacles, the mayhem that my species is capable of committing. I spent three years mired in reporting sex crimes. There is little within me that has not been battered or wrenched or poisoned. But the path that I followed with Miss Sinaloa proved all my background to be so much nothing. I have not entered the country of death, but rather the country of killing. And I have learned in this country that killing is good."

This, and alcohol, wore him down. Like so many of us, Bowden self-medicated with booze. I wish he would have given AA a try. I think he would have liked it. There are some great storytellers in those rooms. But the only time I ever heard him talk about it was when he told me that a close friend of his used to brag about going to AA to pick up women. That was the wrong lesson to learn from a friend who drank himself to death.

When he was at his best, Bowden was the best around, at least in Arizona. But ever since *Blue Desert* and *Down by the River*, I kept wanting more. I got tired of reading the same book over and over again. As I grew older, I lost my infatuation with the relentless prose, which, like Hemingway's, occasionally verged on self-parody, and the fuck-everything-that-moves persona. I wondered if he ever laughed at himself or took comfort in the small acts of mercy and grace that make life worth living.

Hemingway once said that he should have been Faulkner's manager, the closest that tormented braggart ever came to admitting someone was a better writer than he was. Bowden needed a manager. Maybe if the backers of *City Magazine* hadn't been scared off by Keating, Bowden would have had the platform he deserved. But for all his excesses and posturing, there was one constant in Bowden's life, one that's kept me from falling into the abyss. Bowden loved the desert with a fierceness that burns in just about everything he wrote. And he gave me one sentence in *Blue Desert* that became a coda for my own work: "Here the land always makes promises of aching beauty, and the people always fail the land." Bowden's metaphor for those promises in *Blues for Cannibals* was mesquite. He may not have believed in God, or trusted Him, but he believed in mesquite. It's a good metaphor, a tangible metaphor, to believe in. One with rough bark and deep roots, just like him.

TOM SHERIDAN, an anthropologist at the University of Arizona, has written or coedited fourteen books on the Southwest and northern Mexico, including *Arizona: A History* and *Landscapes of Fraud*.

NOTE

1. Azam Ahmed, "Fearing Corruption Inquiry, Former Mexico Party Chief Moves to Block Arrest," *New York Times*, February 23, 2018.

WRITERS ON BOWDEN

America's Most Alarming Writer

JIM HARRISON

Far too long ago, I think it was in the ninth grade, a teacher gave me the work of Joseph Wood Krutch to read. I was immersed in literature and drama, especially my own self-drama, but then one Krutch volume I discovered was devoted to the Arizona desert. I come from an agricultural family, hence was not ignorant of botany, but then every single growing thing in the desert looked alien. Later, in my nineteenth year, I hitchhiked out Route 66 to California and saw the northern edge of some of the flora but was mostly struck by the emptiness and fabulous vistas. I had picked up a ride in Terre Haute, Indiana, from a squirrelly, confessed bigamist (and God knows what else), and he never drove less than eighty until he dropped me off in Barstow, where I headed north to San Francisco to become an official beatnik, of which there were many in 1957.

My first true flirtation with the desert came in 1971 when I traveled to Arizona for the National Endowment for the Arts to read my poems on Indian reservations and at the University of Arizona. It was then on a drive to Douglas with Neil Claremon that I discovered my eventual writer home in Patagonia. On this trip and others in the seventies and early eighties, I met the desert rats Doug Peacock and Ed Abbey and also read part of Chuck Bowden's *Killing the Hidden Waters* that someone had loaned me overnight. As the years passed all of the people I call "edge people," meaning those on the cutting edge, talked about Chuck Bowden, so I started reading him in earnest. You don't simply read Bowden; you become a Bowden addict, and the addiction is not always pleasant.

I will make bold to say that Bowden is America's most alarming writer. Just when you think you've heard it all, you learn that you haven't in the most pungent manner possible. Bowden is an elegant stylist, but then the paragraphs unroll like a bail of razor wire to keep you inside them.

Why is a man out in the Cabeza Prieta at 1:00 am when it's still a hundred degrees? Looking for bats, of course. Who else would call a companion rattlesnake Beulah? Who else would spend so much time in the charnel house, the abattoir, of Juárez where the heads roll like bowling balls and virgins say farewell encircled with burning tires?

Reading Bowden is to ride in a Ferrari without brakes. There's lots of oxygen but no safe way to stop.

Way back in the twelfth century the Zen philosopher Dōgen said, "When you find yourself where you already are, practice occurs." I've long made it a habit to study a place before I make a substantial visit, whether it's Modena, Italy, or Veracruz, Mexico, or the Sandhills of Nebraska. You can't know a place until you look into its history, its botany, its sociological factors, its geology (my weakest point), its creature population, and Native tribes. With minimal research you discover the astounding fact that most people don't know where they actually are. One day in a Patagonia saloon I said that in the late 1800s you could take a small ferry on the Santa Cruz from Nogales to Tucson, and no one believed me....

About ten years ago I finally met Bowden at a party given for the renowned scholar Bernard Fontana. There is a bit of the recluse in both of us, but when I'd drive to Tucson for groceries not available on the border we began to have occasional, then habitual, lunches where we would chat for a few hours about the state of the area, the country, the world in these woeful times wherein you have to be a proctologist to deal with news. At present it is a moral act to get drunk and throw yourself on the earth before a statue of the Virgin of Guadalupe. It is definitely not a moral act to call your broker or erect a worthless fence along the border.

Bowden is unflappable at these lunches, and I am enriched. He never says "I told you so" to the world. He retains the air of the

Charles Bowden at Jim Harrison's winter home in Patagonia, Arizona, 2011

amateur in the old sense, a true lover and student of life. Read him at your risk. You have nothing to lose but your worthless convictions about how things are.

This essay was adapted from the foreword to Charles Bowden's The Charles Bowden Reader *(Austin: University of Texas Press, 2010).*

JIM HARRISON (1937–2016) was one of America's most diverse writers, publishing poetry, novels, nonfiction books, and essays on a range of subjects. Among his best-known books are *Legends of the Fall*, *A Good Day to Die*, *Dalva*, *The Raw and the Cooked*, and *Wolf*. A native of Michigan, Harrison enjoyed winters in Patagonia, Arizona, at a home he and his wife loaned to Charles Bowden in summer.

He Heard the Music

SCOTT CARRIER

When I ask people to tell me their first impression of Chuck
Bowden, they usually start by saying, "He's tall." This is true. But
I think what they're getting at is he had the presence of a sequoia.
Time and space got bigger when he was around. You couldn't see
his roots, but you knew they were very deep. You couldn't help but
wonder, "Where did this come from?"

He was tall enough at the age of fourteen to drive a milk truck, or
maybe a bread truck, from Tucson to Seattle, Tucson to Chicago,
Tucson to New York. His father, Jude, bought the truck and made
it into a camper and filled it with cases of beer. Jude would drink,
young Charles Clyde would drive, and this is where Chuck's roots
started to go down. As a young child, he'd had visions and mystical experiences with animals and music, but these cross-country
trips with his father were where his analytical mind took shape. It's
where he learned how to put the words together, and take them
apart, locked in discussion and argument while passing through
sunsets and moonrises on cornfields, high plains, and Rocky
Mountains. His father was a prosecuting attorney for the IRS. He
went after people who didn't pay their taxes—liars and thieves
against the whole notion of social decency. And he never lost a
case. Do you follow?

When they got to their destination, his father would stay in the
truck and drink and read while young Charles went out exploring.
In Seattle, his dad told him, "You go down to skid row—a navy
fleet's just come in. You're big but you're still a boy, and the people
will see this and take you in. You won't be a threat to them."

In any education, timing is important. Chuck's dad was a good teacher. I don't think he writes about this very much. He tells me stories, and I forget them.

So Chuck walks away from the milk truck, into the bad part of town, seeking to understand—who are all these people? Just what is it they think they're doing? What are those words they are speaking to me? Where is that music coming from?

And this is, I think, when he realized he could see things about people that maybe they didn't know about themselves, wandering around the streets of Chicago, Seattle, or New York.

Who are these people?

He felt hungry.

He wanted to know.

So he began to feed upon them, tasting their lives just by watching, standing close, smelling.

I wonder, though, when he came back to the truck, did he tell his dad what he saw and what he learned?

Is it his father he's been reporting and writing to all along? When Chuck typed at his computer, was he in his mind driving the milk truck back home?

He says he can't write unless he thinks it's music, thereby beating back his own cowardice. He's like Kerouac this way, and also in that his subject is America. He told me once all of modern American writing comes from one line in Lincoln's Second Inaugural Address: "and the war came." His point was the rhythm of the thing. I think some people hear it, and some people don't, and I'm not interested in anything coming from those who don't. Just my preference.

I was at NPR in Washington in 1983, and Alex Chadwick gave me a copy of *Blue Desert*. He said, this guy is a western writer; you're a western writer; read it and tell me if it's any good. I didn't

Chuck Bowden's cassette list of songs for *Blood Orchid*

think of myself as a writer back then, but I took what he said as a compliment and read the book. For me, at the time, everything was opening up. I'd been taken in at NPR and was producing stories that were being broadcast around the country, and people liked them. I was being told that I was a good writer, which I didn't really believe.

So I read *Blue Desert*, and I felt like I'd found the writer I wanted to be like. I think on the first page Chuck writes about the beauty of the desert and how we always fail to live up to it. It was the blues— *Blue Desert*, written in the form of Hemingway's first collection of stories, *In Our Time*. Chuck was improvising on a deep theme that I'd heard in my subconscious but had never seen in print, which was strange because it was all around me. He cut through all the "us" and "them" bullshit and just stayed in the place where we are all in this together. I told Alex that Bowden is a true artist, a genius, and that he should be interviewed for *All Things Considered*. Alex was the producer of the weekend show at that time. But he didn't do it, and I didn't do it because I didn't think I could. I didn't feel worthy. I was doing my thing, and it didn't seem to mesh with interviewing great writers.

More than ten years later, I finally met Bowden when he came to Salt Lake to promote the *Stone Canyons* book with Jack Dykinga. It was in a bar, and I paid my compliments and that was that. Maybe a year later I was down in Tucson working on a radio story and I called him up, three or four days in a row, asking if he had time to talk. I was staying at the Hotel Congress, reading *Blood Orchid* at night. I can still remember that hotel room because I feel like my blood chemistry changed there from reading the book. I was working on *This American Life*, which was a new show back then, and I thought I had to get Chuck on the show somehow. (Ira Glass later called him and interviewed him, but it never got on the air.) Or, that was my excuse to meet with him. Finally, Chuck said let's go to lunch, and we did and then spent the next eight hours locked in conversation, mostly at his house, which was in the pre–Mary Martha Miles stage of its design, that is, dark with some things growing inside that should have been outside.

He'd just started working on *Down by the River*, and he was pretty crazed by what he was getting into. I remember looking at his face split into two sides, one dark and sinister, the other friendly and kind. The *Harper's* article on the dead women of Juárez had finally come out, and I mentioned that I had a story in the same issue, but I think he didn't hear this because a few weeks later he read it, by chance, and left a message on my phone saying how much he'd enjoyed it. My point is that up until he read my story, I was just another media person he was being friendly with, but after he read the story he saw my work as something like his own, sort of, maybe. He said something he liked was my "song," which is the best compliment I've ever had.

So I started learning stuff from him. I think I'd already learned as much as I could about writing, just from reading his books. What I didn't know was how to be a writer. I didn't know how to keep doing it, as a profession. I still don't, because it's hard. Mainly, I guess, I didn't understand the answer to "why do it?" His answer, basically, was "because you don't have a choice." You, for some reason, can hear the music, so you have a responsibility to get it down. You can either decide to do it poorly or do it well. Chuck helped a lot of people do a lot of things, but he expected something in return. Hard work. Good work. He expected you to die trying. Because what else is there? You're going to die, and what will you have left behind?

There's that aspect, the responsibility to do what you are good at, but also Chuck believed very strongly in speaking truth to power. It was in his blood, maybe from his father, definitely a very old gene. He believed in fighting corruption and the evils of power. Somebody has to do it. We can't have a civil society without a healthy press. The watchdog part of the media is essential, and so on. He was cynical of the media's performance, but he was serious about what we're supposed to be doing. I knew what he was saying, but I never felt up to this part of the thing. I still don't. He could take on the drug lords, and he could take on the politicians, but I have trouble enough taking on myself. I lived in fear that he'd be "taken out" and then I'd have to step up and fill in, and I didn't think I could do it. Not because I was afraid of dying, but because I just didn't think I could face evil like that.

We failed as a country, as a culture. Chuck was born soon after the first atomic bomb was dropped on Japan. He grew up during the best of times for America and saw it go down the tubes during his lifetime. He once wrote, after some fires in the Catalina Mountains, that he didn't want to outlive a mountain, but he just might outlive his country. He was like Jack Kerouac in his love of America, but his writing is different because America has changed from what it was in the 1950s and '60s. He'd seen it turn rotten through with greed and fear, and he was strong enough not to turn away or deny this. He was also strong enough not to stop loving his country. He still heard the music. This is why I admire him so much.

SCOTT CARRIER is a Peabody Award–winning radio producer and the author of *Prisoner of Zion: Muslims, Mormons and Other Misadventures*, and *Running after Antelope*. Carrier's pieces have been featured on radio programs, including *This American Life*, since 1996, *All Things Considered*, and NPR's *Hearing Voices*.

Charles Bowden and La Santa Muerte

LESLIE MARMON SILKO

Charles Bowden was an enigma. I only saw him a few times, and in those days Tucson was a smaller town. I probably offended him somehow because I don't recall we ever said more than "hello" to one another the times we did meet. I don't think he liked me, but I didn't care because I liked the way he wrote. Writers sometimes carry on dialogues with other writers by way of books and stories, not conversation.

We had similar interests in the borderland drug wars of the eighties and nineties and in La Santa Muerte, in listening to the dead in the myriad ways they reach us. He was the only person I know besides myself who read *Nunca Más*, the international report on the Argentine "dirty war," as soon as it was available. Maybe we were too similar.

As a child, I preferred to play alone so I could act out little stories I made up. As I was rereading his books for this essay, I realized that Bowden was happiest by himself, lost in thought. He socialized for the sake of getting details for stories—it must have been a great relief to be alone in a solitary space—whether in the blue desert or in a motel room at his keyboard deep into the other dimensions he was able to reach when he was alone. The liquor and other substances were only to aid with the psychic travel. You might argue that hard drink and the rigors of the borderland struggle wore him out but "it was necessary," as his persona CB declares in *Blood Orchid*, because the blood orchids made it so.

Bowden's relationship with Tucson was ambiguous. I don't

think he actually lived in Tucson. He slept here now and then, and got his mail here, but he kept his locations and his destinations confidential. Mysterious and illusive—that was part of his persona that the writer shared with others; it helps explain why the cartels, with their appetites for thrill killing, never got Bowden. His relationships even with friends and companions were ambiguous as well, but his devotion to the blue desert was manifest.

To enter the blue desert, you need layers of low rainy clouds off an eastern Pacific hurricane, evenly spreading blue drifts in intricate layers so that the rising sun's light shines through in blue— every shade of light blue, soaring west of the Sierra Madre to the Pinacate lava flows that edge the gulf shore of Sonora. You need a certain kind of cloud moisture right at dawn. Somehow, the light shines behind the misty rain canopy—a light that is topaz rainy dawn blue.

Toward the end of *Blue Desert*, Bowden confesses that he walked the immigrant trail north, "half to bring notice to the immigrant deaths," but he also writes, "I am going to the blue desert … everything is blue, and a great calm settles over me."

Reentry to the strange noisy world that feeds the blood orchids stuns him, and he fumbles with the pay phone to get an operator on the line. "I begin to grasp what has happened to me. My mind does not work in this world.... I have exited the only ground where I truly trust my senses.... I feel it all slip away and my senses deaden under the blandishments and delights of my civilization."

Clearly, the walks in the desert were the heart of his writing— part elegy, part essay, always poetry. But when I read *Blood Orchid* in 1996, I read it as a novel, a nonfiction novel that was invented by Gertrude Stein in the early twentieth century. *The Autobiography of Alice B. Toklas* was part of a larger paradigm shift and was widely read in the sixties, as the notion of the "objective observer" was challenged. In 1966, Truman Capote published his amazing nonfiction novel, *In Cold Blood*. Other writers followed; Norman

Charles Bowden, book jacket photo for *Blood Orchid*, 1995

Mailer, Tom Wolfe, and Hunter S. Thompson also explored something called the nonfiction novel.

The border in the 1980s was a perfect place to form multiple identities—desert enthusiast, investigative journalist, essayist, poet, nonfiction novelist, and DEA pal. Bowden lived in defiance of borders; academic conventions such as "genre" were trivialities. Bowden was a writer; Bowden wrote. He knew that "facts" can obscure truth and that fiction may illuminate truth. His most impressive desert borderlands character, his most convincing work of fiction, is the journalist Charles Bowden (or CB, as I refer to him), the intrepid narrator of *Blood Orchid, Down by the River,* and *Dreamland.*

In *Blood Orchid,* Bowden mentions that he wrote a novel in 1967, while he was living in California, but set it aside. Still, he was a novelist at heart. Journalism and magazine writing were only a means to the end—to buy him the time to walk in the desert.

The creation of the persona CB was gradual and organic, given the borderland stories he covered. Many writers have supported themselves with journalism from time to time, but only a few, like Bowden, saw their fiction thrive from it.

The persona begins to emerge in *Blue Desert.* An assistant city editor calls him "Captain Death," but CB explains that he doesn't want the immigrants' deaths in the desert to go unnoticed. The origins of Bowden's devotion to La Santa Muerte surrounded him in Tucson when he was growing up. El Día de los Muertos is still widely celebrated in the Southwest, and the devotions to ancestor spirits of the indigenous people are far older than any church.

"The woman with blue teeth" who appears in *Blood Orchid* is, of course, La Santa Muerte. In *Blue Desert,* the corpses of immigrants and narco smugglers accumulated, but it was in *Blood Orchid* that CB embraces her as a lover. Death is unfailing. Death remembers. Death always has time. There is nothing you can do or say that will cause death to forsake you. Before we are born, where are we? Asleep in the dark apron of stars.

Blood Orchid has the complex structure of a nonfiction novel, not an investigative journalist's report. The reader is alerted at once by Bowden's preface, "How it came to pass." These are the words of the narrator of a novel, the main character of the novel, the novelist's persona, Charles Bowden, intrepid journalist of the borderland: "I am hunkered down in a motel room high in the Rocky Mountains. I can only make a stab at writing the truth if I tell others it is fiction—that way no one gets upset with me. I can only start writing if I think of it as music—that way I can beat back my own cowardice. I can only write if I don't think at all. I have changed the names to protect the guilty. But everything happened as it is reported in this book, including things scheduled for tomorrow or the day after that." Meet CB, the persona of Charles Bowden.

I am keen about the dangers.

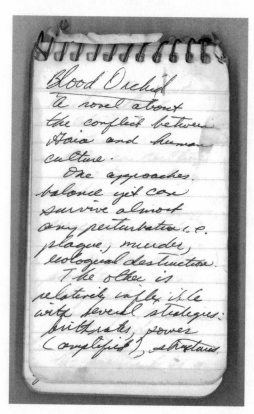

Pages from Charles Bowden's *Blood Orchid* notebook before he had written a word of the book

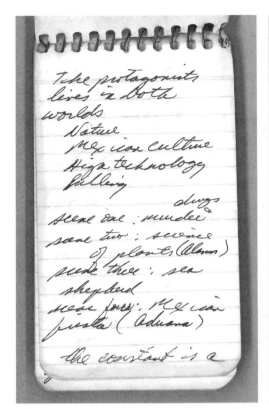

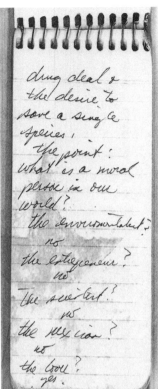

Blood Orchid is about the loss of a "new world" in the Americas. The narrative lines are interwoven at points of tyranny and horror, at the failure of human decency: quotations about the end of the Vietnam War; graphic quotations about torture and murder from *Nunca Más*, the international report on the dirty war in Argentina; the poor victims who lost all their savings and the trial of the Keating Five who got away with their crimes; and the Murdered Child in Tucson.

The quotations from *The Sex Lives of Orchids*, which introduce the chapters, set an underlying narrative theme of struggle between men and women and also reference the cosmological struggle of biological destiny that we humans share with the orchids.

The blood orchid is Bowden's metaphor to account for the slaughter of the buffalo, the murders of millions of indigenous people; for the racism, the cruelty, and the greed that fuel the US government's policies along the Mexican border.

A recurring theme in Bowden's writing is the indictment of government and social mores that institutionalize the exploitation of the powerless. In *Blood Orchid*, quotations from the Vietnam War, the Indian Wars, and the Argentine dirty war of the 1970s appear throughout the text.

Bowden's reporting on the Mexico-US border in the eighties and nineties took him into the dangerous world of DEA undercover agents and the drug cartels, where necessity required him to employ his considerable talents as a novelist. In order to report on the drug trade, it was critical that he shroud the identities of his contacts with fiction by changing details and descriptions and locations to protect "the guilty," as he says in the preface to *Blood Orchid*. He had to protect the cartel jefes and their soldiers, but also had to shield the DEA informants and agents who shared their exploits with him.

The narrator of *Blood Orchid* admits in the introduction, "I can only make a stab at writing the truth if I tell others it is fiction—that way nobody gets too upset with me. I have changed the names and locations at times to protect the guilty. But everything happened as it is reported in this book, including the things scheduled for tomorrow or the day after that."

What is the meaning of "including the things scheduled for tomorrow or the day after that"? I interpret this as a "tell," which the writer included to tip off observant readers that the journalist character CB of *Blood Orchid* is not the same as the writer/author, Charles Bowden.

When I was a boy, I thought the world would get better if people took a good long look at it. Now no one seems to look.

CB is a complex character. He admits his admiration for both Pancho Villa and Charles Keating because they were "men of action." On some points, CB is a curmudgeon who thinks women should wear makeup and high heels; at one point he compares environmentalists with pornographers. This is how you know that *Blood Orchid* is a novel. CB, the narrator/character, is not Bowden, the writer/human being. In real life, Charles Bowden was friendly with Earth First! founder Dave Foreman; and how much did he care about women's high heels?

The writer, the man, Charles Bowden, was reared in Tucson. The few times I met him, he was reserved and laconic in the manner of southern Arizona cowboys, who generally don't say much. Bowden was a listener, not a talker. Those who walked the Pinacate or other wild places with Bowden probably came closest to knowing him.

I must relax. The book is in the can and for the first time in over a year, I'm not looking over my shoulder and I'm not being followed and I'm not carrying a nine millimeter with a fifteen clip and an extra clip in my pocket.

As I reread his books and considered his descriptions of cartel "soldiers" torturing and killing one another out of boredom—killing cousins who owed them money, killing friends for dancing with the wrong woman—I began to suspect that Bowden exaggerated the amount of time he spent hanging out at the narco ranches and drinking with the narco jefes dressed in black at their favorite bars in Juárez. The East Coast magazine editors who bought Bowden's stories loved to hear about CB's adventures, and Bowden didn't disappoint them. After all, he heard stories from ex–county sheriffs, narcs, border patrol agents—easy to do those years he worked at the Tucson newspaper. But, rather than risk his life by showing up one too many times in Juárez to drink with the men in black, Bowden preferred to borrow a storage box of old files, wire-tap intercepts, and undercover agent reports from his pals at the DEA; and when the story deadline loomed, he'd tell everyone he was going to Juárez. His women friends would beg him not to go. This is one of my favorite aspects of Bowden's persona—the way CB used the danger of his work as a "chick magnet" to attract women who wanted to protect him.

So he'd hit the road, but not to Juárez. I suspect that he favored the faded stucco motels bypassed in the sixties on deserted frontage roads along Interstate 10 and I-40. To get his work done, he required a carton of Lucky Strikes, a half-dozen bottles of wine or other "spirits," and a baggie of weed. Then he'd sit in front of the blank page to focus his memory and imagination on the blank sheet of paper, the empty screen, the expanding field of white; a cloud of white light appears in a rush of wind that stirs the white petals of the masses of Casa Blanca lilies.

Suddenly, back he would go, performing the novelist's gambit of astral projection backward, and even forward, to the past or to future locations, to the narco ranches or to the Juárez condos with the narcos and their torture victims. But always he was careful to write fiction—no "facts," so no court in the United States or Mexico could ever touch them.

CB suited the vanities of the DEA, but also of the ones who brought white flowers; they loved reading about themselves. When he'd had enough of Juárez and El Paso, he'd wake up in Tucson at 3 am and write about being in Juárez, at the condo with the "roasted meat" buried in the patio. Years later, Bowden showed a friend a certificate of appreciation from the DEA and joked "here is my death warrant," but he was devoted to La Santa Muerte and she always protected him.

Bowden didn't hide the fact that his DEA contacts were drinking buddies who shared their "war stories" with him; they liked the idea of a writer putting their stories in *Esquire* and *GQ*. They looked out for him. But the cartel members felt the same way. He promised the cartel narcos pure fiction, and he knew better than to screw around. The Juárez cartel saw proof copies of his articles about them before Bowden saw them.

"I am careful," his narrator, CB, tells us, despite the protection he enjoyed from "Don Arturo," from the DEA that he worked with, and from the cartels who were happy as long as he wrote glamorous fiction about them.

His ability to take us there—right to the edge of the shallow graves, to the haunted grief of Phil Jordan for his brother—reveals that Bowden possessed and practiced the novelist's gift of transporting the reader. More than that, we are haunted; we can't forget.

There is the liquor, and there is La Santa Muerte. In *Blood Orchid*, the narrator describes a discussion between himself and a Lakota woman hitching a ride. CB tells her that until the Indians quit booze, "no one will make it and nothing will happen. And I think while I say this that I am angry now and I want a drink." CB doesn't try to hide his bond with alcohol.

The Lakota woman replies that the only way for the Indians to survive these past hundred years was to stay drunk.

"I say nothing to her words. They are the story of every survivor and that is why I know they are true." CB needs to get away from her. He drops her off fast and gets a speeding ticket. "The drinking has been necessary," he tells us.

"We kill what we love." He is mourning the deaths of the springs, lakes, and rivers in the Southwest. CB confesses he doesn't want to give up the comforts of the unsustainable culture he is part of.

"I have to make my own cure," he tells us.

"I have no position on drugs. The blood orchids, I think, make them necessary for many.... I cannot be made acceptable. All this ... stuff gets in the way. This is not what I had planned."

There is a link between La Santa Muerte and the drinking. Robert Sundance, a recovered alcoholic, valued his experiences with the d.t.'s as encounters with the spirit world. Robert Sundance is CB's hero who survived years on the street, kicked alcohol, and devoted the rest of his life to helping others get off booze. Devotions to La Santa Muerte require liquor or other substances to facilitate a shift in consciousness that permits one to speak to the ancestors or talk to the dead.

After 9-11, the DEA faced stiff competition from other federal agencies for funding, because, suddenly, the dominant US fear became Islamic terrorists. Overnight, the fixation on Mexican drug cartels shifted; magazines such as *Harper's*, the *Atlantic*, *Esquire*, and *GQ* began to turn their attention to Islamic terrorists. The grisly cartel murders and gruesome sites where skeletons reached out of the sand could no longer compete with the online beheadings and mass graves and prisoners burnt alive in steel cages. Eclipsed by the Taliban, the cartels also posted videos on YouTube to publicize the horror and terrorize citizens with what became known as "narco porn."

CB reported the border drug war corruption for years, but now he can see that it is impossible for it to be other than it is, and he is old and tired and sick from all the liquor he had to drink to hear the stories from the agents and the narcos. CB, the investigative journalist, begins to break bad.

He started to write the chronicle of betrayed DEA agents and the houses of slaughter in Juárez. He stopped tip-toeing around narco porn and embraced it, embellishing the tortures with details from *Nunca Más*, the handbook of military and police detainments, kidnappings, torture, and murder in Argentina's dirty war in the seventies. Magazine editors loved it.

The result was *Down by the River*, the story of DEA agent Phil Jordan and his murdered brother, Bruno, in Juárez, and of the other DEA agents, cousins, and the journalist CB, who worked with Phil Jordan.

About *Down by the River,* the narrator CB says: "This book is about that world of secret files. Files never seen, files buried alive, files still sealed." Files far more important, but secret, are the DEA files that reveal that the US government knew that Mexican presidents Ernesto Zedillo and Carlos Salinas de Gortari both supported the drug cartels and took millions upon millions of dollars. The US government, for "national security" reasons, never intended to win the "Border Drug War," despite the millions and millions US taxpayers saw allocated to the DEA every year. And yet, the money rolled into the DEA, in part because there was a lurid xenophobic narrative about the borderlands that was reinforced by movies and TV, and also by the press, as the Mexico-US border increasingly became politicized by both US political parties.

Bowden's writing style, an irresistibly rich combination of fifties *Police Gazette* meets Raymond Chandler, keeps the reader going; otherwise, the narco porn in *Down by the River* is unrelenting: the duct tape and plastic sheeting; the shovels and lengths of rope; the rotting bundles—"the cooked meat"—exhumed from the garden patios of Juárez condominiums. The grisly scenes pile one on the other in *Down by the River.* The "narco porn" is intended by Bowden to express his outrage at the hypocrisy and lies: the stench and horror needs to be owned by the "good citizens" and the governments of both the US and Mexico.

Toward the end, the character CB ends up in an unfortunate position, which reveals Bowden's conundrum. We writers are subject to the places and to the prevailing forces of history into which we are born. At the time, Bowden did not see that his writing, because it was "nonfiction," could be weaponized by anti-immigrant political forces more easily than fiction could. So, while he was always clear about his "writing process" (i.e., changes "to protect the guilty," as he put it), Bowden still called himself a journalist, not a novelist, because fiction was dying out—*Esquire, Harper's,* and the *Atlantic* didn't buy short stories anymore.

Bowden's stories reflect the dominant narrative that the DEA used to enflame the US Congress to continue lavish funding for the war on drugs. The cartels liked the way the stories terrified people so that no one gave them any resistance. The DEA knew the war was unwinnable, but they still wanted paychecks, so they played along. This is how the *Blood Orchid* finally won.

We come from green ground teeming with insects and the earth hums now as the summer rains wash the dust from our eyes and we briefly see life before we return to death.

Dreamland is itself a phantasm of narco porn and odd beauty, in which CB's text serves as a center for Alice Leora Briggs's nightmarish and gruesome, but indelible, images. The book is an homage, an offering, to La Santa Muerte, and it is an elegy for all those who have suffered and died in the border drug struggle. It is also an elegy for CB. We see him—the face, the hands—close up; the toll of the miles and the years. We see drawings of him at work and again realize that to write was his greatest pleasure—no need for bars or parties when he could go anywhere in his reveries on the blank page. Finally, it is an elegy for those lost on the desert crossings who died attempting to reach Dreamland.

The devotions to La Santa Muerte are a psychic defense system some people use in the face of terror, torture, and death—to embrace death, as Bowden's meditations and Briggs's images do. Images of Bowden outnumber images of La Santa Muerte—he looks worn and tired, consumed, used up. The writer and his persona have become nearly indistinguishable. And yet CB had one more misadventure left in him—*El Sicario*, with an Italian filmmaker and a born-again cartel assassin. That CB's borderland writing career seems to have concluded with this strange book shows that Bowden never lost his sense of humor or irony.

The woman in the dark with glowing blue teeth at the end of *Blood Orchid* is, of course, La Santa Muerte. "She'll be gentle," CB hopes. And because he would not let the dead be forgotten, she loved him and she was gentle.

Novelist, poet, and writer, LESLIE MARMON SILKO may be best known for her novels *Ceremony, Almanac of the Dead,* and *Gardens in the Dunes,* and her nonfiction books *The Turquoise Ledge: A Memoir* and a collection of letters, *The Delicacy and Strength of Lace,* with James Wright. She reports, "While I was writing *Almanac,* I read all the pieces Chuck Bowden wrote for the *Citizen* and *Weekly,* so I felt his influence." Silko was a MacArthur Fellow ("Genius Grant" recipient) in 1981 and received the Native Writers' Circle of the Americas Lifetime Achievement Award in 1994. She resides in Tucson, Arizona.

The License Plate Said "Hayduke": Chuck Bowden and the Red Cadillac—A Memory

LUIS ALBERTO URREA

> *I try to construct a theory of how a moral person should live in these circumstances, and how such a person should love.*
>
> CHARLES BOWDEN, *Desierto*

I

"Love" might not be the first thing that comes to mind when one considers the often angry, hard-bitten books Charles Bowden wrote. But love was what burned inside him, it seemed to me.

Those who knew him far better than I have told me this more than once. Even the ones who are still mad at him. Even Jim Harrison, after Bowden had left this earth.

I don't think he was claiming to be a moral person, in this quote. But I do believe he was trying his damnedest to live by a code. It just had to be a code of his own devising. I risked calling him my friend.

This is how the thing began.

Early in February of 1993, between 6 and 7 in the morning, my phone rang. I was hiding out in San Diego after a doomed marriage had fallen apart behind me. And my first book had been on the shelves for less than a month. It was a nonfiction account of my previous life working with the disadvantaged people of my birthplace, Tijuana.

I scrambled for the receiver before the answering machine kicked in. The Voice, the voice his many friends and enemies and paramours would never forget, spoke.

"Urrea?" it said.

My first impression: the guy got the pronunciation right. My second impression: he was some crusty tough guy who sounded hungover. Some character out of a B. Traven novel.

"It's Bowden."

Wait. What? As in Charles Bowden?

"Yeah. It's Chuck."

I was immediately pacing the floor.

"Where are you?" he said.

I was trying to wake up enough to understand that Charles Bowden had tracked me down for some reason.

I started to tell him he was one of my prose heroes. Then I remembered to answer his question. "San Diego," I said.

"What the hell are you doing *there*?"

I went into the marriage falling apart explanation.

He cut me off.

"I know about those," he said. "Where were you living before San Diego?"

He said *San Diego* as if it hurt his soul.

"Boulder, Colorado."

There was a long pause. I imagined him taking a drink, or taking a drag on a cigarette.

"Jesus," he said, "talk about a place that makes you want to commit suicide."

Bowden followed this comment with marching orders.

"Where you need to live is in Tucson."

He said something about Boulder being an amusement park for rich people and that it had trucks gluing up picturesque claptrap all over town to make those people feel special.

Both Bowden's and Ed Abbey's books were on the shelf beside my phone. A devil's claw sat beside my computer. Tucson. It would have seemed insane to think I had just heard Chuck suggesting, "Come be my friend." An invitation to take the first step into

Bowdenworld. But that's how I took it. His real friends could have told me he was also saying, "Come here and let me kick your ass."

I had been infatuated with Edward Abbey for years. I was one of those who had camped in deserts often as a kid, and now fancied myself some kind of Abbeyesque long-haul dry-lands wanderer. (I had a much milder demeanor than Ed—every time I reread *The Monkey Wrench Gang*, I grew afraid that the FBI was going to bust through my windows and arrest me for subversion. And then there was that Mexican-hating thing of Abbey's.) But reading his work opened the door to Bowden.

When I read *Blue Desert*, I thought it was one of the greatest American books of the modern era. I distributed Chuck's chapter on bats and their caves to writing students who often stared at it in bewilderment. Like, bats? I may or may not have known that Ed and Chuck were dear friends at that time. Though Chuck would have never stooped to an adjective like "dear." I learned that if he sounded like he could barely stand you, he loved you on some level.

Re: friendship with Abbey, Bowden writes: *He was reasonably polite, didn't shit on the floor, and was well read.*

Selah.

In that first phone call, Bowden announced: "You owe me money."

"I do?"

"Forty bucks."

I must have laughed. I had no idea what was happening.

He said, "I've been up all night rereading your book. And I've bought copies for all my friends."

I somehow knew it was true.

In *The Red Caddy*, Bowden implies that to be an expert on your friend means you were never really that person's friend at all. I didn't know this. I wandered around pondering the weird phone call from the icon. I went to the bookstore to hunt for any new or old Bowdens I hadn't read. They were almost impossible to find,

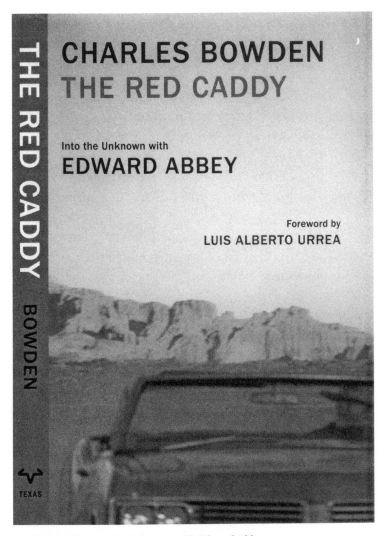

The Red Caddy: Into the Unknown with Edward Abbey

and it made them more appealing. But I was trying to be an expert. That never impressed him.

I had a Jeep, no job, and a little bit of publisher money in my pocket. I packed up and headed for Tucson. Time to meet the master.

I decided to bring an outlaw with me.

This monster of a man had been a biker once, and he boasted of having sex with a woman while stoned and speeding up I-5 on a Harley. He had also guarded LSD loads with a shotgun for the Hells Angels. He sported a Grizzly Adams beard and a head scarf, and was now a born-again Christian who was featured in my border book. Talk about a Bowden character.

Knowing Bowden's penchant for outrage at the vagaries of this world, I also thought he'd be moved to learn that the biker was ultimately too wild for his church. That his beloved congregation had turned on him and turned him out. After years of service feeding the poor in Mexico, he was homeless and living out of public restrooms in San Diego. So I'd gone and collected him and moved him into my back bedroom.

Let's call him Bear.

I called Chuck and told him we were on our way. He did not seem surprised. Over the years, it seemed very important to Chuck that nothing could be seen to surprise him. He allowed books to do that, but few people got the chance.

He told me to meet him at a bar on the corner of Speedway and Campbell. It was in a big hotel because witnesses would make it harder for the narco hitmen to get him. I laughed. What a card. He didn't laugh. He told me there would be a bodyguard. I stopped laughing.

The bar no longer exists. This is fitting. The message of *The Red Caddy*, for all its gloriously hard-bitten prose and philosophical tough-guy narrative, and its often hilarious bluster, is a deep shade of melancholy. A sense of mortality that shadows the pages like the slow creep of dusk sliding over the desert. The bar is gone, its hotel is gone, Ed Abbey is gone, Bear is gone, Chuck is gone, and the bodyguard is gone.

Bear and I walked in and were greeted with a hard-boiled scene from some '50s detective movie. There sat Bowden, back to the wall. Looking wrinkled and beat and nursing a beer. His sideburns were white. I think he was smoking.

Standing to his left, leaning on the wall, was a deadly looking older Mexican with his arms crossed. The man gave us the stink-eye and looked past us. The whole time, he scanned the empty bar for evildoers. "Ex-Federal," Bowden said. "Armed." He shook our hands and called for three more beers. With limes.

He told us some convoluted tale of Mexican narcos who were mad at him over some slight, either in his writing or his general comportment. Perhaps a dustup at a *narcotraficante* ranch, and there might have been a party involved. I don't remember now—I was too amazed by this scenario, and keeping my eye on the gunman. Bowden advised me to always sit with my back to a wall so nobody could sneak up and assassinate me.

I half-expected gunfire to erupt without warning. Which Chuck might have wanted me to think, just to see how I would act. Suddenly, all this manhood struck me as hilariously silly. Chuck gave all evidence of being in on the joke. The prospect of being shot by *sicarios* seemed to make him feel full of pep.

Tucson old-timers, by the way, will know that the bodyguard was the indestructible Art Carrillo Strong, author of *Corrido de Cocaine*.

"You two fed the poor, huh?" Chuck said, staring at Bear.

He was more interested in him than he was in me. Writers? He knew a million. And the writers he knew were not just typists but *pistoleros*. Biker missionary outlaw homeless guys, though, were something new.

Chuck leaned across the table and stared at Bear. He finally said, "Bear, are you a good man?"

"Good?"

Bear twitched and fidgeted and looked away.

"I don't know," he said.

It was a direct kung-fu strike.

Bear drained his beer and went looking for another.

Thinking I'd turn the conversational tables on Bowden, I said, "Was Ed Abbey a good man?"

Chuck looked at his hands splayed on the table.

Then he started to cry.

He muttered something like "Fuck this" and walked out of the bar.

How should such a person love?

I I

I didn't see Bowden again for a year. Eventually, we were both booked to speak at a panel at a southwestern university. I was unsure of my standing with the great man. But he was the kind of guy, in my experience, who liked you to think he lived in the moment and didn't worry about old weepy episodes. When I walked toward the auditorium, he was sprawled on a bench outside, looking more disreputable than he had in the bar. His idea of dressing up. Three women hovered around him, getting autographs. He was in great spirits, flirting in an offhanded way that had them riveted. He greeted me enthusiastically and began an impromptu lecture about the Mexican Revolution that lasted for about twenty minutes. He handed me a copy of Daniel Nugent's *Spent Cartridges of Revolution*. "Read this if you want to understand about revolution," he said. I still have it.

Inside, we sat at a long, swooping table laden with microphones and pitchers of ice water. I remember it as some vast gathering, dozens of scholars, but I'm sure there were only five or six of us at the table and maybe a hundred people in the audience. We each gave our perspectives on the border. Scholars droned on and on, it's true. Footnotes were parsed. Bowden, who never met a gangster he didn't love, even when the killers he dropped in his pages gave every indication of having been kids lounging around a Juárez barrio out of boredom, painted his usual ghastly border inferno. How could you argue with him? He was a force of nature. He was being hunted by narcos, for God's sake.

Being born in Tijuana, and having lived all my life on both sides of the border fence—sometimes in both places at once—I had what I considered to be a saner view of that hideous death trap that so appalled observers of the border. After all, I argued, those of us who live with it every day also see it as a symbol of family, of potential, perhaps even as a place where two cultures might meet each other in partnership as well as in conflict. Witness the Mexican and American kids who regularly play volleyball over parts of the wall. And it was evident that a new renaissance in commerce, technology, culture, and the arts was coming.

I was saying this, apparently to Chuck's exasperation.

Suddenly, he took up his microphone to interrupt me.

"I don't know what planet you're from," he drawled.

Laughter and soft gasps.

I replied, "I'm from the border planet, Chuck. I was born and raised there."

He slumped, disgusted: Urrea scores a kung-fu blow of his own.

Later, he took revenge in Bend, Oregon. We were on a panel with Ursula K. Le Guin and other writers, talking about the future of the American West. I was in the middle of speaking my piece, preaching border glasnost, when Bowden simply sighed into his microphone and groaned, "Oh, God."

Then he went outside to smoke.

III

Once I moved to Tucson, we drifted apart a little. Chuck had become addicted to the ongoing drug war. He had gone from damaging his soul on the southern Arizona immigrant killing fields to feeding on terror and blood with the crime photographers of Juárez. He was wandering in West Texas and southern New Mexico. Rumors of his demise proliferated. His foes and competitors were predicting his fall—surely, Bowden couldn't keep it up.

When he was in town, we spoke. I knew he was a gardener, and had a rumored backyard wonderland. But it felt indecorous to invite myself over to his place, even when he said I should.

Chuck railed against what he called the "Dead Ed Industry." He was drawn to evil and corpses and bad mojo and worse governments, sure. But I am convinced that the Dead Ed freaks had a hand in making him flee Tucson. I had seen the pain he hid with bravado. How does such a person show that he is vulnerable?

He complained that people who had once drunk a beer in the same cantina as Ed were now claiming to be his best friends, and were offering to take people to Ed's unlawful burial spot somewhere out there near the Devil's Highway. "They could just show suckers a pile of rocks in the backyard and say, 'This is Edward Abbey's secret grave,' and they'd believe it." He was furious.

This was when Chuck told me Ed's Red Caddy was moldering away in a dirt alley behind Speedway, the street where we had first met.

"It's covered in raccoon shit," he noted.

Fellow Tucson writer Gregory McNamee confirmed this story. It seemed like some urban legend. If Ed was such a titan, how was his car left out in the dirt? So Greg drove me down the alley one night, and there it was. A well-known book dealer had acquired it. It had become something of a shrine to certain writers, who ogled it and wrote WASH ME in its dust and drank beer in Ed's honor.

It became my habit to visit the car often. I didn't ever tell Chuck, though.

Tony Delcavo, of Bella Luna Books in Colorado, bought the old car. He invited me to help drive it to Denver. That amusing semiepic journey became an essay called "Down the Highway with Edward Abbey." McNamee kindly published it in an Abbey-themed anthology. And here I am, mourning Chuck in print. What a circle.

Charles Bowden. I consider him a master—if not in every book or utterance, certainly a master of audacity. He fought to maintain his integrity. He always tried to tell the truth, even when he lied. Chuck knew things, terrible and beautiful things. I feel richer for reading him and knowing him.

If you listen, you will hear him from the other side, saying "Oh, God" when I say I loved him.

As he wrote about Abbey:

In some way I can't quite put my finger on, he's not quite dead.

This essay is adapted from the foreword to Charles Bowden's The Red Caddy: Into the Unknown with Edward Abbey *(Austin: University of Texas Press, 2018).* Kirkus Reviews *selected* The Red Caddy *as one of the best nonfiction books of 2018.*

Poet, novelist, and essayist LUIS ALBERTO URREA's award-winning books include *The Fever of Being, Nobody's Son, Across the Wire, In Search of Snow, The Hummingbird's Daughter, The Devil's Highway* (Pulitzer Prize finalist in nonfiction), and *The House of Broken Angels.*

Scratchboard Opposites

GARY PAUL NABHAN

When we were both still in our twenties, Chuck Bowden and I showed up at the house of a mutual friend of ours on the same night, both assuming that we would be taking her out for a date. I never figured out which of our calendars was off by a day, or a week, but it didn't matter. While Bowden arrived with a bottle of alcohol and a tattered copy of *Wisconsin Death Trip* in hand, I was no doubt armed with Thomas Merton's *Wisdom of the Desert, The Lives of the Saints*, or a bowl of freshly cooked tepary beans.

Needless to say, I didn't stick around to continue our three-way conversation. It was an excellent moment to learn how to do a disappearing act.

From this story, you might think that the trope I am setting up is one of competition between two desert writers, hikers, lovers, or friends. Oddly, because of either Chuck's largesse or both of us being rather oblivious to social rules and constraints, I don't think either of us thought of the other as in any way a competitor. For the most part, we ran in different fields, played to different audiences, and batted in different leagues. There was room in our worlds for complementary point and counterpoint.

What I most felt about Bowden's trailblazing work as a journalist, nonfiction writer, and scholar-activist is that it was the scratchboard opposite of my own endeavors, for our writings were as different as night and day. While his enduring testament, *Killing the Hidden Waters*, decried the overpumping of desert aquifers and the loss of indigenous knowledge of desert peoples who knew how to survive and thrive without pumping irrigation water, I was inspired by Chuck to seek out the last of the floodwater farmers who persisted in their traditions, the topic of my own book, *The Desert Smells Like Rain*. While Bowden looked to Juárez/El Paso as the "Laboratory of Our Future" for brazen acts of godlessness, I went there seeking out my own Arab-American kin, as well as Crypto-Jews and Crypto-Muslims who put God before anything else. While he scaled the summits of volcanic peaks in the Altiplano of central Mexico, with his sidekick Jack Dykinga, I went there to sample *moles* and seek out the origins of *chile* peppers. There was even a complementarity to our worldviews, a yin and a yang and a live-and-let-live, whenever we got together.

I am not implying that my own modest work will ever be regarded as having the same stature of Chuck's; I am just saying that each of us, as contemporaries and neighbors, wrote in some creative tension with the other. And one time, in Wilson, Wyoming—at the Dinner Party for the American West organized by Terry Tempest Williams for Barry Lopez, Doug Peacock, John Nichols, myself, Chuck, and others to discuss big issues—Chuck sweetly pulled me aside to simply say: "Keep doing whatever you are doing, with the seeds, with the words. I need that light so I don't stumble and fall into my own darkness."

If you have read multiple volumes of Bowdenesque prose, seen his cameo appearances in Day of the Dead videos, or talked to him in bars, I am sure you sensed that his favorite move—his flamenco dance—was simply *to step outside the box*, to ignore all conventions.

If an interviewer asked him which of the Mexican drug cartels would eventually win out and capture the entire pot, he would simply *growl* something like "There *are no* cartels as you are imagining them. *Now that's fiction*. There is only a scatter of independent cells of petty drug lords who sometimes cooperate, sometimes compete, and sometimes kill each other off."

If a radio show host asked him what public policy would help Tucson or Phoenix best conserve its water for future generations, he would argue that residents should turn all their hoses on at peak hours in summer afternoons, and drive the water companies out of their business-as-usual stances.

Bowden could not stay in the box no matter what the topic was, and most of the time that was because he had never been in the box, he disdained it so much. He was metabolically predisposed to being an outsider, a shaman with no community left to heal.

His best writing was as much historic fiction as it was creative nonfiction. His comprehension of Spanish was fair to middlin' at best, and his O'odham *ha-ñeoki* was nonexistent, but he always seemed to catch the drift, *the songline* of where the singer was going, no matter what the language. His understanding of ecological processes was modest, despite his time with the likes of Robert Whitaker and Ray Turner. But what he said about the environmental histories he understood was far more incisive than the way in which the scientists who mentored him could ever articulate.

Like most of us, Chuck's handicaps were also his greatest gifts.

Although we were scratchboard opposites, Bowden and I shared many loves in common. We were both mentored by desert rat heroes such as Julian Hayden, Bunny Fontana, Patricia Paylore, Paul Martin, Ray Turner, Jim Harrison, J. P. S. Brown, and Lawrence Clark Powell. We both loved the quirky music of Warren Zevon and Ry Cooder. We both did time in the Upper Midworst of Grater Chicagoland before settling in the desert for good. Each of us was fictionalized as a protagonist in a Brian Laird mystery novel—"Nate Bowman" for the better, and "Gray Nathan" for wurst. (Well, I did occasionally wear Gray Nathan's Converse All-Stars after the book came out, but no one noticed.)

And our shared affinities for the Pinacate, Cabeza Prieta, Organ Pipe? Well, they became sacred ground for both of us.

Charles Bowden making notes during a three-week hike in the Gran Desierto of Sonora, Mexico, 1985

The last time I saw Chuck was the summer before he died, out just after dawn on the dirt road edging the Nature Conservancy reserve in Patagonia. Both of us had on our binoculars, but neither of us were particularly good birders. It was more the practice than the life list that had wooed us over. And so we stopped and talked for twenty minutes before the sun rose above the cottonwoods and began to scorch the ground around us.

I had encountered him leaning up against a smaller tree, weeping, grieving for the loss of the state's largest and probably oldest cottonwood tree. It had been toppled by winds uprooting it from the soggy soil conditions that follow the onset of summer monsoons. He had visited that tree each summer that he house sat for Linda and Jim Harrison at their little cabin along Sonoita Creek, but now it was toast. We guessed that a cottonwood seed had sprouted around 1908, then survived every fire, flood, and drought of the last century, before it keeled over. His love for that tree—and his grief for its loss—was palpable.

Soon after that, Chuck was gone, and not too much later, Linda and Jim Harrison checked out as well. The cabin that they occupied now lies vacant, its future uncertain, although no greater writing by two timeless Arizona writers has ever come out of the same small square footage.

Now and then when I am passing along Sonoita Creek, I stop and take a look at the large root mass left by that toppled champion cottonwood. It has the memory of Charles Bowden written all over it. We might fear that some of his scratchboard sketches may go out of print during the remaining years of our own lifetimes, but they will never be forgotten. They are too fierce, too heartbroken to ever die a silent death. They will remain in the air, swirling like a dust devil hovering over sacred ground.

GARY PAUL NABHAN knew Charles Bowden for forty years. An Ecumenical Franciscan Brother and MacArthur Fellow ("Genius Grant" recipient), Nabhan's recent books include *Food from the Radical Center: Healing Our Lands and Communities*, from Island Press, and *Mesquite: An Arboreal Love Affair*, from Chelsea Green Press.

Drawn to the Flames: Bowden and Agee, Expanding the Boundaries of American Nonfiction

WILLIAM DEBUYS

You might think, as Charles Bowden did, that the world is a down-spiraling mess, but that's not a reason to read him. The important thing to Bowden was not so much the direction of the spiral as the intensity of its motion. He wanted to feel the gyre. He wanted to see it, taste it, and report it in all its brutality and paradoxical beauty. He was a connoisseur of the actual mess we've made of our world, and he described its flavors meticulously. That's why for almost a generation people have been reading Bowden with amazement, and that's why people will still want to read him today. The wine hasn't changed. It's just aged a little. And the taste is even richer.

Bowden's writing gives off heat. It's the heat of the desert, the heat of sex, the heat of argument. He interrogated everything, following the evidence, hoping to "locate some kind of heartbeat beneath the modern world I live in." He was born in Illinois in 1945, moved to Tucson while still a kid, and was based for most of his life in southern Arizona. The desert that became Bowden's natural habitat was not the ecological desert described as Sonoran or Chihuahuan but the cultural place straddling the life-warping division of the international border, a place inhabited by campesinos, artists, drug runners, fat cats, hunters, and hustlers: *el desierto*. The place got into him. Bowden became the most *mexicano* of gringos. He was a big, bluff white guy, but the spirit of the Day of the Dead, that weird Indo-Iberian decoction of morbidity and ecstatic celebration, sloshed back and forth inside him like a tide.

I asked a mutual friend to describe him. The friend said, "He had an element of confrontation." While other gringos poked around south of the border finding seams in the landscape where they could move safely and unobtrusively, "Bowden would ask, 'Who's the most fucked-up person here? I gotta go talk to him.'" And that's what he did, hazards be damned. One of the ironies of his life is that, after decades of asking questions where a lot of well-armed, hard-eyed people thought he didn't belong, he died in his sleep in 2014, having moved to Las Cruces, New Mexico, to probe the anarchy and carnage of Ciudad Juárez.

Bowden was drawn mothlike to the darkest flames, not just to feel the burn, but to tell the story of their kindling, the light they gave, and the ashes they left behind. His problem, as his friend explained, was the problem of the artist: "How do you get people to see what's there? It's nearly impossible."

But it becomes more possible in the dreamscape of *Desierto*. Bowden gives no chapter headings, no hints of structure, only a collage of stories that mysteriously compound upon each other into a hyperreality of longing, fatalism, and apocalypse, of *el problema*, the violent nihilism of the drug trade, of the surreal greed and egotism of Charles Keating, impresario of one of the greatest financial calamities of recent history, of the mystical yet practical Seri Indians, listening to deer talk one minute and carving junk for American tourists the next. Who is sane? Who is not? The boundaries blur. Cruelty and loss abide. Joy, fleeting, has to be tackled and held.

Follow the money: Americans import drugs, and in exchange they export anarchy, corruption, guns, and terror, not intentionally, at least not most of the time, but as a by-product of their appetites and careless wealth. That's one trail Bowden follows through the desert, an environment that sometimes "is just happenstance, a platform where looting takes place." Other times, the desert is a thing to be obliterated with acres of swimming pools, negated by twining fairways, and denied by an unlimited stream of BTUs chilling palaces clad in Italian marble for the Medicis of today. The present continually quotes the past. So will the days ahead, producing in Bowden's phrase "memories of the future." This is true also of *el problema*: there was always *un problema*. People have always died in the desert for no good reason. People always will.

The money trail is not the only one that Bowden follows; it's not even the main one. He writes, "I have a need for visiting the battlefields of love." The people of *Desierto* twitch with desire; they thirst and lust. Bowden watches them. He understands. He sees life through their eyes. "The whole world is sexual to us, down to the very last stone." Because of which, sometimes they kill, which means that many crime scenes conceal love stories and some of the most savage acts originate, far away, in moments of vulnerability and innocent naked hunger, in moments of tenderness.

It is the tenderness that keeps me turning Bowden's pages. Maybe I have grown inured to the unending brutality of the borderlands, which is meted out casually in government policies no less than in fits of individual rage. What gets to me is the tenderness Bowden finds among the iron-bar realities of *el desierto*. I read him with a pencil in hand, so I can mark the moments:

No one remembers the reasons for his murder. That was years and years ago and the shrine now looks naked in the desert and wants paint and the visit of a fistful of paper flowers.

An image such as that one—and there are many in *Desierto*—halts me in my tracks. I read it again, looking for its magic: *the visit of a fistful of paper flowers*. The tone is exact, the cadence complete, every word necessary. It had to be a visit—something temporary, which time will erase. It had to be a fistful, not a bunch or a handful, because of the slightly sweaty tension in the closed fist, the objection it embodies to letting go of the flowers, to accepting that death is death. A fist is also a weapon. It expresses defiance, if not to the will of God or to fate, then to the sunlight that still touches the face of the bastard who did this deed. And of course the flowers are paper, whether their bearers are rich or poor but especially if they are poor, because nothing else blooms in this desert of loss or retains its beauty under the punishing sun. Paper lasts longer, but not long. A dusty wind blows over the brokenhearted gift. I can see the red crepe flutter.

Bowden reminds me of one of the least appreciated giants of American letters, a writer with an appetite for telling analogous stories from a similarly personal point of view. Like Bowden, this writer worked as a reporter, but was more than a reporter. He styled himself a spy traveling undercover in unsafe territory, and he wrote long, edgy, booze-fueled riffs that brimmed with wild insight and sensuous detail. He disdained the conventions of literary structure and refused to be contained by the standards of so-called journalism because he felt compelled to tell a deeper, wilder, and yes more sexual story about the workings of the world and the fragile, faulted people in it. His masterpiece was not the lyrical novel for which he was awarded the Pulitzer Prize but the sprawling, inspired, rampant creation that dumbfounded critics when it first appeared. *Let Us Now Praise Famous Men* is the *Moby-Dick* of American nonfiction, both in its history of initial rejection and ultimate canonization and in its qualities of "omnivory" as to subject matter and sheer brilliance of expression. Of course I am speaking of James Agee, and I have no idea if Chuck Bowden ever read him, let alone liked him, but in the end they are cousins in style and appetite.

Their subject is the union of opposites, the angels and devils joined at the hip, the beauty married to the beastliness of life. Agee said *Famous Men* was "an independent inquiry into certain normal predicaments of human divinity." Bowden might reject a word such as *divinity*, but not too fast. Like Agee, he saw the holiness of the quotidian, the hunger for transcendence and mercy, the pathos implicit in just carrying on:

There are similar fiestas everywhere in Mexico for different Virgins, for various saints. They exist because people hurt, because work is hard, because women are desirable, because miracles are necessary, because few can stay sober without sometimes being drunk.

Agee would have extolled such observations. He understood the effort and openness, the compassion and years of seasoning required to make them. He was a critic as well as a writer, and his film commentary is as penetrating as his reportage. He died too young to see *Chinatown*, but he would have loved it, especially the final gut-wrenching denouement, when Jack Nicholson interrogates Faye Dunaway about a girl she's been protecting. Nicholson is slapping Dunaway, trying to get the long-hidden truth out of her, and Dunaway, at the edge of incoherence, her head whipping left and right with each slap, is sobbing back at him, "She's my sister, she's my daughter, she's my sister...."

I see Bowden, under similar questioning, admitting another incestuous unity: "It's the hunger, it's the horror, it's the hunger, it's the horror."

In *Desierto* Bowden ultimately confesses the paradox at the source of his fascination, the spark that ignites his fire, the two siblings that make a whole, each also parent to the other. And Agee would understand him, would make the same profound admission: "I am watching ruin, and yet savoring life. I am complete."

This essay is adapted from the foreword to a reissue of Charles Bowden's Desierto: Memories of the Future *(Austin: University of Texas Press, 2018).*

WILLIAM DEBUYS is the author of nine books, which range from memoir and biography to environmental history and studies of place. *River of Traps* was one of three finalists for the Pulitzer Prize in General Nonfiction in 1991.

Wild Gods of Mexico

DON HENRY FORD JR.

Winter 2003
Marfa, Texas.

Finally, we meet. A bookstore. I don't know what he looks like.
I'm a bit nervous.

Like excavating demons, this going back to Mexico shit. I was
fairly well running for my life when I last left the goddamned place.
I see a man enter. A Mexican man accompanying him. The
white guy's hair is long, brown with a tint of gray but not so much.
Button-up 501 Levi's jeans, well worn. Sandals, no socks. He walks
on the balls of his feet, like an excited kid off to have some fun.

He sees me. Our eyes engage. Blue eyes, like Jeff Aylesworth's.
Royal blue. Nobility? He approaches a bit warily and extends a
hand. Long wingspan.

"Chuck Bowden. This is Julián Cardona."

The voice is deep and low, forceful but measured, the wording
precise, delivered in cadence, the accent not unlike that of John
Wayne.

Julián is slender, near six feet tall, but seems small alongside
Chuck. They are obviously comfortable in each other's presence.
His eyes are dark, the face angular, a bit hard.

Stoic.

There's a prominent dent in Julián's forehead, like a chunk of
bone is missing underneath. I wonder if it was a bullet. Car wreck?
Pick ax? Lucky he ain't dead.

Ciudad Acuña, Mexico.

I watch Oscar Cabello watching me. Watching them. He misses nothing. Everybody here has the gift, the intangible that saves lives when the shit goes down. To hear not only what is said, but also what's not said, what doesn't fit.

A pride of lions, if there ever was one.

The beans and the tortillas are superb, as advertised, made by the deft hands of Oscar's mother. Legendary in their simplicity.

Chuck eats ravenously. With gusto, almost snarling like a hungry dog.

The Mexican women can't help but smile.

The trip is on.

I drive. My wife, Leah's, blue half-ton Chevy pickup.

Chuck rides shotgun, Julián in the back seat. Watching me. I watch back, from the rear view. Habit.

Chuck is sick. Eating vitamin C like Tic Tacs.

The talk is of politicians and *narcos* and corruption. I realize I am in the company of serious intellectuals. Nothing of their appearance belies what I hear coming from their mouths. Both have encyclopedic memories. They joust at times. Julián is more than a bodyguard. He's Chuck's sounding board on any and everything Mexican.

I think they must have balls the size of King Kong, coming here with me.

The road from Músquiz to Piedritas is paved much farther than when I last saw it, but the right of ways are grown up with Johnson grass. There is virtually no traffic. Curves appear without warning.

I spot a dead animal surrounded by buzzards and steer to the left. They fly up and then, boom!

Glass and guts and blood and meat and feathers explode into the cab through the passenger-side window, spraying Julián. Chuck is knocked almost into the floorboard alongside me.

"Holy fucking shit. Goddamned buzzard flew right through the fucking window," I declare.

We sit for a while and gather our wits.

Later we begin the ascent over La Cuesta and I feel the tingle. Like silent black wings, swooping by. Some things don't change.

I ask, "Do you believe in God?"

Both Chuck and Julián claim some version of agnosticism.

"Well, how about spirits?" I ask.

You damn well will before we get out of here. If we get out of here, I think to myself.

We're close to the cut-off to Piedritas. There's a hump in the middle of the gravel road, and my tires don't provide quite enough clearance. In places I have to drive on the hump to keep from scraping.

I look up.

A soldier stands in the road.

I spot a camouflaged shooting tower on the left. Another on the right. Both with high ground. Rifle barrels protrude. We drive into a kill zone.

I roll down the window.

The face is dark brown, the accent southern Mexican. Mayan.

A woman soldier with a really nasty looking long automatic rifle watches from the other side. She, too, is dark. Not from around here.

It's easier to shoot people you don't know.

The road is dirt and rocks now, with horrible washouts, large rocks, and other hazards. We pass near an old *jacal*. Goats' skins hang from a fence. A woman works on a skin from her porch, watching us pass. Then we see a man. He leans on a long staff. Dogs pad behind a group of goats as he watches. The scene looks like something two thousand years old.

The man doesn't look a day over a thousand.

Beto, Reynol, and one more sit near the door of the thick-walled adobe. Kerosene lanterns light the room. It's magical inside. The spirit. Almost holy.

Chuck and Julián ask questions, *Los Viejos del ejido* oblige, hats clasped in calloused hands. They trust me, so they trust Chuck.

I think *GQ* has sent Chuck to disprove my existence, but he has done his homework. He read my books. Nobody reads my books, but Chuck Bowden did. Chuck has to know. He risks life and limb to know.

I am perplexed. What kind of man is this?

He pulls a small notebook from his pocket. He always wears the same shirts, bought at Cabela's, I am told. Plenty of pockets, long sleeves. He has made coffee on some portable contraption that spits out espresso. He insists on blackness, no sugar, thank you very much.

"Only notebook you use is the one you have on you."

As he asks questions, he writes the article *GQ* will decline in that little notebook. Somewhat furiously, I think.

That rejected article will someday become the introduction to my book.

The night sky illuminates the light-colored soil. Stars stretch to the infinite.

We sit near ancient rocks for which the ejido is named, silent.

I hear snores from the other room. Chuck passed out immediately, comfortable in these meager surroundings. But he's up early and out again before daylight, soaking up cool desert air. Not only is he comfortable with the place; the place seems comfortable with him.

Beto is on the lead, like a mountain goat, up the trail. Always up.

We're headed to the *tinaja*. I'm heavy, but it's muscle, the result of many hours of training with weights. Habit picked up in prison. But I'm in shape, and well equipped for the brutality of the country—this is my backyard.

Chuck and Julián labor below, steadily climbing but steadily losing ground to Beto.

We stop and wait.

We make it to the tinaja.

I look at Beto. He looks at me.

A chill descends.

There was a day when both of us fucking died here in some alternate reality. I can almost smell the gunpowder.

We climb to my cave.

The *candelilla* mattress looks like I'd slept in it the day before.

Chuck makes it to the tinaja. Huffing and puffing. Coughing, slinging snot from red nostrils. Once he gets his wind he fires up a Lucky Strike. He's bleeding from a toe. Removing thorns. Bareheaded, it's cold, but he's sweating with fever. Sick as a damn dog.

Julián has brushed against a nasty *nopal* with tiny spines that grow in clusters. He's Mexican but he's a city Mexican. Shit'll fuck you up.

It's way too late to warn him.

We climb the path, arrive at the spot where I was interrogated and left blindfolded for four hours. My guard had instructions to shoot me if he heard a shot.

Chuck watches, listens, feels, as I describe the event.

The cavern where the twenty tons of Colombian marijuana was stored—courtesy of the CIA, the DEA, a major Colombian cartel, and a pilot by the name of Michael Palmer, who operated seamlessly among all involved—remains unchanged, but the homemade ladder we used to descend is gone.

Beto offers the ropes he has carried.

I convince them this is something we do not need to do. It doesn't take a whole lot of convincing.

I look for the old junk pile. Chuck wants to see where the crazy kid bangs the iron and sings and screams prayers in the most haunting of ways.

The cemetery remains: vultures adorn stacked rocks, sunning wings in morning sun. But Beto tells us the iron pile became valuable, so someone saw fit to turn the kid's altar into money and hauled it away.

Chuck seems disappointed.

We pull up to the checkpoint. A customs agent peers into the cab. Asks where we have been. And waves us through.

What the hell? No search? And I've spent years in prison.

Chuck gets out his cell phone and calls someone to let them know he is alive.

And then proceeds to try to convince the rest of the world that I am real.

Chuck taught me that all good writing endangers the writer. Otherwise, it ain't worth shit.

I still think there's a God.

But I want to go where Chuck went when I die.

DON HENRY FORD JR.'s memoir, *Contrabando: Confessions of a Drug-Smuggling Cowboy*, chronicling his days as a smuggler, carries an introduction by Charles Bowden.

Crossing the Line

JAMES GALVIN

I like a look of Agony,
Because I know it's true—

EMILY DICKINSON

The poet-philosopher Allen Grossman once remarked, "Life is not a sign, and hence it has no meaning." But there are signs of life all around us—in nature, in art, in all living things that strive for survival, and most dramatically, in suffering and in death. Death is the ultimate sign of life. When I read Charles Bowden's books I am always reminded of the great Mexican novella *Pedro Páramo*, by Juan Rulfo. In Rulfo's book the protagonist wrests his hand from the grip of his dead mother and sets out in search of his father, whom he has never met. All of the characters the protagonist meets exist in a kind of limbo, which suggests that they are all really dead. They are the walking, waking dead. One begins to wonder if the protagonist is dead, but then he dies. When he is buried, he keeps talking. In *Red Line*, Charles Bowden sets out on a similar quest. He wants to understand the life of a dead man he has never met, an assassin in the drug world, who has killed more people than anyone can know, whose weapon of choice is a screwdriver. Bowden feels an affinity with the killer, Nacho, and he wants to understand the forces that turned an innocent into a monster.

At the time of writing, Bowden's own life is a desolate ruin. He has an infant son by a woman he no longer loves. He drinks a lot. He has affairs with women whose names we never know. He drifts in a spiritual desert, a dreamworld, an eternal present. He is a nonfiction version of Rulfo's Juan Preciado, searching the land of the dead for an image of himself. He writes in *Red Line*, "I want out now. Fear is not the right word. The feeling is more compelling than fear. I tell Art we will learn no more, so let's go. He argues. We go to a cheap café near the fence. He thinks we will find more. I know he is right. Three chollos from Buenos Aires sit at a nearby table, their arms dancing with tattoos, the faces a mask. One wears thick black leather bands around his wrists, gleaming studs rising from the dark hide. I think: it is not the fists that are warning me, it is not the guns dangling from the cops' hands, it is not the whiff of muscle coming off the ring of the word 'comandante.' It is the mirror. I am looking into some kind of mirror and if I stay right now I will see something I do not want to see."

Bowden makes no effort to present himself as virtuous, or even likeable. He is objective. He witnesses. Woven into the search for the details of Nacho's life, and Bowden's own search for purpose, are other analogous journeys: following the trail of the miners who crossed the desert in search of gold; tracing the illegal immigrants who risk dying in the desert for a better life; seeking out a mystic archaeologist whose knowledge encompasses the lore of the long-disappeared indigenous tribes who found safety and sustenance where others find death.

To be a proper witness, you have to tell the truth, so far as that is possible. Charles Bowden has a fierce allegiance to truth telling, but unlike a biblical witness, he doesn't know what the truth is. Let me put it this way: in the unlikely event that you find yourself with St. Peter at the gates of heaven, don't bring a lawyer; if, on the other hand, you are accused of a crime and find yourself in a court of law, don't put Ezekiel on the stand. Most of us are changed by what we witness. Bowden is a third kind of witness. He sees reality, and sees that there is no knowledge in it, no discernable purpose. If there is a higher power, its name is hunger. Hunger starts as a physical need, in plants and animals and people. It is common to predators and prey. In people it passes from a literal want to an abstract one, without noticeable or apprehensible shift. The miners who risked death to cross the desert in 1849 had transgressed from hunger to greed. The developers Charles Bowden interviews don't need to destroy the ecological balance of the desert, but they are hungry, not in body, but in soul. As for people driven to flee dire poverty in their homeland, some risk the desert crossing for a life in *El Norte*, where many will serve life sentences as perpetual fugitives and working poor. They will do work that American citizens prefer not to do, and do it for less than the legal minimum wage. Many others will enter "The Life," the world of drugs and death. That original, physical hunger stealthily migrates from body to soul, becoming avarice, addiction, lust, bloodlust, and death. Because of the nature of extended families in Latino culture, no one is untouched by "The Life." As for the journalists who witness the unimaginable torture and death in cities like Nogales and Juárez, who witness the bodies mutilated, killed, and dumped in the desert (as Nacho's was), they too can become addicts. At a certain point, war correspondents can cease to be changed by what they witness. They can live in a limbo of PTSD, and, if they are not themselves murdered, their insatiable hunger for truth can become their heroin. Bowden's own addiction to a certain kind of journalism culminates in *Down by the River*, published thirteen years after *Red Line*.

The desert itself is the apotheosis of hunger, an ecosystem where the life-giving element is the anomaly. Where sun is the enemy. To outsiders it looks near death, but is not so much dead as deadly, and indomitably alive, where living things are, by turns, very slow or very fast, where leaves are thorns, and, even without the mummified corpses, the forces that rule are fanged and clawed. The desert is the perfect analogy for the fugitive soul of Charles Bowden. The desert refuses sentimentality, and possibly even sentiment. The only sin is forgetting.

Bowden was not a nature lover, he was a lover of the desert, a lover of its maws and jaws and hellish heat. Deep ecology was not deep enough for him, redolent as it is of human privilege and human hunger for self-preservation. Environmentalists looked to him for guidance, but he didn't like the nature priests, the self-congratulation. He had no guidance to give them. He fled. He fled into the desert to escape his inner desolation, the damage witnessing, by the end, had done to him. And what, after all, is the distinction between seeking and running away?

"I never walk the line; I cross it," Charles Bowden once wrote. So why is this book called *Red Line*? Two ideas of what a line is, diametrically opposed. One is a limit, the other an invitation. As a writer and as a witness, Bowden understands the importance of living comfortably in ambiguity, paradox, contradiction. He proved his irreverence for the idea of borders, especially the one between the United States and Mexico. He crossed it every chance he got. Like Bowden, the desert doesn't believe it has a border. It's just the desert. And it doesn't have a border between the natural world and the man-made world. Human destruction is part of the desert, as are the corpses of the people who tried and failed to cross it.

There are also those bizarre little desert island towns of failed paradise, inhabited by ghosts from the past still waiting for a future that will never come. And the old Indian village sites, long abandoned, yet still haunted. These are all exterior to the inner life of Charles Bowden. The desert is his refuge from his own inescapable desolation. The border is imaginary and external. The red line is personal, interior, the limit beyond which an internal combustion engine self-destructs. Bowden writes of the thrill of pushing an engine to its limit. But by the end of this lyric essay, all we have is a disarray of blown-out parts, unrecognizable as the complex-centric pieces of a machine designed either for questing or for fleeing, an engine pushed past the red line for no discernable reason beyond the hunger to escape. Juan Rulfo writes, in *Pedro Páramo*, "When I sat down to die, [my soul] told me to get up again and keep on living, as if it still hoped for some miracle that would clean away my sins. But I wouldn't. 'This is the end,' I told it. 'I can't go any farther.' I opened my mouth so it could leave, and it left. I felt something fall into my hands. It was the little thread of blood that had tied it to my heart."

The prose style of *Red Line* is signature. Attention to detail costs more and is worth more than any attending emotion. Every present moment is haunted by all moments past, and by implication therefore, all future moments. The diction, especially the verbs, tend toward violence. The syntax at times winds elegantly serpentine, willfully run-on. At other times, it is as insistently paratactic as an AK-47. The paragraphs at times collide suicidally, and at other times blend narrative threads with no sign of borders. The book tells us as much by how it is written, as it tells us by what it is written about. The only sin is forgetting.

This essay is adapted from the foreword to a reissue of Charles Bowden's Red Line *(Austin: University of Texas Press, 2018).*

JAMES GALVIN is the author of eight books of poems, the critically acclaimed book of prose *The Meadow*, and the novel *Fencing the Sky*.

The Fountain Theatre

FRANCISCO CANTÚ

In October of 2011, I drove to the old town center of Mesilla, New Mexico, to watch a screening of *El Sicario, Room 164*, a documentary about a cartel hitman who tortured and killed hundreds of victims in Mexico. I arrived late and was unceremoniously turned away at the box office. As I stood in disappointment outside the tiny theater, a man lurched through the door and into the daylight, disheveled and dressed in faded jeans, boots, and a vest. It was Charles Bowden, the writer and coproducer of the sold-out film. I approached him timidly and introduced myself, telling him I was a Border Patrol agent who had come from El Paso to see his movie. Bowden looked at me, less surprised than I expected, and patted me on the back. He ushered me inside the adobe building, ignoring the ticket collector who grumbled about the lack of seats, and left me in the care of an elderly usher. She walked with me to the concession stand, where they refused to take my money, and then led me to an empty seat in the back.

I had become familiar with the work of Charles Bowden only a few years earlier, shortly after beginning work for the United States Border Patrol. At the time I was living in a remote corner of southwestern Arizona, trying to come to terms with day-to-day existence in a desert devoid of pity. I began with *Blue Desert*, a collection of essays that includes an account of a forty-mile border crossing Bowden made in the summer of 1983 through the same desert terrain I was then patrolling. "They play a game here but nobody watches from a box seat," he wrote. As someone new to the nature of this "game" and its deadly consequences, I valued Bowden's compulsion to go out and walk along migrant trails, to see and understand things as they were, not as he wished they might be.

In the mid-1990s, on a visit to Ciudad Juárez, Charles Bowden came across a photograph in the back pages of a local newspaper that would change the course of his writing career. The image was of Adriana Avila Gress, a maquiladora factory worker kidnapped, raped, and killed in the still-early years of the Juárez femicide. Haunted, Bowden kept a copy of the picture for years in a folder on his desk. The murders of women in Juárez continued for over a decade, only to be eclipsed by the unprecedented storm of drug war killings that began in 2008. Obsessed with understanding the city's dire social and political intricacies, Bowden eventually moved from Tucson to Las Cruces, New Mexico, barely an hour's drive from Juárez. In his subsequent work, one could sense the darkening of his worldview and the diminished presence of nature. "In Juárez you cannot sustain hope," Bowden wrote. "We are talking about an entire city woven out of violence."

As I read through this bleak turn in Bowden's work, I began to regard his vision with great trepidation. During those years I was careening wildly through the hard realities of the Arizona desert, chasing border crossers and drug runners, offering meager comfort to migrant children and pregnant women, and retrieving from the wilderness dead bodies and stammering men who had forgotten their names in the heat. Grim scenes lingered in my mind and teetered into nightmares. In "Torch Song," an essay on the years he spent reporting on violent sex crimes, Bowden wrote, "I do not want to leave my work at the office. I do not want to leave my work at all. I have entered a world that is black, sordid, vicious. And actual. And I do not care what price I must pay to be in this world." But I was not like Bowden; I feared the price I might pay to remain in such a place.

In his later years, in appearances on news programs and in documentaries, Bowden would sometimes seem on the verge of coming unhinged, as though exasperated at describing, in layman's terms, the scale of destruction swirling across Mexico and the borderlands. As Bowden saw it, the Mexican government, through its deployment of police and military forces and their complicit dealings with drug cartels, was engaged in the wholesale slaughter of ordinary Mexican citizens—a kind of "social cleansing" perpetrated with the financial support of the United States.

Reading Bowden as a young man, I struggled to comprehend how Mexico's shifting colossus of violence could possibly be something designed and orchestrated with intention. Perhaps I was naive, perhaps I was fearful of the implications, or perhaps I was too deeply gripped by the blindness that I had to subscribe to in order to go on working for a government institution that played its own deadly part in the drama. Whatever it was, I felt unable to follow Bowden as his work turned more fully into the darkness; I could not hazard myself to believe something so sinister.

In his book *Murder City*, Bowden declared, "You cannot know of the slaughter running along the border and remain the same person." In 2011, I left the Sonoran Desert of southern Arizona and drove across the Chihuahuan grasslands to work in the city of El Paso. On a nightly basis I beheld the shimmering lights of Ciudad Juárez with staggering dread and compulsion. During the time I lived and worked in El Paso, I never once went to Juárez; I never crossed over to the other side. While Bowden immersed himself in Juárez to bring back dispatches from the abyss, I could only hover at its edge. For me, for most of us, a glimpse of the void is enough, is already too much.

Inside the crumbling one-room theater in Mesilla, New Mexico, the credits rolled and the house lights came on. As the crowds dissipated, I observed Bowden standing in the front row with

Molly Molloy, his partner and production manager for the film. I approached them both and thanked Bowden for getting me into the movie. He seemed to tower above me, but spoke with calmness and measured warmth. He asked how I liked the Patrol and wanted to know where I had been stationed. When I mentioned the western deserts of Arizona, a smile spread across his face. Ah, he said playfully, that's where desert rats go to get a higher education. He went on to describe how the time he had spent at Organ Pipe Cactus National Monument was akin to "bachelor's studies" in desert obsession, which led to "graduate work" in the Cabeza Prieta Wildlife Refuge, and finally, a long and tortured "doctorate" won among the lava flows and dune fields of the Pinacate Biosphere Reserve across the border in Sonora.

Bowden and I stood for a while longer talking about the wild places of the borderlands, about Ed Abbey and the Pinacate archaeologist Julian Hayden and the long lineage of men and women who, like them, found solace in dry places. We didn't speak of our dark work on the border, of the dead migrants in the Arizona desert, or of the cartel killings in Juárez. We talked about landscapes, about plants and vanishing animals, and about walks in the desert far from trails.

This essay was adapted from Francisco Cantú's "Dark Work on the Border," Guernica, *October 22, 2014, guernicamag.com/francisco-cantu-dark-work-on-the -border.*

FRANCISCO CANTÚ is a writer, translator, and the author of *The Line Becomes a River*, a memoir of his time working as a Border Patrol agent in Arizona, New Mexico, and Texas. He is the recipient of a Pushcart Prize and a 2017 Whiting Award. His essays and translations have been featured in *Best American Essays, Harper's, n+1, Guernica, Orion,* and on *This American Life.*

Pure Bowden

WILLIAM LANGEWIESCHE

Charles Bowden was a tall, imposing man and a westerner to his core. He started as a gumshoe reporter for the *Tucson Citizen*, a daily newspaper in Tucson, Arizona. This was in the early 1970s, when the counterculture was still alive, and Edward Abbey was in town, about to publish *The Monkey Wrench Gang*. Bowden was in his midtwenties at the time. He had dropped out of a PhD program at the University of Wisconsin, had traveled for a while, and had dabbled in various political protests—anti–Vietnam War, anti–Jim Crow laws—before landing the job. He was assigned to the city desk, and though he gravitated to Abbey's anarchistic circle, he wrote about mundane matters in ordinary ways, at least for a while. He was married to his second wife at the time and trying to sustain a modest middle-class life, so he could not afford to write otherwise. Years later, in 1998, long after Bowden had liberated himself from such constraints, Lewis Lapham, the editor of *Harper's*, published Bowden's memoir of that pivotal period in his story. The essay was entitled "Torch Song: At the Peripheries of Violence and Desire." In it Bowden wrote,

> I had no background in the business and I'd lied to get the job. I was the fluff writer, the guy brought on to spin something out of nothing for the soft features and the easy pages about how people fucked up their marriages or made a quiche or found the strength to go on with their lives because of God, diet, or a new self-help book. Sometimes they wrote the book, sometimes they just believed the book. I interviewed Santa Claus, and he told me

of the pain and awkwardness of having held a child on his fat lap in Florida as ants crawled up his legs and bit him.

Then one afternoon when the newsroom was mostly empty, an editor at the city desk spotted Bowden and, for lack of a better choice, sent him out to cover a murder. It had occurred in a sleazy motel featuring waterbeds, mirror-tiled ceilings, and pornographic movies. A young stripper from out of town had been staying there with her two-year-old son and some man she had recently acquired; she had gone off to work at a club, and the man had killed the boy by bashing his head against a cinderblock wall. The stain remained when Bowden got there. He returned to the newsroom and wrote an impressionistic piece riffing off a couple of frozen Budweisers that he had found in the room. Then, because he owned the story, he was sent to cover the funeral in a mortuary where, of course, the mother was in attendance. From where he sat he could not see her face, so he studied her profile.

> She has fine hair, a kind of faint red. I once knew a woman with hair like that, and as I stare I can smell this other woman and feel my hands tracing a path through the slender strands. I can smell the soap, the scent of the other woman; the small smile and fine bones and clean, even teeth. In my memory the coffin is open, the boy's small face very pale and blank, and he is surrounded by donated teddy bears that come from a town that told itself these things are not supposed to happen, and if such things do happen they're not supposed to happen in our town.

Again, this was Bowden writing for *Harper's*, long after throwing off constraints. He guessed the police might take the woman out the back door to keep her away from cameras and the press, so he positioned himself there.

Sure enough, suddenly the metal door opens and two cops burst through with the lap dancer handcuffed and sagging between their grip. The light is brilliant at 1:15 pm and merciless as it glares off the woman. Her face is small, with tiny bones, and her age is no longer possible to peg—somewhere between nineteen and one thousand.... A moan comes off her, a deep moan, and I sense she is unaware of the sound she is making, just as she is unaware of what has happened to her. The only thing she knows is what I know. There is a toddler in a box with teddy bears, and the box sits in a room full of strangers from this town where she has bagged a job dancing for other strangers.

Bowden wrote it up. He became the newspaper's crime reporter and stayed on that beat for three years, too long for anyone who expects to emerge unscathed. During that time he quit the job twice only to return. He started taking hundred-mile hikes through the desert mountains to work off the poison, a habit he maintained for the rest of his life. In *Harper's* he wrote, "I would write up these flights from myself, and people began to talk about me as a nature writer. The rest of my time was spent with another nature, the one we call, by common consent, deviate or marginal or unnatural." Many of the crimes he covered involved sex. He gradually came to see blurriness in the distinction between, if not victims and aggressors, at least criminals and the rest of humankind. He left his second wife. He wrote, "The marriage ends because I do not want to live with her anymore, because she is a good and proper person and this now feels like a cage. I do not want to leave my work at the office. I do not want to leave my work at all. I have entered a world that is black, sordid, vicious. And actual. I do not care what price I must pay to be in this world." Or so he thought at the time. The crimes he couldn't handle or get beyond were those involving children. One of them had led him to the crime beat, others had followed, and a final one—the abduction, rape, and murder of an eight-year-old girl—had left him drinking whiskey and silently crying late one night in his backyard. Looking back, he listed five truths for a crime reporter.

1. No one can handle the children.
2. Get out after two years.
3. Always walk a woman to her car, regardless of the hour of the day or night.
4. Don't talk about it; no one wants to hear these things.
5. No one can handle the children.

He wrote, "Theories don't help, therapies don't help, knowing doesn't help. The experts say they have therapies that are cutting recidivism, and maybe they do, but I doubt it. I live with what I am and what I saw and what I felt—a residue that will linger to the end of my days in the cells of my body." One key to understanding his work is precisely that.

Bowden didn't quit just the newspaper business; he ruthlessly ditched regular paychecks, withholding taxes, dinners at six, Sunday brunches, and any pretense of normal life. He was brave, maybe a bit nihilistic, and certainly reckless. He condemned himself to the uncertain and lonely existence of an independent writer and to a vow that he seems to have taken: to express himself with utter frankness, holding nothing back, even in the cases when (number 4) no one wants to hear these things. His work is often perceived as dark. To make matters worse, it evolved into books and essays primarily about northern Mexico and the border with the United States—subjects that are often distasteful and notoriously difficult to sell to New York publishers, their advertisers, and the public.

Bowden is now recognized as the real thing and one of the best writers of our time, at least among a circle of like-minded people. There is no evidence that this would have made him proud. It is

hard to make a living as a goddamned writer's writer. All his life
he barely scraped by. But he had made his choices, and he stood
by them. He was a lover of many women, sometimes several at
a time. He was a drinker and smoker. He was a gunman. He was
contrarian, a libertarian, and by many accounts a difficult man. He
disdained the bourgeois sensibilities of mainstream environmentalism. He disliked nature writing for its lack of women, sex, and
booze. He hated the US-Mexico border and the uniformed gate-
keepers there. Unlike Edward Abbey, he did not believe in protecting pristine spaces from the ravages of the poor. He believed
in racial mixing. He believed in graffiti. He believed in social justice. He was a man's man. And yes, absolutely, he was a writer. He
wrote more than twenty books, and though some became known,
they did not sell well. He was a writer because he felt no need to
apologize for any of this.

Which brings us to *Blood Orchid*, first published in 1995, when
Bowden was fifty years old. It describes itself as an unnatural history of America, which explains nothing, except maybe to hint
that it is not another sexless nature book. Far from it. The book is
probably Bowden's purest work. I mean that in the sense of Pure
Bowden, as in Bowden Unfettered. It is a lament, an objection, a
travelogue, a meditation, an exhortation, a call for change, a call
to arms. An unnatural history? More like an iconoclastic one. Here,
for instance, he weighs in on the drug war:

> It is obligatory to deplore the drug business. I will not do this.
> Once it was simply a way for people with no future to find a fu-
> ture by smuggling and selling drugs.... Then ... this drug business
> became the premise for war. People pissed into cups as part of
> their employment application, were taught to wipe their asses
> with the Bill of Rights, had their homes and haunts searched, and
> forfeited what property they had when the suspicion of drugs
> crossed their lives.... Hardly anyone objects.

But I do. I object to gun control, liquor laws, urine tests, fingerprints, computer-filed credit records, dog licenses, driver's licenses (let the highway be the judge), mandatory use of seat belts, mandatory installation of air bags, the DEA, FBI, CIA, NIA, INS, BIA, IRS, FAA, the National Park Service, Bureau of Land Management, Department of Defense, curfews, blue laws, the omnibus crime bill, cooling off periods (some like it hot), the draft, riot statutes, transactional immunity, nonprofit organizations (if the government approves of their actions, it is a moral certainty I will not), RICO statutes, Department of Justice strike forces, obscenity laws, fagophobia codes, burial codes, tax exemption for churches, narcs, taxes, and borders as defined by the authorities.

The list is typical of the book's abandon. In *Blood Orchid* as in his life, Bowden cast caution aside and challenged the assumptions that generally go unquestioned. He was serious about it, too. Readers might question his reasoning, but he obviously meant every word he wrote. Not that he lacked humor. He mentions an unhappy response to his work that he received from the editors of a German magazine who had sent him to Argentina to write about adventuring in the mountains.

I have a fax in my pocket—they love to rocket faxes from their dark bunkers where they recline in lederhosen while slowly turning *Untermenschen* on a spit—and it is to the point. The *Volk* are nothing if not exact.

Where are the mule rides? Where are the men and their camaraderie? Where is the heroic toil against the great mountains? I know, you will say these are very German questions. Well, our readers are Germans and you should remember that.

But Bowden was not an adventure writer. And with *Blood Orchid*, it is clear that as he wrote, he did not give a damn whether readers accompanied him for the ride. The book has little obvious structure, and though it has plenty of content, at any moment in the narrative the specific subject matter is often obscure. The book requires a particular way of reading, a self-abandonment to Bowden's manner of expression, and a willingness to let his words wash through the mind. Readers who learn how to approach the experience will ultimately be glad that they did.

This essay was originally published as the foreword to a reissue of Charles Bowden's Blood Orchid: An Unnatural History of America *(Austin: University of Texas Press, 2018).*

WILLIAM LANGEWIESCHE has been a professional airplane pilot, globe-trotting correspondent for *Vanity Fair* and the *Atlantic Monthly*, and author of acclaimed books *Outlaw Sea*, *Aloft*, and *Finding the Devil*.

Street Reporter on *La Línea*

PHILIP CAPUTO

I met Chuck Bowden roughly twelve years ago, at Jim Harrison's house on Sonoita Creek, near the close-to-the-border town of Patagonia, Arizona. They were out on Jim's patio, looking at and talking about birds. Songbirds that were migrating northward from Mexico into the United States and beyond. Dozens of them, representing many species from vermillion flycatchers to yellow warblers, were flitting in the cottonwoods and underbrush bordering the slender creek.

Chuck was as ardent a lover of the southwestern deserts as Ed Abbey, though he loathed being thought of as an environmentalist, characterizing environmentalism as a pursuit of middle-class whites who drive Volvos. That said, his bird-watching seemed out of character to me. I knew him through articles he had written and his 2002 book, *Down by the River*, as unflinching an account as I'd ever read about the deceit, treachery, and corruption that afflicts *la línea*, the line, the frontier between the United States and Mexico, and between public lies and private truths. To quote from his *New York Times* obituary, *Down by the River* was—is—"a blend of biography, history, narrative journalism and essayistic expression that spins outward from a single, seemingly unremarkable crime along the Rio Grande: the murder of a man who had no apparent involvement in the border conflict but turns out to have been the brother of an official at the Drug Enforcement Agency."

In appearance, Chuck lived up to the image I'd formed from reading his work: he was an intimidating presence, topping out at around six feet four, with a lanky build, a voice that sounded like a good imitation of Zeus pronouncing your fate, and icy blue eyes whose stare seemed capable of penetrating solid lead. What they did penetrate, to a degree few journalists can match, were the fictions created by governments, by official spin-meisters, by cops and crooks and crooked cops, by corporate spokesmen, public relations shills, and by ordinary people—the crap we all feed to the world and to ourselves. This is to say that he possessed the device Hemingway termed an essential in the writer's toolkit—a built-in, shockproof bullshit detector.

He and I had one affinity—both born in Chicago, home of the then-biggest stockyards in America, a city that knew bullshit when it smelled it. I remember thinking, as he, Harrison, and I sat down to talk, "Don't try to flatter this guy, don't try to present yourself as anything more, or less, than you are, don't tell him what you think he may want to hear." Not in those words, of course, but that was the gist. Harrison had invited me over because he thought Chuck could be of help to me. I was working on a novel set on the border, and I had an assignment from *Virginia Quarterly Review* to write a piece about border problems—drug smuggling, illegal immigration.

I thought I knew a few things about those issues (I'd been living in Patagonia part of the year for several years and had traveled throughout Mexico), but as Chuck delivered a brief seminar in that oracular voice of his, I learned that there is a wide gulf between thinking you know something and actually knowing it. It's been too long for me to remember specifics from our conversation. I came away aware that the "problem" was far more complicated than I'd imagined, and, what's more, with an impression that maybe I ought not to look at it as a problem, which implies that there is a solution somewhere. I may well be wrong about this, but I don't think Chuck believed there was.

The border, to him, was a condition to be endured, not a problem to be solved. He was a fine journalist with a novelist's sense of the tragic. We live in a fallen world, filled with sorrows and losses that must be suffered—even as, paradoxically, they must be resisted. It was this outlook that made his books and articles unique, suffused with tones of sadness, bitterness, and menace, but never with a false or compromising note in them.

Later on, he gave me a hand reporting on the Mexican drug wars for the *Atlantic*, generously sharing his sources in Mexico. He also put me in contact with his longtime companion, Molly Molloy, a researcher at New Mexico State University and a simultaneous translator so skilled she could easily have worked at the UN. That assignment took me into Juárez, then the deadliest city on earth (more killings per year than Baghdad), and one that he described brilliantly in his 2011 book, *Murder City*.

There was another way in which he exhibited the novelist's sensibility—his concern with moral evil. He was, I think, fascinated with it—the heart of darkness, the abyss. And some of us who knew him were concerned about him. You can look into the abyss for just so long before it looks into you—a spiritual danger, if you will. But the physical dangers were greater. Chuck was casting his gimlet eye into the world of *sicarios*, professional killers who settle accounts for the *narcotraficantes*. These killers make La Cosa Nostra's hitmen look like a sewing circle, and we worried that Chuck was going to get himself killed. He didn't, and produced, with Molly Molloy, *El Sicario: The Autobiography of a Mexican Assassin*, a chilling, firsthand description of a contract killer's life and work. An undercover Border Patrol agent whom Bowden and I both knew told me it was the scariest book he'd ever read.

The irony that Chuck died while taking a nap is almost too much to accept as true.

To be candid, there were moments when I thought his skepticism tipped over into cynicism, when his outrage at injustice curdled into a kind of angry hopelessness. But those lapses were few and were balanced by his compassion for the poor and the oppressed, for everyone who had been dealt a bad hand by the universal cardsharp. He was a complicated man, with sides to his personality and temperament that I'm sure I never saw. In the end, he reminded me of the best street reporters I'd worked with when I was newspapering in Chicago—hard, tough, intolerant of the public relations goo that passes for wisdom in our age, but a man with a heart, dedicated to speaking truth to power.

Born in Chicago in 1941, PHILIP CAPUTO has published sixteen books of nonfiction and fiction, including his best-selling memoir of Vietnam, *A Rumor of War*. He has written numerous articles for *Esquire*, *National Geographic*, the *New York Times*, the *Washington Post*, the *Atlantic*, and *Virginia Quarterly Review*. Caputo is cowinner of the Pulitzer Prize and winner of the George Polk Citation.

No One Gets Out Alive

RICHARD GRANT

When I heard that he'd died—peacefully in his sleep aged sixty-nine, and not gunned down by cartel assassins, as so many had predicted—I bought six yellow peppers and a bottle of cheap hearty red wine. He disapproved of white wine, finding it pale and insipid. In his writing and his life, he was a champion of boldness, lushness, vibrancy. Why drink wine that looked like watery urine, he argued, when you could drink wine the color of rubies and blood?

Charles Bowden was the name on his books and magazine stories, but in person he was always Chuck. Tall, rangy, and rugged, he had blunt handsome features, blue eyes that seemed to devour his surroundings, hair that wanted to climb back down his collar into the 1960s. Some genius said he looked like Robert Mitchum crossed with Neil Young, and that can't be improved upon as a physical description.

He was always deeply tanned. He would lie out in the desert sun for hours, smoking unfiltered Lucky Strikes, and reading big scholarly books about his latest obsessions, which ranged from medieval trade routes to rattlesnakes, American jurisprudence to Italian food. It was a way of feeding his intellect, decompressing after writing, and drinking in heat and light through his skin. He had no fear of skin cancer, lung cancer, or other ways of dying. "What's the difference," he would growl. "No one gets out alive."

He went to bed early after copious amounts of wine, got up at three in the morning, and went straight to his keyboard with strong black coffee. He wrote for eight or nine hours on a normal day, fifteen or sixteen hours if the crunch was on, and he almost never took a day off or a vacation. By this method, he produced twenty-six books of utterly distinctive nonfiction, and hundreds of magazine articles. At his best, in *Desierto: Memories of the Future* (1991), or *Down by the River: Drugs, Money, Murder, and Family* (2002), he was searing, incandescent, incomparable, a hard-nosed reporter who wrote like a poet or a fire-breathing prophet, and seemed wired into the deepest currents of his time. At his worst, he was overblown, macho, teetering on self-parody—too many perfumed whores and fierce dark hungers in the midnight streets.

He was always willing to risk his life to get the story, and the deeper he got into the Mexican drug world, exposing cartel bosses and the role of the army, the more urgent and extreme that risk became. Bodyguards accompanied him on occasion. He started keeping guns within reach at all times. His contacts in the US Drug Enforcement Administration said there were three contracts out on his life. If Chuck Bowden ever wanted to commit suicide, people said, all he'd have to do was stand on a street corner in Ciudad Juárez and wait for half an hour.

Risk was there in his prose, too. He gambled with structure and tone. Writing about a brilliant, charismatic, amoral financier, he interspersed the story with observations on mountain lions, suggesting that both were predators following their instinctual desires. In 2007, in an essay for *Esquire* called "The Bone Garden of Desire," he constructed a mosaic of vignettes about food and death. When your friends are dying, he advised, go into the kitchen, cook well, savor the flavors on your tongue. So I lay the yellow peppers on the blue flames of the stove, and start chopping the onions, carrots, and other vegetables.

He grew up in Chicago, and it was still there in his accent, and his no-bullshit attitude, but he lived most of his life in Tucson, Arizona. When I pitched up there in the early 1990s, as a fledgling journalist and uprooted Englishman, we became friends. We shared an irreverent outlook toward rules and authority. We both liked drinking and books and the outdoors. In the early years of our friendship, there was a strong element of mentorship on his part. I seldom left his house without important books to read, sage advice, an idea for a story, a useful contact, and some insight that he'd tossed off ringing in my head like a gong. He taught me most of what I know about Mexico and the Southwest, ecology and the environment, US politics, history, crime, and journalism. But the deepest lesson I absorbed from him had nothing to do with words or ideas.

I had never met anyone whose senses were so hungry and alive. Even when interviewing a cartel enforcer about the unbelievable atrocities he had committed, Chuck's fingertips would be registering the texture of the tabletop that lay between them, because he was incapable of ignoring such a thing. He lived in a place where the thermometer stays above 100°F for months on end, yet he disapproved strongly of air-conditioning, because it cocooned people from the physical reality of where they lived. He wanted to melt into the heat and become one with it. He thought sex in the summertime was all the better for being sweaty and overheated, and he thundered against air-conditioning for ruining it.

Unless he was working, cooking, or sleeping, he was seldom inside his house. His real home was in the backyard, where the walls were painted in bright, Mexican-inspired colors. Hummingbirds dive-bombed each other at the feeders, the males flashing iridescent green, purple, and ruby at their throats. There was shade from a spreading mesquite tree, and the beds were planted with cactus and succulents. When the night-blooming cereus unfurled

Charles Bowden in his garden, 2002

their outrageous flowers in midsummer, Chuck would hold parties in their honor, and plunge his face into the spreading, heavily
scented white blooms with the purest ecstasy.

He relished intense heat, bitter cold, thunderstorms, and reek-
ing pitch-black bat caves. He craved sensory bombardment and
loved everything that amplified the feeling of being physically alive,
right here, right now, in the present moment. Television bored him.
It was a cold dead machine dispensing clichés and imitating life in
two dimensions. He never went to the movies, to gaze at a screen
with a herd of silent strangers in a climate-controlled room. He
loved wine, but he had no interest in identifying its characteristics,

or analyzing its nuances. If it was big and red, sluicing across his palate, and coursing through his bloodstream, he was delighted by it.

For me, a generation younger, and far more colonized by technology, media, and marketing, Chuck's sensory awareness offered a kind of refuge, a last-ditch hope of an honest connection to a real, living world.

The people with the sharpest senses of all are those still using them for their original purpose. In Tanzania, I spent a few days with the Hadzabe people, who hunt their meat with bows and arrows; gather wild honey, fruits, seeds, roots and tubers; and live in caves or temporary huts. Their DNA comes straight down the main line from the earliest *Homo sapiens*, who evolved nearby in the Rift Valley, and their lifestyle has changed very little over the millennia. The hunters could identify sounds that I couldn't hear at all, because the animals making them were nearly two kilometers away. They could spot stationary creatures hiding in thorn-scrub patches that I couldn't see with binoculars, even as they pointed and pointed, and then gave up laughing. It was the same in Mexico with the Tarahumara tribe, in the Kalahari with the San people. To them, I was an oaf who stumbled around half-blind and half-deaf in a kind of fog.

Chuck Bowden had an analogous experience while hiking in Madera Canyon in southeastern Arizona. Birders were there from all over the United States and Canada, in hopes of seeing a spectacular migrant called the elegant trogon, along with elf owls, painted redstarts, sulphur-bellied flycatchers, and fifteen species of hummingbird. Chuck started talking to the birders, and they started pointing out birds to him, except that half the time Chuck couldn't see the birds, even when they loaned him their binoculars. It would take him a few minutes with careful direction to find the telltale ear tuft of a sleeping owl in a thicket seventy yards away, but they had spotted it almost instantly. They could differentiate tiny variations of plumage coloration on birds darting around in the treetops. Because of their superior vision, the birders were having a richer, more vibrant sensory experience than he was.

Back in Tucson, Chuck bought himself a good lightweight pair of binoculars, and set about learning the 250 bird species that frequent southern Arizona. Unlike most of his obsessions, which flared and subsided, and were replaced by the next one, watching birds became a steadily accumulating source of pleasure. He didn't tick them off lists. There was no goal in mind. He was in it for the visual delight, and he never stopped marveling at their ability to fly.

In time, we both left Tucson. Chuck moved to New Mexico, and I went off to Africa and New York, and then Mississippi. We stayed in touch through irregular e-mail exchanges, and occasional telephone calls. I stopped in to see him a few times when driving across the country, and once bumped into him by accident in a small town in West Texas. We still had that ease in each other's company. We still had the ability to entertain each other, a key aspect of male friendship. The mentorship had faded away over the years, and a kind of camaraderie had expanded to fill the space. But it was still an unequal relationship.

He was older, wiser, smarter, more talented, forceful, and charismatic. He still did most of the talking, and most of the interrupting. Even when he was dismissive and scornful, to me or someone else in the room, I never called him on his rudeness. It was part of his arrogance, and he needed every ounce of arrogance to keep doubt away and keep writing what he truly believed.

Chuck was rough and surly around the edges. When I first met him, his house was the lair of a beast who worked and drank and smoked and never cleaned. He complained of jealous women looking through his kitchen windows, trying to catch a glimpse of their rivals. Rather than put up blinds or curtains, he smeared the window glass with pork fat to foil their prying eyes.

He drank instant coffee, and subsisted on cheap Mexican food and thrifty stews. Wine came from a box or a jug, except on special occasions, or when checks arrived. As a writer, he was a regional cult figure, and he lived without complaint in the poverty of that position. Then a woman moved in. The house became clean and civilized, and Chuck decamped to a shed. He started winning awards, and writing big articles for national magazines such as *Esquire, GQ, Mother Jones, National Geographic.* He was making some real money now, and he used it to buy time. He needed the time to work on his books, which mattered more than anything else in his life, but never provided him with a living.

Words flowed out of him relentlessly. One reason he drank so much wine was to staunch that flow, and get some respite. Sometimes he'd write twenty thousand words in a few days, sitting there at the computer in a kind of trance, not really looking at the screen. Phone calls lasted two hours on average, and he dominated conversations. His monologues were brilliant and bombastic, loaded with erudition, peppered with wit, nimble-footed in making connections and leaping to conclusions.

Money also allowed him to explore his sense of taste. Food and cooking became the great new obsession. Delicious fragrances emanated from his kitchen, and he slavered over cookbooks at night. The late Marcella Hazan was a particular favorite. Her recipes were designed to express the flavor of the main ingredients as fully as possible, rather than disguise and manipulate them, in the way of French haute cuisine. He persuaded a magazine to send him to her cooking school in Venice, and he returned with a new passion for espresso, and a simple, perfect, sublime recipe for roasted yellow pepper soup.

———

I remember the look of innocent pleasure on his weathered face as he watched the hummingbirds, the unabashed sexuality as he plunged his face into the crotch of a flower, the scabs and lacerations on his legs after his long marches across the desert. Rather than walk around the patchy vegetation, Chuck would walk through it, refusing to deviate his course, and presumably enjoying the sensation of thorns and twigs raking across his skin.

He had the most interesting and original mind that I ever got to know well. It cut right through the conventional wisdom and surface veneer to the stark uncomfortable truth. His intellectual honesty compelled him to fully acknowledge the horrors and pointlessness of the human experiment in this world, but he never lost his sense of wonder or curiosity. Even as he catalogued the monstrous dystopias emerging from social and political collapse in Mexico, even as he prophesied the bleakest of futures for our ransacked planet, his love of life was undiminished—mainly because he could take such pleasure from the color of a bird's throat, the feel of a woman's thigh under his fingertips, the rain falling like arrows on the desert as the sky convulsed in thunder.

Considering how much time we spent drinking together, over the course of twenty years, it's odd that I didn't know him better. He had that old-fashioned masculine privacy about his innermost feelings, except for anger, which he couldn't contain. He loathed hypocrisy, pretension, piety, and smugness, especially when they emanated from the rich and privileged. Dishonesty caused his anger to flare, because he was deeply moral. Finding so many human institutions lacking in morality, and engaged in deception, he was an iconoclast and provocateur. On literary panels, or at any kind of formal event, he was a loose cannon, who felt almost honor-bound to insult somebody, or perhaps everyone in the room, with some growling cantankerous remark, or fuck-you cigarette.

The world will be a more boring and polite place without him, at least for me and those who knew him, or followed his writing.

A few iotas less of truth will be spoken to power. He was a lion and a screech-owl, a hard charger, and a rough glass of cheap red wine.

This essay was adapted from Richard Grant's "A Sense of Chuck," Aeon, April 6, 2015, aeon.co/essays/in-memory-of-charles-bowden-a-writer-and-a-sensualist.

RICHARD GRANT is a British journalist who currently lives in Mississippi. He writes for *Smithsonian* magazine, the *New York Times*, the *Guardian*, and other publications. His last book, *Dispatches from Pluto: Lost and Found in the Mississippi Delta*, was a *New York Times* bestseller.

CODA

Here Stands a Reporter

TOM ZOELLNER

I first knew Charles Bowden through his words, and those words were sharp, exhilarating, repellent, and completely fascinating. Dark elemental forces coursed through his work. Nobody could write about the American desert like him because nobody could quite defamiliarize it as he could—to depict its civilization in ways that were completely truthful and yet strange and mystical.

In Bowden's vision, Mexican migration was really about lust; the urbanization of the Southwest was really about desperate love. His 1987 book *Frog Mountain Blues* came out when I was a high school senior in Tucson, Arizona, and I bought it in hardcover—a considerable expense for me at that time—because it was about the Santa Catalina Mountains, where I had done a lot of backpacking. But this was not the placid nature essay I had been expecting. Bowden took aim at the guilty conscience of the West; this was Emerson wielding an axe handle. "The stone skyline exists in every car sold, every house slammed against the desert floor, and every steak sizzled over a mesquite fire in a cowboy restaurant," he wrote.

I decided I wanted to be like Charles Bowden when I grew up. I had ambitions to be a newspaper reporter; he had been an expert one, writing about local crimes in horrifying draughts of copy for the afternoon *Tucson Citizen*. Finding of fact was his foundation; the rest was gorgeous interpretation. In his own cantankerous way, he had an attitude like Albert Camus, who always insisted that he was not a philosopher, but a journalist, first. Except that Bowden also hated being called that, too. He told the *Arizona Republic* in

2010, "I'm a reporter. I go out and report. I don't keep a [expletive] journal."

Imagine those words spoken in a cigarette-tempered Chicago monotone, through bad teeth, on a sandstone patio looking out onto desert plants, and you have an idea what it was like to spend a tipsy afternoon with Bowden at his small bungalow just southeast of the University of Arizona. This was a man who had spent long periods of time living out of his car or sleeping in the desert, and his house on Tucson's Ninth Street had been a filthy mess until his longtime partner, Mary Martha Miles, put her civilizing influences into it. She wiped the translucent pork grease off the windows, put in decent furniture, made it smell like something other than a freshman dorm room. With her New Orleans–bred sense of hospitality and her own voracious reading habits, she made the endless work-and-play binges seem bearable and even normal.

He typically left her side at 3 am, crept out to his converted garage, turned on classical music and worked through the dawn and early daylight, argued over the phone with New York editors until noon, and then drank red wine in his reclining chair in the afternoon and held court with a revolving cast of Tucson eccentrics—crack-addicted prostitutes, politicians, scientists, artists, and, of course, reporters, members of his own tribe, to whom he could be exceedingly kind. He had taken an interest in me as I was working on my first book, and he penned me one of the most generous lines of praise I have ever received.

Listening to Chuck could be exhausting. He had theories for everything that was hidden, and while some of his ideas were opaque, he spoke in the same twisting beats of his prose. I occasionally caught exact phrases that I'd read in his work. "You follow?" he asked incessantly. "You follow?"

His garden had standing water in the fountains, and mosquitoes buzzed around us. "You know what's really causing that?" he said to me, his unfiltered Lucky held aloft as I slapped at a fresh bite.

Charles Bowden at work in his writing studio, 2002

"That's ovulating females at work. They're taking their revenge on us. You follow?" The natural world, in all its austerity and violence, was never far from his thinking. "We do not know who we are until we look at the mountain," he wrote.

Just as he could treat his guests like interchangeable sycophants, Bowden appeared to care little for how his work was received by the mandarins of national media. If editors wanted to let the gas out of his sentences, he only shrugged and said it wasn't his business. He claimed to have ignored his reviews (though Mary Martha thought it strange he could quote all the negative ones from memory), saying that the only point of writing was in service to the reader. It was part of his duty, he felt, to expose the comfortable reader to the nastiness that lay out of sight: the sex crimes in Miracle Mile hotels, the drug tortures, the bodies rotting in the sun, the blood smeared on the firmament. Writing was an intensely physical act for him that often made him feel like dying; the agonizing labor over his sentences was the most overwhelming compulsion he knew. He drove himself to the point of physical collapse.

His biography was a hornbook of migration and compulsion. Bowden was moved to Tucson from Chicago when he was twelve because his father, Jude, a lawyer, was fascinated with cowboy literature and wanted to move his family to the "wide open spaces." The rocks and air and plants of the Southwest made an immediate sensory impression on Bowden and he wound up a chronicler of Arizona himself, though not in the arrows-and-teepees style that his father had adored. His thinking was shaped by the headstrong adventures and conspiracy mongering of the 1960s, a decade in which he plowed through the University of Arizona in less than four years (a feat nearly impossible today) with a degree in history, attended antiwar marches, watched Janis Joplin sing on the streets of San Francisco, and smoked his share of marijuana, then did work toward a PhD at the University of Wisconsin–Madison before flirting with a life of scholarly comfort teaching history at the University of Illinois–Chicago Circle. That last job was not for him—too much pretense, not enough grit.

He moved back to Tucson, bounced around various staff jobs at the U of A before landing at the Office of Arid Lands Studies, where he was fired for producing an introduction to a bibliography of water policy that was just too rangy and lyrical. That unwanted document was the seed of his first book, *Killing the Hidden Waters*, published by the University of Texas Press. It also marked the public launch of "the Bowden sentence"—his immediately recognizable mixture of the tactile, the prophetic, and the doomed. It followed him like creosote.

About a cave of bats near Morenci, Arizona, he wrote this: "The sound tightens now, a shrill spike of screeches and squeaks. The mites scramble across the skin. The larvae writhe like shiny stones at our feet. We stand inside a brief island of life, a hiding place of our blood kin." In the hands of another writer, this scene might have come across as hopelessly purple, or composed under the influence of Queensrÿche. But Bowden made it work because of his ferocious sense of connection with the natural world, and his way of forcing the reader to see herself or himself as a part of it.

He could be mordantly hilarious. A buffet dinner in Laughlin is a "casino cheap feed." Of the abundance of Mercedes in Palm Springs, he writes: "It is not easy being both rich and original." About a load of cocaine dumped into the Sea of Cortez that killed two hundred porpoises, he wrote: "The law of the sea has always been there is very little law at sea." He said of himself that he "was born to fill the cheap pages of newspapers," a reference to his stint as an inverted-pyramid-shunning crime reporter for the *Tucson Citizen* in the early 1980s, a time when he almost single-handedly made child-sex crime a major issue of local discussion and when he drove himself to the edge of sanity by living in a constant mental world of kidnappings, throat slicings, and eight-year-olds with gonorrhea of the mouth. "I have entered a world that is black, sordid, vicious," he wrote in *Harper's*, years later. "And actual. And I do not care what price I must pay to be in this world."

His personal life was famously disarrayed. Few people ever saw him wearing anything but a brown safari shirt. He could bore and frustrate some of his closest friends with his monologues on what was right and wrong with the world—tangled discourses peppered with obscure philosophical references and quasi-paranoid theories in which you were expected not to speak but listen to the Great Man hold forth. They got worse later in the afternoons as he got drunker. The same impersonal lust that perverts held for children was what Bowden felt for grown women—this is part of what drove his post-*Citizen* crack-up—and he justified his peccadillos with appeals to evolutionary appetites.

He had multiple girlfriends of the wrong kind, both secret and open; a love of cigarettes, thick coffee, and liquor ("strong waters," he called it); a yen for disappearing into the desert for weeks at a time; a compulsive need to push himself and his body's engine until it hit what he called the "red line" of extremes. But under the image of a rawboned priapic ecowarrior was a yearning for a life of tranquility, a quest for decency, a deep conservatism of humane values. I didn't understand everything he said, but on that one: yes, I follow.

This irreconcilable tension fueled his best work. In *Blood Orchid*, his wandering but brilliant meditation on the human conquest of America, he wrote: "Now I dream of the soft touch of women, the songs of birds, the smell of soil crumbling between my fingers, and the brilliant green of plants that I diligently nurture. I am looking for land to buy and I will sow it with deer and wild pigs and birds and cottonwoods and sycamores and build a pond and the ducks will come and fish will rise in the early evening light and take the insects into their jaws. There will be paths through this forest and you and I will lose ourselves in the soft curves and folds of the ground."

The last sentence is telling. Did Bowden have a death wish? Did he want his own downfall, even despite his lusty ways and bottomless need to get it all down on paper? He would have shared this brew of libido and Thanatos with John Keats and—arguably—his friend Ed Abbey. Going over repeatedly into Mexico (the parts not listed in *Lonely Planet*) to ask probing questions of assassins and drug couriers is not playing the right side of the actuarial tables. There were said to be enough connected people in Juárez who wanted him dead that all he needed to do to commit suicide would have been to walk down certain streets in broad daylight. He treated his own body like a skateboarder treats asphalt. I rarely saw him without a cigarette, either fired up or ready to go, and his tolerance for vast quantities of red wine of any quality (he was not picky in this department) was enough to inspire as much pity as awe. Yet he was up at 3 am most mornings, at his word processor, emptying himself, feeding that gut craving, which for him was even stronger than the pull of food, sex, liquor, friendships, or the reckless marches through the Cabeza Prieta desert that used to consume him for weeks at a time. He was drowned in the beautiful sentences that were his supreme repository of self-adoration—he almost never wrote in any style other than the first person—and also his most generous gifts to everyone who came across him and to readers who will continue to find him.

Bowden is lost in the soft curves of the ground that he cherished. He gave the desert a narrative it desperately needed: he helped us see the "hidden waters" of love and blood that create what we see around us, and, in so doing, he became one of the most blindingly original literary voices of the last century. His influences remain. Here stands a reporter.

This essay was adapted from Tom Zoellner and Luis Urrea, "Charles Bowden: Tom Zoellner and Luis Urrea Pay Tribute," September 1, 2014, latimes.com/books /jacketcopy/la-et-jc-charles-bowden-tom-zoellner-pays-tribute-20140831-story .html; and "Remembering Chuck Bowden: Friends Say Goodbye to a Southern Arizona Literary Titan," September 11, 2014, tucsonweekly.com/tucson/remem bering-chuck-bowden/Content?oid=4826242&showFullText=true.

TOM ZOELLNER is a former reporter for the *Arizona Republic* and the author of four nonfiction books, including *A Safeway in Arizona: What the Gabrielle Giffords Shooting Tells Us about the Grand Canyon State and Life in America.* He is an associate professor of English at Chapman University and serves as the politics editor of the *Los Angeles Review of Books.*

Packing Chuck's Legacy

MARY MARTHA MILES

Chuck Bowden was "packing" the first time he came to stay with me. He explained, very matter of fact, that two of the three Mexican men he had interviewed for a drug story in the last few months had died in one-car crashes. He simply said, "If I die in a one-car accident, someone will die with me."

For the next thirteen years, after I left Nebraska and my teaching position at a small rural college and came to live with Chuck in Arizona, it was always like that. No drama, just simple straightforward killings, threats, and violence. After calls from the DEA to tell us Mexican drug cartels had placed one or more contracts on Chuck's life because of what he had written, Chuck placed handguns in every room of our house. And most years Chuck kept a gun in our small blue truck, except when he traveled into Mexico. I got used to moving aside the handgun in the bathroom linen cabinet so I could reach a bath towel or my good face cream.

Besides the guns, there were other precautions. When Chuck was doing dangerous work, he was careful never to tell people, other than myself, where or when he was going, and he certainly never said whom he was meeting. Our landline was always blocked, so that no one could identify our phone number.

Chuck was the most observant man I ever met. He always sat in a corner when we were eating in restaurants in Mexico, his back to the wall. He noticed everyone and everything around him.

He was a fast, extremely competent driver. Twice when I was with him in Mexico, he evaded cartel men who were chasing us toward the border with their guns drawn. He listened to his intuition. He escaped carnage more than once by leaving a place when his intuition said to get out. Chuck made the point that he was always careful, never brave.

I became used to the varied guests sitting on our patio in Tucson. Often during the day his old trusted friends such as Arturo Carrillo Strong, a retired Tucson narc, and Roy Elson, a retired politician, both of whom had lived on the edge, would come by. They'd sit down under the old mesquite and drink black coffee and tell stories. One week we entertained three guests over three evenings—a drug lord, one of the richest men in America, and a prostitute—Tuesday night, Wednesday night, and Thursday night. We averaged between two and three hundred guests a year—but I only counted the ones who had something to drink or eat. So many wonderful photographers, writers, artists, and good friends, in addition to narcs, DEA agents, Border Patrol agents, publishers, killers, and drug addicts shared our evenings. Chuck was happy—a glass of red wine in his hand, good food that we'd cooked for our table, sharing stories and the beautiful garden we created together. And everything was presided over by a large black standard poodle named Sam. Chuck adored that dog.

There was travel. Some years Chuck would spend twenty weeks on the road following stories, putting a minimum of ten thousand miles per year on his truck. He only flew if he absolutely couldn't drive. He was at home behind the wheel, and it gave him time to think. He always drove a small truck because he said driving it made people trust him more. At six foot four inches, he could be intimidating. He always underplayed his height, wearing jeans, sandals—boots and a down vest if it was cold—and always the same type shirt. I ordered new shirts every year from Cabela's in Nebraska—cotton canvas with lots of wide pockets that buttoned for his notebooks.

Chuck always carried small spiral notebooks for his interviews. He rarely made notes while he talked with people. Instead, he would sit down afterward and record the conversation in his notebook. And, he never used a computer for interviews. The trick to getting people to talk to you, he said, was to sit down and listen over a shared meal. Over the years, he had meals in just about every setting you can imagine.

It was such joy for Chuck to interview and write about intriguing people in the United States and England and Europe. At other times the world was a dark place where he witnessed and wrote about the horrors of the drug trade. He always said that he was going to quit that world because he knew it was destroying him— that he was waiting for a younger writer to come up and eat his lunch. But no one was ever hungry enough. And so he stayed at it longer and longer.

Chuck's desert walks were his meditation. Taking a sleeping bag and a small backpack containing water, a little food, a one-cup espresso pot, and a good thick book, he would drive far out to where he'd never see another person. There he would walk and walk, cactus snagging his legs and ripping his shirts. At night he'd throw down his sleeping bag, never sleeping under a tent. There were times when he'd find a rattler huddled up against the bag for warmth, but that never seemed to bother him.

No matter his travels or how many people he had been up with late the night before, when he was home Chuck was at his computer by four o'clock each and every morning. He never used an alarm. Chuck said that just before he woke, he could see words scrolling across a computer screen. When that happened, he would leave our bed, make coffee that a spoon had no trouble standing up in, and walk out through the garden to the computer waiting in his backyard office. There he would write and edit for at least three to five hours, until a publisher in New York or somewhere else would weigh in. Afternoons were for research, more phone calls, and more research. I never saw him write a magazine article for which he hadn't read at least one book for each and every paragraph. And he researched mountains of books and articles for each of the books he wrote. His personal library held several thousand volumes, and book write-offs were always one of the biggest items on his annual tax returns. At four in the afternoon, he would drive to the market to pick up his daily bottle of red wine and whatever meat or fish he wanted to cook for our main supper dish.

My mornings started later. Tea, breakfast, wandering the garden to greet new blooms were the gentle start to my day. By then Chuck had come up from his office, and he placed at least twenty or thirty pages on the dining room table for me to edit. During our first year together, I edited with a red pen, but Chuck kept saying it looked like I'd bled all over his pages. So I finally switched to black.

Besides editing, I took on the tasks of restoring the house after years of neglect and acting as Chuck's hostess. Then, slowly, I began taking care of the business side of Chuck's writing—working with his agent, accountant, and editors. Chuck would do the initial edits on his books and magazine articles and then turn the project over to me. I met and worked with so many talented people at several major publishing houses, magazines, and university presses—while Chuck wrote.

Thirteen years, eleven books, and more than a hundred magazine pieces later, Chuck left me in the spring of 2009 and moved into the home of our friends, the writer Jim Harrison and his wife, Linda, in Patagonia, Arizona. The house was empty because the Harrisons spent half the year in Montana. After six months Chuck asked to return to our Tucson home. I told him of course, but first he would have to enter an alcohol rehabilitation program and deal with the abuse he had exhibited toward me during the last few years we were together. He refused. From then until his death in 2014, he split his time between Patagonia and Las Cruces, New Mexico.

For a year, Chuck would e-mail me each day new pages for *Dakotah*, his work in progress. He had been writing the book, and I had been editing it, for a year before he left Tucson. Chuck assumed I would continue to edit it—and I did. Once the book was done, the editing stopped. For the next three and a half years until his death, he didn't send me any new work.

Chuck's will made me both his executor and the trustee for his literary estate. It was an old will, one that he had made when we were first together. So, I assumed he'd just not gotten around to changing it. That wasn't the case. Three of Chuck's good friends— none of them knew each other—swore that Chuck had told each of them exactly the same thing: he didn't know what Mary Martha thought of him (and I certainly didn't think a lot of him by then), but he knew that I would take care of his work. And, with the help and kindness of many people, I have.

Jim Harrison sat down with me as I was trying to decide what path to take for Chuck's eight unpublished manuscripts and his backlist of twenty-six published books. Jim told me, "The only thing an author really cares about is staying in print." I made this my lodestar.

Patrick Lannan of the Lannan Foundation in Santa Fe offered any help I needed. He sent Anthony Arnove out from New York and Sarah Knopp from the Lannan Foundation to look at eight unpublished manuscripts (four that Chuck had written in his last five years, plus four that he had written earlier). Sarah and Anthony spent a week in Chuck's office reading and assessing.

Chuck's editors from all over the country advised me that a good university press would be the best venue for getting Chuck's unpublished work into print and keeping his literary legacy alive. I had already worked with the University of Texas Press at Austin, one of the very best university presses in the country, so I approached the director, Dave Hamrick, whom I had known for years as someone who was always true to his word. Dave was enthusiastic about taking on all of Chuck's work. So, with Dave, Sarah Knopp, and Tim Schaffner, Chuck's first literary agent and treasurer of the Bowden Literary Trust, we arranged for the University of Texas Press to publish Chuck's work in perpetuity.

Chuck was a fascinating, driven man. He was a fine writer whose work always came first. The years I spent with him were among the most interesting and most difficult of my life. I loved him.

MARY MARTHA MILES, a college English instructor, radio disk jockey, and writer, is coeditor, with Erin Almeranti, of *The Charles Bowden Reader*, published by the University of Texas Press.

Why We Carry On

ALAN WEISMAN

Writing is a precarious way to make a living at best, and some-times it gets just plain dumb. Among the dumbest things I ever heard was what a New York agent once said about author Charles Bowden.

At the time of the aforementioned stupidity, I had known Bowden about six months. We'd met over the phone when mine rang in Prescott, Arizona, one morning soon after publication of my 1986 book, *La Frontera*.

"Weisman?" growled a basso profundo. "Chuck Bowden here. You know you just wrote the best goddam book about the border ever." Steamrolling over my attempted thanks, for the next half hour he parsed my book in a stream of vocabulary so rich I felt incoherent by comparison.

Years later, Luis Alberto Urrea told me practically the identical story. His own call from Bowden awoke him at dawn; Chuck had stayed up all night reading Urrea's 1993 book, *Across the Wire*. But by then I'd heard it often. A dumbstruck young newspaper reporter named Luke Turf once described staggering from bed to see who was pounding on his door at 7 am. An outsized, rangy, sandy-haired guy in denim, his face craggy as a cliff, was waving Turf's *Tucson Citizen* story about brutalized jailed illegal immigrants, yelling that he'd gotten it right. Turf, who had just moved to town, had no idea how Bowden had found him.

The list goes on. And each of us felt not merely complimented, but anointed: One of the best around had just affirmed our worthiness as writers by acknowledging us as his colleagues. Which was why what Chuck told me that day in 1987 was so completely ridiculous.

We were in his office at *City Magazine*, a publication as outsized as its editor—him. A former *Tucson Citizen* reporter himself, Chuck had learned while covering the collision of splendor and seaminess in the Southwest to wield his commanding physical presence to disarm interviewees, and he wanted his magazine, which measured 11 × 14 inches, to be the biggest thing on the newsstand. At age forty, after years of newspaper work and two haunting books, *Killing the Hidden Waters* and *Frog Mountain Blues*, a widening circle of western literati were already referring to him by the l-word: *legend*. When he was approached to head a new Tucson magazine, he accepted on one condition: no editorial meddling by the owners.

It was a deal that for two years produced some of America's finest local journalism, until the day the owners asked him to ease up on some of their biggest advertisers—golf courses, if memory serves, although by then many sanctioned perps such as developers had been nailed in *City Magazine*'s crosshairs. That same afternoon, Bowden walked out. Two issues later, the magazine folded.

On the occasion I'm referring to, I'd come because Chuck was excerpting a portion from *La Frontera*, in which a prominent Nogales, Arizona, border merchant gloated about favors exacted from female Mexican customers in exchange for debt forgiveness. By publishing it in a southern Arizona magazine, where plenty of people who knew the guy were bound to see it, I suspected that Chuck was hoping we'd both get sued and reap the ensuing publicity.

We talked about the years I'd lived in Mexico. "I need to spend more time there," he kept saying. Eventually and memorably he would, and would write an astonishing number of seething, relentless books about it. But that day he confessed that he was having trouble getting any visibility beyond the immediate region. His own two books had been published by southwestern university presses with predictable limited distribution, and it looked like his next, *Blue Desert*, would be relegated to the same.

"Ed Abbey had me send it to a New York agent. The agent called it 'bad Edward Abbey.'"

Anyone who knew Abbey knew that *Killing the Hidden Waters* was one of his favorite books, and Bowden one of his favorite authors. Both incomparably original, all Bowden and Abbey had in common was the land each revered and wrote about, and mutual admiration. That Chuck Bowden's prose struck some agent as remotely similar to Edward Abbey's reflected the basest of Manhattan publishing sensibilities, deadened or deluded by what passed there for literary fashion.

A couple of books later, someone at W. W. Norton & Company would do right by Bowden. What followed was a torrent of work from major publishers over a quarter-century that exalted the rapture of the southwestern United States and northwestern Mexico, even as it exhumed appalling numbers of tortured bodies strewn there. But labeling Charles Bowden a western writer would be as confining and misleading as branding William Faulkner a southern writer. Faulkner set his books in the South he knew best, to tell universal stories. Bowden embraced the desert as hard as anyone possibly could, yet his power was not just in evoking a place, but our times. *Harper's*, *Esquire*, and *GQ* didn't use him continually because he was a regionalist—nor was that why *Orion* gave him the 2010 Orion Book Award (for *Some of the Dead Are Still Breathing*).

At his best, Bowden ranked among the greatest American non-fiction writers of my time. I don't say that lightly, especially about someone whose entire oeuvre was in first person: too many writers use it because it's easiest to write in the person in which we live, *I*, or because they're narcissists. Chuck did it because it worked: a

Charles Bowden, about 1970

gourmand and gourmet cook, a prolific gardener, at times a (self-confessed, in print) Lothario, he combined a boundless appetite for engagement with an uncommon gift for eloquence and a predilection for rawness, in order to portray things far bigger than himself. Even when he'd obsessively repeat himself in fury over the wreckage of places he loved, he could make it imaginatively new each time. Sentence for sentence, his was one of the strongest voices ever put to paper that I know.

Nearly every obituary I read after his unexpected death in 2014 lifted quotes from his books, but as I explained to some young writers who had seen a eulogy I wrote, Chuck Bowden's words properly belong in the context where he so carefully placed them, draft after draft. Do him justice and do yourself a favor, I'd recommend, by revisiting his work or discovering it, if you haven't already. Start anywhere—the informal trilogy of *Desierto*, *Blood Orchid*, and *Blues for Cannibals*, which can be read in no particular order, or any of his incandescent books set in Ciudad Juárez, culminating in *Murder City*.

I also advised them to never try to imitate him—no one possibly could—but to learn from his fearless commitment to saying exactly what needed to be said ... no, I'll rephrase that: Chuck Bowden wasn't fearless. He was scared plenty—but he had the courage to never turn away, regardless.

Over the years, I'd sometimes crash on his couch when I came through Tucson—me and every other writer. Then, while writing my book *The World Without Us*, I ended up living just a couple of blocks away. Chuck had just finished what some consider his magnum opus, *Down by the River*, set in El Paso and Ciudad Juárez, and was already plotting his next. Nights on his back porch, overlooking his beloved cacti collection, we'd drink ourselves to the bottom of many bottles of wine, shuddering over monstrous things we'd covered, mulling how to describe the unspeakable. I'd walk home on the hot streets, inspired by his sheer existence. He would fade away reading a cookbook—"my idea of pornography," he'd say—and then be up before dawn to brew first an espresso, then more trouble with the English language.

Damn, I still miss him. Everyone who knew him does. But there's his indelible body of work to remind us why we do, and why we carry on.

This essay was adapted from Alan Weisman's "Charles Bowden, 1945–2014," Orion, *September 5, 2014, orionmagazine.org/2014/09/charles-bowden-1945-2014.*

ALAN WEISMAN's most recent book, *Countdown: Our Last, Best Hope for a Future on Earth?*, won the 2014 Los Angeles Book Prize. His book *The World Without Us*, an international bestseller translated into thirty-four languages, was named best nonfiction book of 2007 by *Time* and *Entertainment Weekly*, and was a finalist for the National Book Critics Circle Award.

I Have Had to Make Up My Life As I Went Along

CHARLES BOWDEN

I have had to make my life up as I went along. I suppose we all do that but I seem to have been less skilled than some. I never found what others call a vocation or way to describe myself until I was in my thirties and that sensation was fleeting. I'll try to explain.

In the beginning the world was blue and green and the air raw with March and sunshine. I was maybe two and I have never forgotten the green grass, the roar of blue sky overhead and my mother hanging clothes on a cool sunny day. Later, we left the farm for the city and I learned the boredom of dense colonies of humans. There is a usage in English—the natural world—that I have never felt comfortable with. I don't consider my own species unnatural. But I do recoil from the monotony of life where they dominate. Years ago, I spent an hour in a bat cave at dusk. The floor of the cave was guano, the air felt like acid from the constant shower of urine and 25,000 bats clung to the ceiling. I climbed a mountain of guano to get close to them and as darkness claimed the mouth of the cave, they dropped down, swirled around me and left. All this reminded me of human cities—throbbing with life but limited in variety, messy but alive.

I think I have always sought borders to escape this sense of limits and monotony. I have spent almost all of my life in check-out lines with people of various colors. I have sought the edge of human communities and still found it necessary to flee them at times. This hunger has not simply colored my life, it has directed it.

Decades ago, I was working on my doctorate in American his-

Charles Bowden, Texas Book Festival, 2010

tory and I went to Mississippi with a caravan of other students to deliver clothing and other castoffs to people on the delta. That is when I met Fannie Lou Hamer and others. The bad violence had ebbed but there were still night riders and spasms of fear. What struck me was the other America—black, submerged, poor and rising. I had seen extreme poverty in Mexico but this did not help me accept a similar poverty in my own nation. I remember joining a basketball game at an encampment of protesting field hands and how my ribs ached afterwards as the players took a shot at finally slamming a white person. I remember riding around with SNCC people and how they had entered a world I did not know the name of. They lived with threats of death but they were free.

A few years later I was teaching in a university, and then I walked out on that career. I did manual labor for a year, wound up on a daily newspaper for three years, left that and founded a magazine, left that and became a freelance writer. All these things are simply scraps of facts. I think I kept trying to close the gap between my species and other species and between the rich and the poor in my own warrens of life. And I did this by the only means I had, the pen. I don't really think writing is that important, but it is something I can do. I think the people and places and throbs of life I have written about are more important than I am or ever will be.

The border and drugs and murders and the violence of nations are things I did not seek but could not ignore. When I was about thirty-five I outlined ten books I hoped to write. They were all about animals and plants. I never wrote a single one. Things got in the way of my schemes, things like the ground under my feet, the writhing of Mexico under the expansion of the drug industry and then the savagery of both the global economy and the senile Mexican state. At the time, I had no idea what was going on. I simply saw death and violence being ignored and so I went into it. I have not controlled events in my life, they have controlled me and this has turned out to be a blessing. People certainly had more to teach me than I ever had to teach them.

My father when he was old and dying told me that about the time you figure out life, you die. I think he did not get it quite right. I think a person can actually figure out life early on, but the trick is to act on this knowledge. The people I met in Mississippi in the sixties like Fannie Lou Hamer and the SNCC workers knew what to do and why. They taught me without even paying much attention to me. You either try to make things better or you wind up living without joy or much hope. My work, with all its sputterings, has been about a desire to have things make sense and to ease the pain I see around me. This is hardly a bold claim. I have never seen a person tending their garden or a bird on a nest who did not know this simple lesson I struggled to learn.

The newspaper stories, magazine articles, books and speeches have all been details in one piece of work. I have been lucky on a couple of counts. Nothing I have done has really pleased me. I can't believe that I will ever do anything that lives up to my hopes. And everything I am working on at the moment captivates me. Also, I come from people who have little interest in old age. You almost have to club them to get them to give up even their vices, and it is impossible to get them to be idle. So I figure I will keep doing what I do with an ear cocked to bird song and an anxious heart each spring eager for the first buds of leaf and flower.

Other people made me better than I could have ever been on my own. And I doubt any of them knew what I had taken away from knowing them. Every time I have choked in life when facing a moral decision, my parents have come back from the dead. Once, when I had to walk away from a financial deal that I knew in my bones was wrong, I realized, after the meeting where I had refused the offer, I was wearing my father's shirt, the only thing of his I had retained. And I don't think I ever faced someone in need without hearing my mother's voice, in a stern midwestern tone, admonishing me that people need help. Both of them would be puzzled by this accounting of my behavior, since I was the rebellious child and the one that caused them serious worry. And to be blunt, every time I have felt I might cave in to fear, Fannie Lou Hamer has loomed before me and I have thought of her being beaten because she wanted to vote and I have told myself I had no right to give in to fear because if she could keep the faith, I had no excuse.

I had a friend once, Edward Abbey, who noted he'd never heard a mountain lion complain about its fate. Fair enough. But still I think besides acceptance we can nudge things down the road with a few gardens, symphonies, good meals, and some laughter.

The whippoorwill's name reflects the sounds we hear it make. But studies show there are two more notes to its song beyond the range of human hearing. Scholars wondered if other birds heard these notes, and recordings of mockingbirds, a species that mimics the songs of other birds, revealed that they did. I think I want to hear these missing notes about the border and the ground about us when I write and bring the full song to the attention of others.

My life has either been a series of train wrecks or a trip that keeps jumping the tracks in order to get where I am going. I'll let you know which as soon as I know.

Written as a ninetieth birthday note to Father Peter (James Hinde), 2013. Along with the note, Chuck carried a crepe myrtle sapling across the border in his backpack to Casa Tabor in Ciudad Juárez. Fr. Peter (Order of Carmelites) cofounded Cristianos/Cristianas por la Paz en El Salvador (CRISPAZ) and, with Sr. Betty Campbell (Religious Order of the Sisters of Mercy), cofounded Tabor House. (Bowden's essay is courtesy of Molly Molloy. © The Charles Clyde Bowden Literary Trust, Mary Martha Miles, Trustee)

Charles Bowden, Gonzales, Texas, at Don Henry Ford Jr.'s home

Acknowledgments

Foremost, we thank our exceptional crew of contributors for their chapters in this book. "Sure, I'll do it for Chuck" was a familiar refrain. Mary Martha Miles, trustee of Bowden's literary estate, encouraged us from the beginning and helped us along the way. Tim Schaffner helped bring out-of-print manuscripts back to life. Patrick Lannan and the Lannan Foundation underwrote the Bowden book series at the University of Texas Press.

At the University of Texas Press we continue to be inspired by director David Hamrick and to rely on Allison Faust, assistant to the director; Sonya Manes, our copy editor; and designer Matt Avery. The Texas team is tops.

Photographs from the Wittliff Library's Charles Bowden Collection are used by their permission and Mary Martha Miles, literary trustee. Joan Scott standardized our photographs.

At the Wittliff Library, Steve Davis and Lauren Goodley provided enormous assistance and sound advice. Lauren and Joel Minor organized the Charles Bowden Collection (MS 112), and its finder's guides, now online, are indispensable. We highly prized and relied on the efficient skills of independent researcher Mary Elizabeth García.

Readers who have original photographs, correspondence, memorabilia, or other artifacts related to Charles Bowden may contact The Wittliff Collections about donations to its Charles Bowden Collection in care of Steve Davis, Curator, The Wittliff Collections, Alkek Library, Texas State University. 601 University Drive. San Marcos, Texas 78666. Ph. 512-245-2313.

The Wittliff Collections are dedicated to collecting, preserving, and sharing the creative legacy of the Southwest's literary, photographic, and musical arts, and to fostering the region's "Spirit of Place" in the wider world. The Wittliff presents major exhibitions year-round; hosts readings, artist talks, lectures, and other events; publishes significant books from its holdings; and makes its collections available to statewide, national, and international researchers.

A description of the Charles Bowden Papers is available on the website thewittliffcollections.txstate.edu under the Research tab. You may also schedule a research visit using a form on that page. Funding for research travel is available through the competitive William J. Hill Visiting Researcher Travel Grants; applications are due in January each year.

Copyright and Credits

PHOTOGRAPHERS' CREDITS

41 Robert L. Bartley, chair of Pulitzer feature writing committee, letter to Charles Bowden, April 19, 1984 (The Charles Bowden Papers, The Wittliff Collections/Texas State University, box 3, folder 8. © The Charles Clyde Bowden Literary Trust, Mary Martha Miles, Trustee)

45 Charles Bowden, *City Magazine* editor, and Richard "Dick" S. Vonier, *City Magazine* publisher, about 1986 (The Charles Bowden Papers, The Wittliff Collections/Texas State University, no. 112, box 7, folder 5b. © The Charles Clyde Bowden Literary Trust, Mary Martha Miles, Trustee)

66 Cover of *City Magazine* featuring Charles Bowden and Art Carrillo Strong's story "El Nacho," September 1987

67 Cover of *City Magazine* featuring Charles Bowden and Dick Vonier's story "Charlie," about Charles Keating, August 1988

71 Ray Carroll, Charles Bowden, and Arizona Senator John McCain, at a fundraiser for the senator (By permission of The Charles Clyde Bowden Literary Trust, Mary Martha Miles, Trustee)

81 Charles Bowden showing his desert-plants garden in bloom (© Kasey Anderson)

98–99 Charles Bowden at Alamos, Sonora (The Charles Bowden Papers, The Wittliff Collections/Texas State University, box 101, folder 18 © The Charles Clyde Bowden Literary Trust, Mary Martha Miles, Trustee)

102 Charles Bowden and a gray hawk, San Pedro River, Arizona, 1986 (© Rich Glinski)

104 Letterpress broadside: "Lies In The Desert," by Charles Bowden, 2003 (© Ken Sanders and Ken Sanders Rare Books; used by permission)

105 Letterpress broadside: "Killing Is Fun," by Charles Bowden, art by Alice Leora Briggs, June 2009 (© Ken Sanders and Ken Sanders Rare Books; used by permission)

125 Charles Bowden, "Rednecks for Social Responsibility," 1987 (© Jack Dykinga)

149 Charles Bowden fording Paria River in winter, 1986 (© Jack Dykinga)

150 Charles Bowden and Jack Dykinga retracing John Lee's winter trip down the Paria River, 1986 (© Jack Dykinga)

153 Charles Bowden, hiker, 1986 (© Jack Dykinga)

155 "Predator's View," Chuck's favorite photograph by Michael Berman (Charles Bowden, *Inferno*, with photographs © by Michael Berman. Austin: University of Texas Press, 2006, 57)

box 102, folder 7g. © The Charles Clyde Bowden Literary Trust, Mary Martha Miles, Trustee)

297 Charles Bowden at work in his writing studio, 2002 (Photo by Steven M. Johnson. The Charles Bowden Papers, The Wittliff Collections/ Texas State University, box 2069, folder 25a. © The Charles Clyde Bowden Literary Trust, Mary Martha Miles, Trustee)

311 Charles Bowden, about 1970 (Photographer unknown. The Charles Bowden Papers, The Wittliff Collections/Texas State University, box 101, folder 12. © The Charles Clyde Bowden Literary Trust, Mary Martha Miles, Trustee)

315 Charles Bowden, Texas Book Festival, 2010 (© Parker Haeg)

319 Charles Bowden, Gonzales, Texas, at Don Henry Ford Jr.'s home (© Julián Cardona)

Index

Note: page numbers in *italics* refer to images.